To: Brother
Brother in Christ

It is my prayer that the inspired words on the pages of this book will be a blessing to your life.

Blessings in the name of Jesus!

Love and prayers,
Willa D. Turner
07/2/17

POWER *to* OVERCOME

MY LIFE STORY

WILLA D. TURNER

WESTBOW PRESS®
A DIVISION OF THOMAS NELSON
& ZONDERVAN

Copyright © 2017 Willa D. Turner.

All rights reserved. No part of this book may be used or reproduced by any means, graphic, electronic, or mechanical, including photocopying, recording, taping or by any information storage retrieval system without the written permission of the author except in the case of brief quotations embodied in critical articles and reviews.

This book is a work of non-fiction. Unless otherwise noted, the author and the publisher make no explicit guarantees as to the accuracy of the information contained in this book and in some cases, names of people and places have been altered to protect their privacy.

Scripture taken from the King James Version of the Bible.

WestBow Press books may be ordered through booksellers or by contacting:

WestBow Press
A Division of Thomas Nelson & Zondervan
1663 Liberty Drive
Bloomington, IN 47403
www.westbowpress.com
1 (866) 928-1240

Because of the dynamic nature of the Internet, any web addresses or links contained in this book may have changed since publication and may no longer be valid. The views expressed in this work are solely those of the author and do not necessarily reflect the views of the publisher, and the publisher hereby disclaims any responsibility for them.

Any people depicted in stock imagery provided by Thinkstock are models, and such images are being used for illustrative purposes only.
Certain stock imagery © Thinkstock.

ISBN: 978-1-5127-5708-8 (sc)
ISBN: 978-1-5127-5710-1 (hc)
ISBN: 978-1-5127-5709-5 (e)

Library of Congress Control Number: 2016915328

Print information available on the last page.

WestBow Press rev. date: 3/13/2017

To My Gifts from God, My Children: Therese (Truly a Miracle), James Jr., Christopher, Ithiel, Emell and Aprille

My Wonderful, Chosen-daughter–Cynthia

My Precious Step-daughter–Gail

In Loving Memory of–

My late, great, beloved, handsome husband–James H. Turner, whom I affectionately called "Honey." He was not only the best husband a wife could have, but he was also my best friend, my lover, the father of all my children, my pastor, my superintendent and a lover of people in general. He was a humble man. One who could be touched by the young as well as the old, the rich, the poor and all nationalities. My husband was an anointed man of God who loved winning souls for Christ. He would work with a lost soul for as long as it took to bring that soul to Christ–time didn't matter when it came to a person's salvation, deliverance or healing. This powerful gospel preacher reached thousands for Christ in his lifetime, and his impact on all who knew him is still felt.

With Grateful Appreciation to the Following:

Aprille Turner, MAE–Picture Inserts

Pastor Grace Hinton–Sponsor

M. Ojinga and Dionne Harrison MD–Sponsors

Bria Arline, B.S.–Editor

As the hart panteth after the water brooks,
so panteth my soul after thee, O God.
Psalms 42:1

Keep Striving

As the deer runs through the woods–sometimes at play, other times running from the hunter who seeks his life–he gets worn and looks for a place to refresh himself. He seeks out the brooks along the way, that he may be strengthened until he reaches his final destination.

    We are also on a journey. We didn't come here to stay but are passing through on our way to a better country. There will be many obstacles in our paths. But if our souls keep thirsting for the living God, He will give us the strength we need to fulfill our purpose of glorifying Him and winning souls to the kingdom.

CONTENTS

Chapter 1	Early Childhood	1
Chapter 2	On the Farm	6
Chapter 3	Growing Up	14
Chapter 4	High School	18
Chapter 5	College Years	25
Chapter 6	Single and Saved	32
Chapter 7	A Dream Come True	39
Chapter 8	Wife–Pastor's Wife	51
Chapter 9	A New Edifice	60
Chapter 10	Mother Through Prayer	66
Chapter 11	House of Our Own	76
Chapter 12	Loss of My Child	89
Chapter 13	Parenting Others	100
Chapter 14	Founder of Churches	103
Chapter 15	The Move to Raleigh	119
Chapter 16	The Beginning of the End	130
Chapter 17	Darkest Day	137
Chapter 18	Life as a Widow	141
Chapter 19	Starting over at Fifty	159
Chapter 20	Making It Through Prayer	172
Chapter 21	A Necessary Move	177
Chapter 22	Return to Raleigh	190
Chapter 23	My Miracle!	194
Chapter 24	Broken Contract	199
Chapter 25	Letters, Tributes & Poems	212
Chapter 26	Devotional Readings	236
Chapter 27	Memorial Ceremony	251

Conclusion 261

CHAPTER 1

Early Childhood

Many, many years ago in a little town called Trio, South Carolina a pint-sized, wide-eyed, hairless, black girl was born. Her parents named her Willadine Shirley Ann McCrea. Gwendolyn was to be a part of her name also, but her father said he couldn't pronounce it. The new mother, Lula Mae McCrea, was proud of her baby girl. The father, James Bennett McCrea, was hoping for a boy. As he left Charleston, South Carolina to go home that weekend, he told his friends at the navy shipyard where he worked that if the baby were a boy, he would leave his car for his family's transportation. But if it were a girl, he would drive his car back. Well, he drove his car back to Charleston.

    I was born in the same house that my mother grew up in. She stayed with her grandparents while waiting for me to be born. Shortly after I was born daddy decided to move back home to earn a living as a farmer. He took us from Trio to the little place called Taft where he grew up. Taft was in a small community on a rural route about fourteen miles from the nearest town, Kingstree, S. C. I grew up there on a fifty-two acre farm.

    Willadine was the first of six children born to Bennett and Lula Mae. The others were Willie James, David Franklin, Felesha Belle, Thomas Jefferson (TJ) and Francis James. Francis was the first child born in a hospital. He was premature and spent three weeks in an incubator at the hospital after Mama came home. One day shortly after Mama came home, she told me, "Dean, every time I sit down, someone sits down beside me."

    "Mama, there is no one in here but us," I told her. We found out later that her blood pressure had risen so high it was causing her to hallucinate.

Francis had been home for a few months when he caught a cold. Mama and Daddy took him to the doctor on a Thursday, where they found out he had bronchitis. The doctor gave him some medicine and sent him home. Mama and I were sitting on the front porch swing that evening. Francis James was asleep on Mama's bed. We were talking when a woman in a long, flowing gown came walking towards us. She held a little child by the hand. They turned into our lane and came right up to the front porch. But they didn't stop. Instead, they passed us as they went around the side of the house to where we had our bedrooms. I asked Mama, "Did you see that lady and the little boy?"

She said, "No." I told her they had passed in front of us. She said, "I didn't see no lady." We got up and went around the side of the house, but we didn't find anything. I told her it was as if the lady and child were floating. She said, "Girl, you didn't see anything." To this day, I am convinced the vision was real. Francis died in Mama's arms the following Sunday morning at the age of six months. It was sad around the house for a long time. Mama later told me that what I saw was a token of an angel coming to get Francis James.

One of my first memories as a little girl was watching our house being moved. I was fascinated as our house rolled along on logs as mules pulled it down a hill to be closer to the road.

My first Christmas memory is the year I received a toy that consisted of a large Mother duck with about four baby ducklings waddling behind her. As I pulled the string that was attached to the Mother duck, the Mother duck clucked and waddled and the baby ducklings clucked and waddled behind her.

One year my brother and I received a red bicycle for Christmas. It was probably my brother's bicycle because it was a boy's bike. We had so much fun taking turns as Daddy and Cousin Thomas Wilson was teaching us how to ride that bike.

My father owned a general store. I remember it being filled with sodas, cookies, candy, hash, crackers and lots of other things. One night Willie and I wanted something from the store. Daddy said if we could reach the key, we could have what we wanted. The key was kept on top of the "safe"–the china cabinet. We climbed up to get it and were hanging on when somehow we pulled the cabinet down. We were not hurt, but Mama picked up a tin tub full of broken dishes and glasses. It was her fine stuff she used when the preacher or company came for dinner. We were both sorry to have broken the dishes, but we were also afraid we were going to get a terrible beating. Thankfully, Daddy and Mama decided not to whip us.

When I was five years old, Great-grandma Sarah passed away. I will never forget the night she died. No one we knew had a telephone then. Someone from Trio had to come and get Mama, and she took me with her. When the undertaker arrived, they zipped Great-grandma Sarah up in a shiny, black bag and placed her on what seemed to be a long bed with wheels. When they rolled her near the door, I said to Mama, "She moved!"

Mama said, "No she didn't girl. She has been dead for a while now." I still believe the zipper moved. It was as if a hand inside the bag had pushed against the zipper.

My great-grandparents, Edward and Sarah Gibson, reared my mother and her three sisters and two brothers: Sara Lee, "Little" Sarah, Pauline, Edward (Eddie or Gip) and James. My mother's mother, Lynn Orean, died when Mama was about twelve, and Mama's father, Dave, died when Mama was thirteen. Great-grandma Sarah was a loving, caring woman who was always kind to us. She was tiny and pretty. I remember how gracefully she walked in her high-top, laced-up, black, leather shoes. We used to love to visit Papa and Grandma Sarah. But after she got sick, Grandma Sarah didn't leave the bed. Mama's sister, Aunt Pauline, lived with Grandma and cared for her. Grandma used a straw to take her food as Aunt Pauline fed her out of a heavy bowl.

We still went to see Papa from time to time after Grandma died. I remember riding in the back of the wagon from Taft to Trio to visit Papa or gather fruit. Mama never got her driver's license, so she drove the mule and wagon when she went without Daddy. In the fall, we came back from Trio with big, tin tubs of scuppernong grapes and pears. Some grape vines wrapped around a four-corner, wood railing, and the grapes hung high enough for us to walk under them. Mama called these supports "grape harpers," which were actually trellises. She made jelly out of the grapes and canned the pears in jars. The jelly and pears were delicious with hot biscuits when we sat around the fire on cold, wintry nights.

Papa's house was huge, with high ceilings. It had a parlor where we couldn't play, a living room, three bedrooms, the dining room and the kitchen. Except for the dining room and the kitchen, all the rooms had fireplaces. Beautiful flowers and many trees covered the front yard. I remember the persimmon tree well because one day I bit into a persimmon that wasn't ripe. I was afraid my jaw would lock. Persimmons are sweet and soft, though, when they are ripe.

There was a long porch around the left side of the house. A well was not far from the porch, and I used to watch Papa draw water from it with a tin bucket. The water was cool when he first drew it. Just out the backdoor, the shade from the tall pecan trees overshadowed the ground. A path led from the backyard to the outhouse and on down to Papa's store. I liked getting candy and cookies and drinks from Papa's store. Uncle Lucius and Aunt Sarah Lee lived right across the road from Papa's farm, so we got to play with our cousins Annie Mae, Lucius James (LJ), Yvonne and Clara Belle when we went to Trio.

It was a four-mile stretch from our house to St. Mary's Church where we attended. St. Mary's School was right across from the church. I remember walking to school with the bigger children down a dirt road. At the edge of the schoolyard stood an outdoor spigot which never stopped running. The water was always cold and refreshing. St. Mary School was a one-building school with many rooms heated by potbelly, wood-burning stoves. All grades were taught there. Professor Lawrence, who was known as "Prof" to many people, enforced strict discipline. But we loved him as a wonderful principal and teacher.

Children started in what was then called "little first" and continued to the twelfth grade. I am sure little first was really kindergarten. I remember Mama bragging about how I made little first and big first in the same year. Most of the children had to finish little first the first year and then move up to big first the next.

The lunchroom was a little ways off from the school. Schools served real lunches then—good old southern, home-cooked meals. Some of my favorite dishes were fried chicken, homemade macaroni and cheese—not boxed stuff—fresh collard greens, corn bread and sweet potatoes. When we didn't have money for lunch, I had to carry biscuits and some of the apples and pears Mama had canned. Even though the meal was good, it was embarrassing to take a brown-bag lunch for me and my brothers. Since I was the oldest, it was my responsibility. The school had outdoor toilets, one for the girls and one for the boys. The basketball courts were outside too since none of the black schools had gyms then. I tried out for the basketball team but never improved enough to play in the games. I ended up going as the water girl. I was skinny and fast on my feet, which came in handy for the annual May Day 100-yard dash. The day before we got out of school for the summer, we celebrated May Day with sack and egg races, wrapping the maypole, horseshoes and all kinds of games.

CHAPTER 2

On the Farm

Lula Mae and James Bennett McCrea (Mom & Dad)

Mama told us about a time when we were small. She and Daddy had been working in the fields. She had put Willie, who was still a baby, in the carriage and parked it behind the truck for shade. But he woke up and started crying. She had just taken him out when Daddy got in the truck and backed up without looking. The truck smashed the carriage to pieces. Mama said that the Lord spared Willie's life that day.

I learned to cook when I was around nine years old; I had to stand on a chair to reach the stove. That old stove turned out some good food. Mama would put the meal on and tell me what to do with it. On her way out to the fields she said, "Don't let that food burn." Even though I still had to watch out for my younger brother and sister, I never let the food burn. I was proud, and Mama was too when she returned.

Almost everything we ate grew on the farm. Before we had electricity, Mama canned fruits, vegetables, jellies and preserves in jars using her big pressure cooker. It had a gage on top that looked like a big stopwatch and held eight-twelve quart-sized jars. We had pecan, apple, plum, peach and fig trees, strawberry vines and nearby blackberry and "huckleberry" or blueberry bushes and hickory nut trees. Nothing can top the fruit, jellies, jams and vegetables Mama canned. We always had plenty of eggs and poultry from Mama's chickens, turkeys, ducks and guinea hens. The duck eggs had yolks of a deeper yellow than that of the hen eggs and made a richer tasting cake. Mama milked the cows for fresh milk and homemade butter. She sterilized the milk by heating it on the stove to a certain temperature. When it had cooled down and sat for a while, the cream rose to the top. Then she spooned it off and filled a glass jar with the cream. We churned the cream by shaking the jar until the cream turned to butter. If one of us got tired, someone else took over until it was ready.

We grew sugar cane also. We children liked to chew the canes to get at the sweet juice. Daddy made syrup by taking the sugar cane to the mill for grinding, and we ate the smoothest, sweetest syrup for our flapjacks. We also made our own grits from our corn crop by shelling the dry corn off the cob. Then, Daddy took the kernels to the mill to be ground. When he brought it home, we separated the grits from the meal with a sifter or sieve. We grew mainly yellow corn, so we ate yellow grits and yellow corn meal.

We grew two cash crops–cotton and tobacco. At harvest time, each person carried a burlap bag which held about twenty-five pounds of cotton. As we filled the sacks by hand, we kept emptying them onto sheets made of burlap at the end of the rows. A good picker filled at least two sheets of cotton, which together weighed two-three hundred pounds. When we had gathered so many pounds, Daddy took the load to the cotton gin. The cotton was then separated from the seed, baled and paid for by the pound.

We had a lot to do when the tobacco was ripe. First, the men and boys pulled the tobacco from the stocks, leaf by leaf, and laid them in what we called a dray–a long, narrow, wooden box which held several arm loads of leaves. When it was full, someone took the dray to the barn where we waited to tie the tobacco on sticks. The stringer tied the tobacco onto the sticks as the hander passed it to her. Each stick held about fourteen bundles of three or four tobacco leaves, seven bundles tied on one side and seven on the other. When the stick was full, someone hung it in the barn. At sundown a fire was started in the kiln attached to the barn. Someone added wood until the kiln was hot enough to cure the tobacco, being careful not to make it too hot so that the tobacco would not dry too fast. The tobacco took about two days to cure. At the end of the second day, we put the fire out and left the sticks to cool overnight. Before dawn the next morning, someone took the tobacco from the barn and put it in the pack house, where we removed it from the sticks for grading. First grade was the heaviest, light-tan leaves; these leaves brought the most money per pound. Second grade, the deep-brown leaves, weighed a little less. Third grade or trash tobacco was the really dark leaves; it took a lot of these to make a pound. After we separated the tobacco, we used one leaf to tie bundles of about six dried leaves. Then we stacked them by grade on burlap sheets about the size of a king-sized bed. Daddy drove his big truck loaded down with tobacco bundles to Lake City to sell at the tobacco market.

One day Daddy took me with him to the tobacco market in Lake City, South Carolina. I was excited to be riding with him in his big truck. The boys were the only ones that got the chance to go with him to the market most of the time. Mama packed us a lunch, and we left early in the morning. The trip was an hour drive, but we had to be there early for the bidding. I was fascinated by the men talking. They didn't seem to take a breath as they bid on the tobacco. After the sale, we ate our bologna sandwiches and drank Red Rock sodas before getting back on the highway for home. I have never forgotten that day. I enjoyed it so much that I still call it, "A Day with my Dad."

In later years, Papa went blind. But he knew each of us by voice. Once, my cousin Yvonne led him through a path across the field. There was a hole in the path. She went around the hole but led Papa right into it and he fell. Papa always got a good laugh out of telling that story, and we did also. He had a slight speech impediment, which caused him to stutter a little, making it funnier when he told it. On the days we went to Trio to work Papa's farm, I left the field a little earlier to cook Papa's dinner before we left for home. Later, he married Mrs. Lizzy, who cared for him until he died. He was over ninety years old at his death in the early '60s. But his mind was still sharp, and he still looked good. He was a gentle, kind, loving person. I still smile when I think of him. He was a devout Christian and a deacon at St. John AME Church, where he was affectionately called "The Preaching Deacon."

When I was a child, sometimes the store came to us. I remember how the iceman came every Thursday to fill our icebox. He brought us a huge block of ice. After the iceman came, we had fun chipping pieces from the block with an ice pick to make ices with Kool Aid. Mama loved fishing, and so did our neighbor, Mr. Johnnie Beaufort. They would go to the river, which was a long ways from where we lived, to fish. But when they didn't catch enough fish, we got some on Fridays when the fish man came. The rolling store was another excitement. It drove by our house once a week also. Everybody ran out to meet the store on wheels. We had saved our nickels and pennies to buy ice-cold sodas, candy, cookies and bubble gum. Pennies and nickels went a long way then. A dime's worth almost filled our little, brown bags with cookies, candies and a soda. My cousin John (June Bug) always seemed to have something left over when all of ours was gone. We used to ask him for some of his candy, but he wouldn't give us any. He gave some to his dog while we watched. We did finally get over it, but we still tease him whenever we get together for family reunions.

No electricity meant we used kerosene lamps. It was my job to keep the lampshades clean. They were made of glass and got smutty over a period of time, especially if the wicks were not trimmed. You wouldn't be able to use the lamps when it got dark if the lampshades weren't cleaned. I made sure the lampshades were clean each day before the sun went down, and I don't remember breaking one.

From May to August, we went barefoot. The only time we wore shoes was on church days or when we got a chance to go to town. Some of our games were different than games today. My favorites included: hopscotch, marbles, jump rope, dodgeball, softball, jack rocks, drop-the-handkerchief, tug-of-war, hide-and-seek, checkers and old maid. We climbed trees and rode bicycles. The boys liked swimming in the irrigation ponds. We made our own balls out of the twine we used to tie the tobacco. The girls made dolls from grass. We washed the dirt out of the roots, which we braided as the doll's hair. We tied a piece of cloth around the green leaves to make a body and little pieces of cloth to look like bows and ribbons. If it rained or was the end of harvesting season when we weren't working in the fields, we read a lot. Mama had a big, black, family Bible and a lot of Bible story books around the house. I read all of them to my brothers and my sister. Outdoor toilets, clothes washed in big, black pots and ironed with smoothing irons heated on the stove, tin-tub baths and hard days in the field may seem unthinkable today. But our days were also full of laughter.

My mother put the fear and love of God in us early in our lives. She wouldn't let us fight or call each other bad names. And we would get a whipping for fighting, stealing or sassing. If an adult falsely accused us, we weren't supposed to talk back; Mama said we were to tell her, and she would take care of everything. Sometimes when Mama was gone, we fought. But we wouldn't let her know. If she found out, she would make us hug and kiss while we were still mad at each other. Mama expected us to be truthful, even if doing so got us into trouble. She used to say our eyes gave us away when we lied, and she wouldn't stop whipping us until we told her the truth. As she beat us, she would say, "If you lie, you will steal. If you steal, you will kill. So I am not going to let you get away with lying."

One day while Mama was gone, Franklin wanted some bologna. He wasn't supposed to take any without asking. So, he bit a few pieces out of the end of the leg of bologna and put it back. When Mama came home, she went to get it for supper. "Who bit this bologna?" she said. Franklin said, "The rat did it." His teeth left prints on the bologna, and she knew it was Franklin because the gap in his front teeth was wider than any of ours. She got him good for lying on the rat.

Mama taught us The Lord's Prayer and "Now I Lay Me Down to Sleep." She knelt down with us bedside our beds and taught us until we learned to pray them by ourselves. We could add whatever else we wanted to say to these, and she prayed the grown-up prayer. Many nights she asked, "Did you say your prayers?" If the answer was yes, then we were okay. If the answer was no, she would say, "Get out of that bed right now and say your prayers."

In our house, going to church and Sunday school was not a choice, and we had to be ready on time. Mama also made sure we went to catechism class on Saturdays. Mrs. Scott came by and picked us up. Sometimes we were the only children there. When we got upset and asked Mama why we had to go when other parents didn't make their children go, she said she did not have anything to do with what other parents did. Her children were going. Mrs. Scott was very strict; she told your parents if you misbehaved, which made some of the children dislike her. We learned speeches for Easter, Children's Day and Christmas. Mrs. Scott always seemed to give me the longest speech. When we recited, Mama beamed and told us how well we did. One Easter, Willie had to sing a song. He did well in practice. He still did well when it was time for him to sing for real, except he didn't wait for the music. After finishing the song, he sat down while Mrs. Scott was still playing. We all laughed.

Besides being a mother and teacher, Mama was also a good nurse. When I was about eight years old, I began to have terrible headaches and dizzy spells. Sometimes while I walked, my head would feel heavy all of a sudden. I staggered back and forth, and my head hurt until I was in tears. I always seemed to be sick with those headaches. There were days when the principal had to bring me home from school. The doctor said I needed glasses. They put eyeglasses on me, but my headaches would still come and go. Mama stayed by my bedside all night long, giving me home remedies and praying for me. Usually I did not fall asleep until daybreak.

One day a bad storm came up. Mama was almost through with dinner, and we kept telling her we were hungry. She was mixing Kool Aid in a glass pitcher when a bolt of lightning shot through the window, shattering the pitcher and splattering Kool Aid everywhere. No one said anything else. We all went and sat in a corner, even Mama, until the storm blew over. Afterwards, Mama fixed our dinner. But she said that it was the last time she would try to do anything while the "Lord was working," no matter how hungry we were. It was a blessing that Mama was not hurt or killed. From then on we remained quiet during a storm. I've seen lightening hit a tree and split it or strike a field, leaving a big, brown spot. When we were at Aunt Louvenia's house during a storm, she put all the windows down, pulled the shades and put sheets or blankets over the mirrors. When the storm blew over, we were about roasted.

One Sunday afternoon Daddy and Mama left us with Grandma Belle, Daddy's mother, while they went visiting. Grandma's sister, Aunt Beulah, was home from Washington, D.C. For some reason, I showed out that day. I sassed my grandma and talked shamefully. I remember Aunt Beulah asked, "Is she always like that?" Grandma said, "No, because she knows that Bennett wouldn't stand for this." That statement brought me back to my senses. As the sun was setting, I knew Daddy and Mama would be back soon. I apologized and begged Grandma not to tell Daddy about how I acted. Thankfully, Grandma said that she wouldn't. A bond formed between my grandma and me that day, and we were close until her death. I loved her and knew I could trust her with anything. I have always regretted the way I acted, especially in front of Grandma and Aunt Beulah. I apologized to Grandma over and over again, even as a young woman with children of my own. Grandma was a special person, and of course she had forgiven me long ago. I got the chance to prove that I was a better person than the little girl who showed out that day, but Aunt Beulah never got to know the real me. She went back to Washington, and we never saw each other again. I remember how crushed I was when I got the news that Aunt Beulah had died.

In the mid-'50s, we got electricity. With each new machine, like our new refrigerator, ringer-washing machine, electric stove and radio, we were ecstatic. Our family got the first TV in our neighborhood, and all the neighbors came over at night to watch. It was like we were celebrities. The first movie I watched on TV involved a little girl who was kidnapped and later killed. I cried and cried because I thought the story was real. Mama convinced me that it was "play acting," and I was better.

After we got the refrigerator and freezer, Mama froze lots of fruits and vegetables. But she still canned some things because they tasted better that way, especially the peaches, pears, tomatoes and corn. My family added butchering days to our calendar. We had separate days to process our hogs, cows and poultry, and we had roasts, steaks, beef and pork liver, ribs, chops and plenty of other meats piled in the freezer. Before the freezer, Daddy had our meats salt cured; afterwards, he took them to be packaged for freezing. I actually liked the fresh or frozen meat better than the salt-cured meat. Mama made link and patty sausages as well as hog-head cheese and souse meat. I used to turn the meat grinder handle for her. Mama even made chitterlings. She washed, scraped and cleaned the pork, washing it inside and out over and over again. Her chitterlings were the only ones I would eat because I knew they were clean.

I helped when it was time to clean the chickens. Mama put each chicken in a dishpan and poured hot water over it, and I picked off the feathers. Next, she held the chicken over an open fire outside to singe the little hairs off before she washed it down with baking soda. She kept all the pieces: neck, feet, liver and gizzards as well as the legs, thighs, wings and breast. Before butchering, Mama put chickens, ducks and turkeys in what she called the fattening pen. She only fed them cracked corn and water; she said she was cleaning them out and getting them ready for us to eat. Nothing from the stores compared to our fresh poultry. Once after a chicken's head was chopped off, the chicken still jumped around for a while.

They used hot boiling water and a razor to scrape all the pig's hair off, and then they hung it from a tree by its hind legs. Then they split the pig down the front and cleaned all the insides out before washing it thoroughly. The liver they put in a tin pan and sent in the house for me to cook. They left the intestines in a pail full of water and put them aside for Mama. Then they would take the pig down and place the head in another pail for Mama to clean and make into hog-head cheese. We ate every part of the pig that could be cut up and used. The same thing was done with the calves, but except for the liver, we didn't keep their inners.

I always stayed inside with the blinds drawn on butchering days. If I saw the animals being killed, I wouldn't be able to eat the meat. Once I walked outside to find hogs hung by their legs from the tree. They had dug out the hogs' insides and were hosing them down. My stomach felt queasy, and I ran back in the house.

CHAPTER 3

Growing Up

The day had finally come—my thirteenth birthday. Where I grew up, a girl's thirteenth birthday was a momentous occasion. It was on that day that she became a young lady, which meant she got her first pair of stockings and a pair of shoes with little heels. Some even got the chance to wear lipstick. I could only hope Daddy would change his mind about lipstick or red nail polish and short pants. But I got a wonderful surprise when Auntie Becka came. My daddy's sister Rebecca lived in Lake City, South Carolina. She bought beautiful clothes for her children, Ruth, RJ, John (June Bug) and the twins, Bobby and Betty. Ruth was a little older than I, and I used to get her hand-me-downs. Well, this time Aunt Becka bought something just for me—the prettiest pair of black suede pumps and a pair of stockings. I put them on and strutted. My skinny legs let wind in my stockings, and the seams never stayed straight. There were no panty hose then, and we held our stockings up with garters. I had to twist the elastic and stockings together and make a knot, and still they didn't stay in place. Those stockings and I had a time. But still, stockings and heels at last!

Mama always made our birthdays special, and we had as much fun on each other's birthday as on our own. First, Mama made our favorite cakes. Mine was chocolate layer. And we had ice cream and Kool Aid. Mama could make the best Kool Aid. She put the ice (if we had some left in the freezer) and sugar in the container with two or three different flavors of Kool Aid. Then she rolled two or three lemons until they were soft, diced them and dropped them in right before she added the water. She was the best in the kitchen. Oh, how good it was and how sweetly Mama smiled when she saw how much we enjoyed it. I'm not sure who smiled wider, Mama or I.

My birthday was the beginning of grown-up surprises. Over the summer, changes started showing up in me. I was filling out in areas where I had been flat before. I didn't like tomboyish things like climbing trees as much. And I cared more about how I looked–the way my hair was fixed or the clothes I wore. There were new, confusing feelings I was ashamed to talk about with anyone. Finally, I went to my mother. She didn't answer me, which was strange, and I didn't have the nerve to ask again. But my biggest change happened at the end of the summer. I wiped and wiped, but it would come again. I couldn't remember falling or hurting myself. When I saw I couldn't make it go away, I told my mother. She told me, "You just got your period," and that it was a sign of growing up. Then she told me how to take care of myself. I didn't like this thing, but according to my mother, I was stuck with it for many years to come. I couldn't figure out why I had never heard about the period. Most of the girls at school were ashamed to talk about it. After summer break, one girl asked, "Did ya'll get your period over the summer?" Almost everyone answered no. We all confessed later, one by one, that we did.

My mother and I sat up many evenings in our screened-in porch after all the other children had gone to sleep. We talked while we waited for Daddy to come home. We didn't turn the lights on because she didn't want Daddy to know that she was afraid. She knew the sound of his car from anyone else's, and when she heard it, I scurried to my room and she went to hers. To this day, those conversations have helped me. One night Mama told me that she had sought more of the Lord for much of her life. Papa and Grandma Sarah and other devout Christians in the AME Church taught her and her siblings to fear the Lord. But she wanted more than what she was receiving in the Methodist Church. During a time when she was seeking the Lord for more of Him, a little Holiness church not far from where she lived was holding a revival. It was conducted by Mrs. Carrie Broughton. Mrs. Carrie and Mrs. Annie Holly were notable, soul-stirring preachers of that time. Mama and her siblings worked hard in the fields all day and then begged Papa to let them go to the revival at night, which he did. She said it was there she got saved, sanctified and filled with the Holy Ghost. She gave up dancing and playing cards and later married my father, who was also a Methodist. But she said that she still had a longing. More than one time during our late-night talks on the porch, Mama told me that the Lord spoke to her in dreams. I remember one dream she told me she had over and over. In the dream Jesus told her that she had to be immersed in the water. She said this dream could only mean one thing. "I've got to be baptized," she told me. She had been sprinkled on the head in the Methodist Church. Yet she said that wasn't enough. I don't know if she asked my dad to take her to be baptized or not. I just know somehow she got word to a local Holiness pastor that she wanted to be baptized. The preacher, his wife and another man picked us up in a pickup truck. I was around twelve or thirteen years old at that time. I remember Mama riding in the truck's cab with the preacher and his wife while my brother Willie and I rode in the back. We drove to a pond behind the old, white church. I was afraid that snakes or frogs would come out. But if my mother was afraid, I didn't know it. That day she was immersed in the water. When she came up, the way the sun hit her face made it seem like she was shining. She cried and praised the Lord for some time. Her dream and restlessness never came back. It was an experience I have never forgotten.

When the spirituals came on the radio, Mama would start shouting and praising God. It was funny seeing her praise the Lord outside of church. I wouldn't let her see me laugh. But when I went to my grandmother's house, I showed Grandma how my mother was acting and laughed and laughed. Years later Mama and Mrs. Mary Burgess, Mrs. Martha Tisdale, Mrs. Anna Dukes, Mrs. Viola Seabrooks and some other ladies were allowed to have a part in the fourth-Sunday morning services. Those ladies prayed, testified and praised God with all their might.

Mama and I grew closer after she talked to me about growing up. I loved and respected her as my mother, and she loved and guided me as her daughter. But we were more like sisters. I told her everything, even about my first kiss. She then warned me that kissing would lead to other things—I couldn't take fire into my bosom without being burnt. "I want you to be a virgin bride," she said. She also told me that if I ever got pregnant, never get rid of the baby because it might be my only seed. Mama's dream for me became my dream for myself, and it guided me as I started seeing young men.

Junior started coming to see me when I was fourteen, but my father told him that he couldn't come back until I was fifteen. He waited three months and came right back. We sat out on the porch swing and talked about wild hogs, hunting and the like all Sunday afternoon. But I was about as interested in him as I was in those things. My mind was on this guy named James (Jag). James was a good looker and popular, especially with most of the girls. I wrote him a letter, which my mother found in a book I had left on the table. She didn't say a word. Instead, she went and got a switch from the hedge bush, came back inside and started beating me. She beat me until my skirt fell off. And she talked all the while, saying she was sending me to school to learn and not to court. The letter didn't have much on it. The main body read, "Roses are red, violets are blue, sugar is sweet and so are you." I was miserable then, but years later Mama and I laughed and laughed about it. I still smile when it comes to mind.

O'Neal came to see me for a short while. He was actually my daddy's choice. One Sunday another guy named Leroy came to see me before O'Neal got there. O'Neal got so mad that he walked up and down the little country road in front of our house, shooting his gun in the air as he went. As far as I was concerned, that was it for our relationship.

CHAPTER 4

High School

I started at Blakely High School in the eighth grade. Blakely was a newly-constructed, brick building with electric lights, an inside cafeteria and gymnasium. It had bathrooms and central heat–that was progress. Our principal, Mr. Cooper, loved the students. And we loved him. We were also glad to see his wife, Mrs. Hannie, when she subbed. She was a nice, pretty, smart lady. I used to say to myself, One day I am going to be a teacher like Mrs. Hannie and smell just like her when I walk down the halls.

I enjoyed school and the work usually came easily to me. We had great teachers. Our science teacher, Mr. Woods, was one. He told us war stories and spoke to us in the little German he'd picked up while deployed. He didn't play when it came to learning, but he made us believe we could learn anything. I loved his class except on days when we had to dissect frogs because I couldn't stand the smell in the science lab. I took home economics and got better at sewing and cooking. I loved spelling, English and math, especially algebra.

Our basketball team was second to none. My cousin LJ was on the boys' team. He could make a basket from half court. When he did, our side of the gym cheered until we were hoarse. He was amazing, especially since he was about five feet, five inches tall.

We didn't carry sacked lunches in high school. School lunch only cost twenty cents. Everyone's favorite was the fried chicken lunch, which included macaroni and cheese, fresh collards and cornbread. Many times I didn't have lunch money. But on the days we were having fried chicken, I asked everyone I met in the halls for a penny. By lunchtime I had twenty cents. We all asked for lunch money before going to bed. When Daddy said he didn't have any, Felesha (Lish) and TJ waited until he was asleep. Then they got his wallet out of his pants' pocket. Many times he had over two hundred dollars. They took enough for their lunch. Those two never got the kind of whippings Franklin, Willie or I did, and we were afraid to pull some of their stunts.

I think I was in the tenth grade at the time. Some girls and I were in our homeroom talking and having fun before the bell. Then someone said, "I smell garlic." I closed my mouth and sat quietly. Soon I walked out of the room and went to my locker. I looked for something that would get rid of the odor. The only thing there was my Evening in Paris deodorant. I bit off its end and held it in my mouth for as long as I could. Then I ran to the bathroom to spit. It was nasty. But no one mentioned garlic when I got back to the classroom.

Around my house you couldn't complain of ailments or act sick without Mama coming with the garlic bottle and a spoon. She grew garlic in the corner of the garden. She would cut up the bulbs and put them in a jar with water to keep in the refrigerator. All winter she said, "Come on and get your garlic so you won't get sick." I had been escaping this morning ritual, but that day she caught me. When I got home, I told Mama that I was too old to go to school with garlic breath. If I had to take it, please give it to me at night. That started a nightly ritual for us. I don't like garlic or Castor oil or any other of my mother's remedies to this day.

During high school, I participated in many activities and plays. One of my best experiences was being a member of the Glee Club. We traveled to nearby cities for competitions. I was also active in my church. I had the chance to represent St. Mary AME Church at the State Sunday School Convention on several occasions. My biggest encouragement for everything was Mama. I don't know how many times she gave her last so that we had what we needed to flourish. Another special person in my life was Mrs. Eva. She was the church secretary and worked with the 4-H Clubs for our local schools. Because of her I had access to many opportunities that otherwise I would not have had. I raised chickens and won prizes and ribbons at county and state fairs. I also sewed dresses and cooked and entered my creations in fairs, where I won awards. Mrs. Eva also took us to summer camp. She was like a second mother to me.

It was my job to fix breakfast during the winter months when there were no crops in the field. One day when I was through serving breakfast, I didn't have enough time to get ready myself. I missed the bus. When Daddy got up, I was getting ready to walk to school. He wanted to know why I had missed the bus. I told him, and he gave me a beating I never forgot. He took me to school battered, bruised and bleeding. I was ashamed to go to class. So I went to Mrs. Davis' classroom in the elementary hall. She cleaned me up. After I stopped crying, I went to class. Mrs. Davis was my daddy's first cousin. Though he never said a word, I am sure she gave him a good tongue lashing. I never knew whether I got a killing that day because I missed the bus or because I was getting ready to walk to school. Young girls were not allowed to walk anywhere by themselves back then. And if we had a friend who got pregnant out of wedlock, we had to cut all ties.

About two days or so after that incident, I got so sore that I couldn't walk. There wasn't a bruise where I was hurting. I ran a temperature and my head hurt. In those days you had to be about dead before you went to the doctor. My mother made a poultice of baked sweet potato, lard and some other ingredients. She wrapped it up in a big, green leaf from a plant that grew at Grandma's front step. Then she laid it on my throbbing pelvic region. The green leaf wilted, so she had to keep changing the dressing. She said the leaves drew out the fever. The wound healed after draining. After a day or two I could walk again.

There was another time when I had a sore on my leg from a mosquito bite that I had scratched. It wouldn't heal. Mama wouldn't let me wear anything but white socks next to it. I wanted to wear red socks one day because my outfit was red. But Mama said that the colored socks would cause infection. Well, I put on the white socks first, then the red ones, turning the white bobby socks over the red. I ended up with red and white socks to match my outfit. It wasn't long after that when girls were coming to school with blue and white, green and white or red and white socks on to match their outfits. I had started a trend without trying.

Fashion wasn't the only reason I got noticed at school. I had always been a fighter. When I was younger, I only fought when someone bothered my siblings. I was used to beating everyone I tackled. But I got beat good one time the year before I began high school. The girl was big boned and had muscles like a man. I was small, but I had a big mouth and was not scared of anyone. After that girl whipped me, I knew I had to do things differently. The next time I got to running off my mouth I was in high school. Again the girl was bigger than I. I jumped on top of her, throwing her off balance. She fell on the floor. I began boxing with both hands so fast that she couldn't get in a punch. Someone pulled me off, and we scattered. If the teachers caught us, we'd be suspended. After that I decided to stop running my mouth.

Summer break was days away when two boys got into a fight. One stabbed the other with a fatal blow. We were standing outside the gym when the injured boy ran by us, collapsing by the water fountain. One of the teachers tried to stop the bleeding, while others sent us to class. An ambulance was on its way, but it had to travel fourteen miles to get to us. Before we got out of school, a voice over the intercom announced that he had died. It was a long time before we got over his death. Many of us blamed ourselves. We had learned basic first aid in health class, but everyone had stood there in shock. We found out later that there was nothing we could have done because the blade severed the aorta.

The boy who'd done the stabbing had always been in trouble. But he had been trying to avoid a fight that day. He put distance between himself and the boy who kept following him. In order to ward off his antagonist, he got a knife from a friend who was in class. The friend did not ask any questions when he sent the knife. The article in the newspaper called the weapon a "Saturday night special." The one who borrowed the knife and the owner of the knife went to jail.

I met Joe Nathan when I was fifteen. We went to the same school, but I'd never noticed him. When he came along the birds began singing, and they sang often. We started going out together. Our relationship grew quickly, and I was deeply in love by the time I turned sixteen.

In those days male friends visited on Sunday afternoons and possibly one night during the week. But he would have to leave by nine or trouble would follow. When Joe and I went out, we had to be back by midnight. Like some of my friends, I had to go out with an escort. My brother Willie usually came with us. There were times when we left home together, and then Willie switched cars later to be with his friends. We got together before going home. When I was double dating, he could stay home. Soon my friends Connie and Ethel and I became a threesome. Connie was in love with a boy named Clarence, and Ethel was in love with a guy named Isaiah. Most of the time Ethel and I double dated with her friend Isaiah and Joe Nathan because our parents were stricter than some of our other friends' parents. For instance, we didn't have keys to get in our houses like other girls who could stay out longer.

Our dates started with us stopping where we'd told our parents we were going. But many times we went other places afterwards. We loved to dance. When things stopped hopping at one place, we went to another. We had favorite night spots in Andrews, Kingstree and Lanes.

I always had my parents' permission when I went out. Yet it seemed as though I always got a whipping when I got home, especially when my brother was not with me. I would have understood why my father whipped me if I hadn't come back on time. But even when I arrived on time, I got a killing. Once I made up my mind–the next time I'd do something to earn a whipping. But I couldn't when the time came. Joe Nathan and I had a lot of fun together, and I decided how he made me feel was worth the pain.

Though there were bad days, the years I spent at Blakely High were the best school days of my life. I had Joe, good friends and good grades. Life was perfect.

I was a rising senior, and school was out for the summer. Joe Nathan decided to go to New Jersey to work. He said he was coming back to marry me. After my heartthrob left, I lost myself in work. I worked harder that summer than I ever had. I strung tobacco until two or three handers could not keep up with me. I graded and tied dry tobacco at the same speed. When it came time to harvest the cotton, I worked harder. I was sixteen years old, five feet five inches tall and weighed about ninety-eight pounds soaking wet, but I picked over 200 pounds of cotton per day. It must have been love that kept me from complaining that the sun was hot enough to make heat waves. Most of the time we met Daddy's goals in picking cotton to keep from being punished.

We used to run whenever Daddy would get ready to punish us. Willie and I stopped running because the punishment would be worse if we ran. Franklin never did get the message. He was short and moved quickly–no one could catch him. Daddy was going to beat him one day. Franklin ran. When he saw Daddy was gaining on him, he jumped into a pond of water where Daddy said water moccasins lived. Daddy went back home so that Franklin would come out of the pond. It was dusk before Franklin came to the edge of the yard. Daddy sent one of us out to tell him to come on in because he wasn't going to bother Franklin. Daddy didn't run after him anymore.

It was shortly before I began my senior year when some words were exchanged between Daddy and Mama. I had seen my father fight my mother many times over the years, but this time was the last straw. Usually I ran to get Grandma, and she got Daddy off Mama and gave him a good talking to. But he did it right in front of Grandma this time. Mama said, "Call the police." I didn't wait for another word. I sprinted the four miles to Foxworth Store. After I explained what happened to Mr. Foxworth, he took me to his house near the store and dialed the police before giving me the phone. I was afraid to go back home, so I caught a ride to my uncle's house in Trio. Uncle Lucius and Aunt Sarah Lee came for me whenever things got bad for me at home, and I usually stayed with them for a few days. My uncle took me back home later that evening. The police had come, but Daddy had run down into the woods. They would not go after him because Mama wouldn't sign the warrant. Uncle Lucius offered to help Mama get to D.C., where her brother Edward lived. She didn't have to keep taking those beatings, he said. I told her I would keep my brothers and sister until she got settled. Mama was a beautician by trade and had a lot of talent. She could start a beauty shop, and it wouldn't be long before she got it up and running and would be able to send for us. But she said no to Uncle Lucius and me. She wanted to keep the family together.

I was sorry for calling the police on my own father since Mama wouldn't leave. I had been trying to help her. But since she would not leave, I decided I couldn't watch this scene again. Even though I wanted to finish school, I decided to go with Joe Nathan when he came back for me. The only person who knew my plans was Mama. She kept trying to change my mind because she wanted me to finish high school and go to college.

But Joe Nathan did not come back that summer. When school opened, I didn't go. I kept picking cotton. Daddy and my siblings thought I was being "smart," for helping without being asked. Mama knew what I was feeling. She talked me into going to live with her sister Pauline and my uncle James and their two children in Greensboro, North Carolina. A few months back, Aunt Pauline told them that if they let me live with her for my last year of high school, I could go to NCA&T College without having to pay out-of-state tuition. Mama said, "I want you to leave home right, so let me talk to your daddy." Daddy agreed, and I was ready to leave for Greensboro. We didn't tell Daddy or the others the real reason I was leaving home.

Mr. Cooper heard about my plans. He sent word asking me to finish at Blakely because I was up for valedictorian. I was honored by his request and by the fact that I could have been valedictorian. But I was convinced this move was something I had to do.

A few days later, I left home on a good note. Cousin Winston picked me up and took me to Greensboro, where I entered Dudley High School. I was three weeks late and had some problems in math. I was a wiz in algebra. But when someone told me geometry was a requirement for graduation, I said, "G who?" With some help from my teacher, I caught up with the class. I didn't know it then, but I had made the best move of my life.

Even though I missed my mother, sister and brothers, living with Aunt Pauline and Uncle James was wonderful. They showered me with love and kindness. I calmed down a lot while living with them. When I lived at home, I tensed up when my father's footsteps sounded into the house. I used to bite and peel my nails until they bled. My father was a good dad when I was small, but he changed when I became a teenager. I couldn't understand why.

It snowed in Greensboro every Wednesday the first three weeks in March. I wasn't used to snow. It was beautiful, and I played in it with my little cousins, Clayton and Cheryl, like I was as young as they.

I wasn't valedictorian. But I graduated with a B+ average out of a class of 229 in June of 1961. Mama and Daddy came for my exercises, and they brought O'Neal with them. I didn't go back home with them after graduation because I wanted to spend the summer helping Aunt Pauline. She was expecting a baby soon. That handsome baby boy, Lionel, was born in July.

CHAPTER 5

College Years

September 1961

My freshman year began well. College life was fun and challenging. A&T College ran on the quarter system then, and tuition was ninety-three dollars per quarter. My parents helped me with tuition, and Aunt Pauline supplied me with clothes, food and a place to live. The people she worked for gave her nice things. The price tag still hung from some of the clothes, and most of them fit me. I couldn't resist some of the pretty, smaller shoes, and for the first time in my life I developed corns on my toes. I liked most of my classes, especially typing and shorthand, and worked hard at them. Joe Nathan contacted me. He said he still wanted to marry me and promised to wait until I finished school. He called and wrote often.

In the summer of 1962, I went home to work on the farm to help pay for my tuition. Joe Nathan came home in July. We spent all of one Sunday afternoon together reminiscing about old times. I still loved him very much. He told me that he would not leave without me this time, and I decided school could wait. When I told my mother I was going to get married, she tried to talk me out of it. "I want you to have a college education," she said. But Joe didn't come back Sunday night as he promised. Monday came and went, but no Joe. I had no idea what happened. On Tuesday my friend Gert and I visited our friend Lula, who was home from Washington, D.C. for the Fourth of July. During our visit, Lula said to me, "You know Joe got married." I didn't believe it, not after all the things he had said to me.

Instead of staying home and working on the farm, I went back to Greensboro, got a job and lost myself in work for the rest of the summer. I worked all day and then went to the movies, staying until the last show. I didn't say much when I was home. Aunt Pauline asked me one day, "Did you see Joe when you were home?" As I told her what happened, I began crying and couldn't stop for a while. In the fall, I kept working and going to school. At one time I worked two jobs and went to school full time.

I went home again the next summer to help on the farm. One Saturday I got into it with my father. I had asked him to pay my brothers, sister and cousins for working that morning. Down through the years, we always got paid for working on Saturday mornings until noon. Then we would change and go to Mr. Cooper's store. Daddy decided not to pay the children this time. I asked him to please pay the children because they all looked forward to going to the store. The next thing I knew, I was trying to shield my face from a broom handle. My arm and hand were swollen the next day, and I had to cradle my arm across my stomach. After we got back from church, Grandma sent for me. She said, "Let me see your arm." I didn't want her to touch it, but she took my arm and messaged it with some liniment. Then she pulled it. The swelling started going down by evening, and the next day I said good-bye to my family. I told my father not to send me another dime because I would never come home to work again.

Usually I didn't know what I'd said or did that had earned me my father's anger. Sometimes I locked my fingers together to stop my hands from shaking while I got myself together. I was known everywhere as a well-mannered, smart girl. I tried hard to please Daddy, but I never could. Mama always made excuses for Daddy, telling us that he was our father and we had to respect him. One day when I asked Mama why Daddy was mean, she said she felt like it was because his father left them when Daddy was young. While all of his friends were still in school and free, he had to quit school and farm the land so that he, his mother and his sister had food money. They never saw or heard from their father again, but it was rumored that he was in Maryland with another woman. I knew Daddy could be nice because he was when we were younger, and he was really nice to his sister's children who lived with Grandma. If my father had been a drinking man, he probably would have killed all of us.

Back in Greensboro, I got a job and sent myself to school from then on. There were times when after paying my tuition, I didn't have money left over for paper. I could have asked my aunt for money and gotten it, but she was already doing enough. Sometimes as I walked down the street on my way home from school, I asked the Lord to let me find a dime for a pack of paper. And He would. Then I went up the street from where I lived to Mr. Bradshaw's store. Mr. Bradshaw let me have the packs of paper without paying the penny tax. I saved money when it came to books. A&T had a system where we checked out books for our courses at the beginning of the quarter and turned them in when the class finished. Working and finding time to study was difficult, though. I made A's and B's in my major subjects. Sometimes I stayed up all night long, trying to understand courses I didn't think had anything to do with Business Education. I wasn't financially able to experience dorm life, but I was content to be in school. I certainly didn't miss out on friends, fun or school pride. When I was there, A&T's drill team was second to none. And did they look good in their Air Force-blue uniforms as they showed out in a square downtown. Everyone tried to get a good standing place. Sometimes it was cold enough to see your breath. Still the crowd stayed until after A&T had performed.

I took the bus to my job on the evenings when I worked. I had to walk a little way from the bus stop. One night footsteps sounded behind me. I was being followed. I ran with an arm full of books till I got away. The stalking continued, and my friends told me to call the police. It happened again. As soon as I got to work, I called the police. I reported what was happening and what time I got out of school each day and the route I took to work. The next day as I crossed the railroad track, the man appeared. Moments later a police car turned the corner. They stopped and talked to him. I did not have that problem again.

Willa D. Turner

College Friends (left to right): Gertrude, Dorothy & Dean

Once I went downtown to enlist in the Air Force. I only thought about it because I liked the Air Force blue. The recruiting officer was out to lunch, and I never went back. When I told my brother Willie about it, he said he would have disowned me as his sister if I had joined. I was surprised, but he never explained.

It was during class one Friday when it was announced that our President Kennedy had been assassinated. A student stuck his head in the door and told us the president was dead. Classes were canceled. A weight hung on our hearts for a long time. I'll always remember President Kennedy as a great man who was doing great things.

I had the pleasure of knowing quite a few memorable people at A&T, including one special person. The then-student Jessie Jackson acted as our campus civil rights leader. Those participating in a nonviolent protest gathered at the Student Union Building, and Jesse gave us instructions. He told us if someone spit on us, we couldn't spit back. If someone hit us, we couldn't hit back. We looked up to him and followed his instructions to the letter. Because of his leadership, we were able to accomplish our goals in the face of opposition. Once a group of us found ourselves in trouble. We were sitting in front of the Carolina Theater on Green Street in downtown Greensboro one Friday evening. We locked arms, forming a human chain.

The police came. They grabbed us, carting us off in patty wagons. There were so many of us that the jail overflowed. They had to lock us up in an old, out-of-use, county nursing home. I hadn't told my aunt what I was doing before I left home. She wouldn't have wanted me to go. Aunt Pauline found out when she saw me on the six o'clock news. People from the city and community brought us toiletries, food and anything else we needed. We had to stay for a few days before we were released. Later, all charges were dropped. After integration, I went to all formerly-restricted places. It was great to have a part in changing history.

Because of my job schedule, I only went to church on Sundays. When I quit one of my jobs, I started going to church on Friday nights. It was April of 1964, my first Friday night service, when Minister Turner walked in carrying Bishop Wells' briefcase. I was in the second auditorium, sitting in the back row with my friend Syretha. I leaned over and asked her, "Who is that?"

She said, "I haven't seen him in a long time. I wonder where he's been."

"Where who's been?" I said.

"That's old James Henry, Dot's old boyfriend." When he walked in, I knew he was going to be my husband. But when Syretha said he was Dot's old boyfriend, I pushed him out of my mind because Dot was her first cousin.

I had finished singing in the choir for Sunday morning service, and I was thirsty. I went to the water fountain for a drink, and I found him standing nearby. We started talking. He lived in Southern Pines, and Bishop Wells was his pastor. Minister Turner had returned home from a tour of duty in the Air Force and had recently accepted Christ. Bishop had suffered a stroke a few months ago. So Minister Turner, who had recently accepted his call to ministry, was driving Bishop to check on the different churches in the Greater North Carolina Jurisdiction, over which Bishop presided as prelate.

On each visit Minister Turner made to Greensboro, he sought me out. I had a lot of male friends between 1962 and 1964. But that was all they were, friends. I always thought of Joe Nathan. I wasn't going to make the same mistake again. Whenever Minster Turner came, we talked, and he witnessed to me. But he didn't take me out. Once when he was witnessing to me he said, "You're too pretty not to be saved." Well, he had my full attention then. I told him about Joe after a while, how I still ached when I thought of him. He listened and said, "I'll make you forget him." I never dreamed how well he'd make good on his promise.

It was the second Sunday in November of 1964. I was sick with the flu, but something urged me to go to church. I caught the last morning bus. I sang on the choir, all the while feeling terrible. Elder Cureton preached from I Kings 18:21. When he said, "How long halt ye between two opinions? If the Lord be God, follow him. But if Baal, then follow him," it was as if someone slapped my face, waking me from sleep. I gave my life to the Lord at Wells Temple Church of God in Christ, 409 Asheboro Street, Greensboro, NC. Oh, what a change came on the inside of me on that wonderful day. Old things were truly passed away, and I was convinced that I was brand new in Christ Jesus. I told Bishop Wells what happened, and he instructed me to continue seeking the Lord for the baptism of the Holy Ghost. Mother Boyd and the other saints said, "Keep on seeking until the Lord fills you." I had to have the Holy Ghost. I kept praying.

Nearly three weeks later during our December revival, I kneeled by my bedside. I promised God I would serve Him until I died if He would fill me with the Holy Ghost. The Lord filled me with the Holy Ghost and gave me the sign of speaking in tongues as the Spirit gave utterance. I praised God, and it was like my feet were in the air. As I said, "Thank you, Jesus," another language began flowing from my lips. I didn't know what the words meant, but I couldn't help but speak them. When the saints took me home, I was still speaking under the anointing of the Holy Ghost. I went to sleep an hour later and still awoke several times to find the Spirit's power on me, and I couldn't help speaking this heavenly tongue. The same excitement bubbles up now as it did when I was first filled. Thank You, Jesus!

After I received Christ into my life, Minister Turner and I started dating. We were both in school; he was a student at Sandhills Community College in Southern Pines. Still, the miles could not keep us from seeing each other.

I lived with Uncle James and Aunt Pauline until the summer of 1965. I spent part of my summer vacation in Washington, D.C. When I came back, my aunt and uncle had moved across town. To get to school I would have had to catch the bus, go down town and then take a transfer to campus. So at the invitation of my friend Lue Belle, I went to live with her and her husband Robert and their two beautiful daughters, Linda and Wendy.

I worked as Secretary of Wise Photography Studio while at A&T, and I was always either in front of a camera or in the darkroom developing pictures.

CHAPTER 6

Single and Saved

After college I received a stenography position in Winston-Salem State University's business office. I was enjoying my new, full life with Christ. But I was realizing I had things on which I needed to work. I told jokes all of the time. Sometimes I laughed more than the people listening. I was telling a funny story at work when the Spirit convicting me that my storytelling was actually lying. Telling jokes came naturally to me, and I struggled to quit. I went on a fast to stop, and the Lord delivered me. I don't tell jokes nor laugh at them to this day. Although some people say that there is nothing wrong with a good, clean joke, it would be wrong for me to tell one or laugh at one since the Lord convicted me. But I get as many laughs out of some funny truths, like stories from church. Once there was a man at the altar. When he heard he was supposed to open his mouth to accept the Lord as his Savior, he stood there, mouth wide open. Then someone told him to open his mouth and pray with sincerity and faith. I had a good laugh later.

When I started working in Winston-Salem, I carpooled with a man who ran the university's bookstore. One morning began fine; we rode together without an incident. But at the end of the day, he picked me up with alcohol on his breath. I clutched my bag while he drove all over the road. I found myself in this situation again and again. Many times instead of home, I found us pulling up in front of a bar. He always told me that he would be right back, and I waited in the car, wishing no one would see me. I couldn't stand alcohol when I was unsaved. In college I double dated a few times with a girl who drank Black Label like it was a milkshake.

After she had a few glasses, she slouched down in her seat with her legs wide open. I was embarrassed for her, and I knew I never wanted to act like that. It wasn't long before I stopped double dating with her and her friend. I praise the Lord for saving me.

Eventually I suggested I drive home in the afternoons, which worked for a while. Then one day as I drove, his hands became reckless. I swerved all over the highway trying to keep his hands off me. I had had it. Robert worked in downtown Greensboro, so I started catching a ride with him to the train station. I took the train from Greensboro to Winston-Salem; Winston-Salem State University was right across the street from the station. The arrangement was perfect.

My brother served in the U.S. Army. When he was deployed to Vietnam, he left his car in South Carolina. I arranged to keep it and started driving to work. One day at church Elder Spruill told me that he prayed for me every morning. I was glad he was praying for me, but then he said why. He said I sped past him on the same curve every morning. When I got Willie's car, I always seemed to be running late. After our conversation, I tried hard to leave on time. I had a great deal of respect for Elder Spruill. What a powerful preacher. When I was a lost soul, I still found myself standing when Elder Spruill preached. Once I told him that whenever I got married, I wanted my marriage to be like his and Mother Spruill's. They had a lot of children, but you could see they were still in love.

I would have gotten saved sooner, but I didn't want to give up dancing or wearing pants, lipstick and nail polish. One day someone told me I didn't have to give up dancing, just change partners. The silent partner was Jesus Christ Himself. When I made the decision to live for Christ, I started dancing for the Lord instead of for the devil. I gave up pants, nail polish and lipstick because I loved God more, and I never missed them.

The saints used to sing a song that went like this:

> This is the Church of God in Christ.
> This is the Church of God in Christ.
> You can't join it.
> You've got to be born in it.
> This is the Church of God in Christ.

I wouldn't sing that song when they did, though I wanted with all my heart to belong to the Church of God in Christ. After some time passed, Bishop explained the lyrics. I thought you had to be born into the church as a little baby. But the song meant you had to be born again into the church through salvation. You might say I was almost as bad as Nicodemus. I rejoiced when I learned the meaning of that song.

At the close of one of our Tuesday night services, Bishop Wells said we were going to the mountain on Friday. We were going to pray all day. I took Friday off from my job. Lue Belle got off hers too and asked Robert for the car. We talked about how wonderful it would be on the Asheville Mountains in prayer with our pastor. We even had Syretha, who had been in church much longer, confused. Percy, her husband, was going to let her ride with us.

As we planned our lunch the night before the trip, we realized no one knew what time we were supposed to leave. I called Bishop. When I asked him what time we were going to leave for the mountain, he got quiet. Then he started chuckling. I couldn't understand what was so funny. He called Mother Wells to the phone, and when I told her what I had called for, she started laughing. She gave the phone back to Bishop Wells, who had composed himself enough to explain that "going to the mountain" meant fasting and praying all day. Of course, he told the story in church, and the saints had a big laugh. I was too embarrassed to laugh then, but I did later. I still fast Tuesdays and Fridays because, as Bishop told us, on those days saints in the Church of God in Christ all over the world are in one accord. I also add special days when we are asked to fast or whenever the Lord leads me.

I met Bishop Wells in the summer of 1958 when I went to visit Aunt Pauline and Uncle James. Their church was in revival at the time, and they took me to service with them. I remember walking into the big tent on Gorrell Street, where Bishop Wells was conducting revival services. The choir sang like how I imagined angels would. Then Bishop stepped up to the pulpit. No one I knew preached with such power and authority. The Holy Spirit's anointing flowed from him. I never got over that revival. When my friends got back from New York in the fall and tried to teach me the latest dance steps, I showed them the holy dance.

Bishop and Mother Wells loved people. They always treated you like you were precious, especially when Mother Wells smiled her beautiful smile at you. After the Lord saved me, I had the occasional privilege of driving Bishop and Mother Wells to Wells Tabernacle in Southern Pines for service. Once I took a curve too fast and Mother Wells gasped. I couldn't tell by Bishop's reaction whether he was scared or not. Bishop had a way of taking your mistakes and teaching a lesson. I learned something that morning, and curves have my respect to this day.

The Wells had a beautiful home on South Benbow Road in Greensboro. Folks from the church loved going over there. Sometimes I typed for Bishop Wells or ironed for Mother Wells. When it was time for dinner, Bishop called us over the intercom. Mother Wells always set the table and made sure we ate with the right utensils. When I eat alone, I still use a one-place setting on the table. It seems as though the food has a better flavor that way. Bishop and Mother Wells liked to outdo each other in the kitchen. Several Convocation Sunday afternoons saw their home and yard filled with saints over for dinner. On Tuesday and Friday nights, Bishop taught us the unadulterated Word of God. On services where Mother Wells stepped up to the microphone and sang, the glory of the Lord came down. I loved it when she sang, "Everything in You Got to Come Out if You Want to See the Lord." All the lying, all the hatred, all the backbiting…had to come out. She always testified to the goodness of the Lord. Whenever Bishop had to travel to preach in another city, all the young people wanted to ride in the Cadillac with Bishop and Mother.

Sis. Deulah Spruill led our choir, a group of beautiful voices which seemed to come from heaven. As we sang praises under the anointing of the Holy Ghost and Bishop preached, the anointing filled the sanctuary. People ran to the altar, crying to be saved. There were many services when the clock wore on because Bishop wanted the Lord to have His way. It wasn't anything for a shout to break out which lasted for about an hour. Those who wanted to leave did. Many of us stayed to praise God and left later. We could hardly wait for the Young People's Willing Workers (YPWW) meeting or for the Sunday night service. Many times we had dinner at the church. Mother Haygood, Mother Peay and Mother Noland would be in the kitchen cooking some of the best food you ever ate.

Sunday night services were less formal than Sunday morning services. The ladies left their hats at home and filed into the sanctuary, ready to give God all the praise. We broadcasted our Sunday night services, and it wasn't uncommon for people listening to our singing to decide to drive to the church. I was told some people jumped out of their cars and ran into the sanctuary, leaving their car doors wide open. Bishop preached like the heavens had opened up and several got saved. When Bishop was out of town, we called each other to make sure no one took a break.

I loved being in church, but testimony service was a little difficult for me. I sang on the choir, but I wasn't as good as others. My friends Nancy and Yvonne were wonderful singers, and some of us asked one or the other to sing our songs during testimony service. But Bishop told us that if the Lord gave us a song, we should sing it. So the next time the Lord gave me a song during the testimony service, I began to sing. I nearly cracked my knee caps together, but I kept on singing my own song. Soon the fear went away. I sang and testified, and the Lord blessed. I found the more I sang the easier it got, and the more I told of the goodness of God, the more He gave me to tell. God is awesome!

There were nights after service when we weren't ready to go home. Bishop let us remain if we got one of the brothers to stay with us. A brother and a missionary named Mother Boyd would stay, and together we went down in prayer. The Lord blessed. Often Nancy would start praying and singing as the anointing invaded the room. Oh, what a time! What a time! We left for home as late as three o'clock in the morning. The Temple was a special place, where the Lord did pour out of His Spirit.

When I was growing up, my mother warned me about many things. She told me that even in the church, not everyone had the same spirit. My mother told me, "Never take money from men," because they would probably want something in return. She also told me to watch what I ate or drank when I went out on a date. She said boys were known to slip "mickeys" in girls' drinks. She said if I ever left my food or drink for any reason, throw it away when I returned. Well, I always followed Mama's advice. But I never foresaw this one experience.

A friend had asked me to ride with him to Durham to visit his grandparents. Before we got out of Durham on our way back, he pulled into a dark area. I asked him where we were and why were we there. The fight was on. I told him if he didn't take me home, I was going to tell Bishop Wells. That didn't seem to make a difference, so I prayed within myself. I told the Lord if He would let me get home the way I came, I would never make this mistake again. The Lord gave me physical strength I'd never had before or had since. When the man saw he was not going to win, he took me home. I was sore in my chest for a long time, but thank God for giving me the strength to prevail. More painful than the soreness were my shock and disappointment. We had been friends a long time. He used to pick me up for school and take me to work at times. The man was an elder in our church, and we had been to gospel singing shows together. He had proposed and given me a ring. But I realized I didn't love him except as a friend, and I gave it back. If I had heeded the warning of my pastor, I wouldn't have found myself in that spot. But I was too close to the situation to see straight. I learned a lesson that night—not everybody who says he is saved knows the Lord.

I thank God for placing another elder in my life. Minister Turner was ordained an elder in 1966. Our relationship took off after I got saved. When we went out together, he treated me with respect and courtesy. Most of our dates ended up at Bishop's house. When Elder Turner visited Greensboro, he'd have to see his pastor. There were times when he'd have to reschedule our date or couldn't see me at all. He'd call saying he thought it best to talk over the telephone, but he would see me later. Most times I understood.

When Elder Turner came for services, we sat and praised God together—if Bishop allowed us. Most of the time Bishop called from the pulpit, "Come on up here, James Henry. No courting in here." And he would head up to the pulpit. We had great times when Elder Turner visited to conduct revivals. We all knew prayer time wouldn't be cut short. He loved to pray. He cried out to God under the anointing. Elder Turner preached and labored on the altar with lost souls for as long as it took for them to surrender their lives and accept Jesus Christ as their Savior.

I enjoyed driving some of the older mothers to church on Sundays. We had some sweet mothers at Wells Temple. One wonderful woman was named Mother Prince. She used to tell me to take my time talking with my friends after church. I also worked with the Busy Bee Club, sang on the Celestial Choir and served as the Sunday school secretary.

Willa D. Turner

Bishop Wells called Elder Turner "his son." He loved Elder Turner because of Elder Turner's commitment to the Lord. One day Bishop called me over to his house for a long talk. He told me Elder Turner was not courting just to be courting. And, very importantly, he approved of our courtship.

Elder Turner told me that he wanted me to be his wife in the spring of 1967. We drove to South Carolina so that he could meet my parents. My family loved him, especially my mother. We were officially engaged that weekend when he gave me a ring. On Monday I showed it to my friends at work. They teased me about it coming out of a Cracker Jack box, but I didn't care because the man I loved had done his best. But they were glad for me and congratulated me. And they gave me wedding tips I took into my marriage. One woman told me to never leave my husband, no matter how mad I got. "Every time you leave, you lose something. It is best to stay there and work it out." She had left twice, and though she went back, she regretted leaving. Another friend told me that she already had two boys before she knew a woman was supposed to "get a feeling." She told me all about that.

When we talked with Bishop Wells about our wedding plans, he was pleased. He told Elder Turner, "You are getting the cream of the Greensboro crop." I was moved by his words, and I still smile when I think of them. We set our wedding date for the fall of that year.

Miss. Willa D. McCrea

Elder James H. Turner

CHAPTER 7

A Dream Come True

Waiting for the Arrival of the Bride
Left to right: Barbara, Syretha, Yvonne, Janet, Catherine and Lue Belle

Willa D. Turner

The Bride to Be: Miss Willa Dean McCrea

September 16, 1967-

My wedding day

This day was one of the most important days of my life. Excitement grew as the hours on the clock ticked away. My friend Janet fixed brunch for me and brought it to my apartment. I lay in bed as she served me. She told me that I was supposed to stay in bed until it was time to leave for the church. So I did.

    I began dressing about an hour and a half before the wedding. Enthusiasm, joy and, of course, nervousness bubbled in me as I thought about the ceremony and a new life with the man I loved. When I finished, I went to get my father's approval. He was changing into his tuxedo in the next room. He stepped out, his pant legs hitting him about halfway up his legs. Somehow he had gotten my brother's tuxedo. TJ was getting dressed at Aunt Pauline's house, which was all the way across town. What were we going to do? It was almost time to leave for the church. About that time Bishop Wells' son Billy arrived at the house to pick us up in his father's big, black Fleetwood Cadillac. But we couldn't leave with my father dressed like that!

By then I was frantic. I couldn't be late for my wedding. Billy called my aunt's house; my brother had already discovered the mix-up and was on his way. He arrived a few minutes later, but in his haste he had left the buttons for the shirt. "Now what are we going to do?" I asked. Billy said, "I'll take care of it. Do you have any pins?" Thank God, we did. Billy pinned that shirt on TJ, and we were finally ready to leave for the church.

I rode to Wells Temple Church of God in Christ, 409 Asheboro Street, Greensboro, NC, in style. My heart cut a flip when I thought about my tall, dark, handsome man, James H. Turner, waiting for me. It seemed as though Billy was driving too slow. As we pulled into the church grounds, the photographer and the wedding party were waiting for us.

Our wedding was held in the main sanctuary. The great moment arrived an hour late. Yet I didn't notice as I marched down the aisle, holding on to my father's arm with my beautiful white wedding gown flowing behind, a virgin bride filled with pure joy.

Mr. James Bennett McCrea and Daughter

Guests packed the church. My mother-in-law to be, Missionary Lula Belle Turner, had come down from New Jersey and sat in the front row. Elder Turner's Aunt Betty, his cousin Odell and other relatives and members of Wells Tabernacle, Southern Pines, North Carolina and members and friends from his other church, Temple COGIC in Rockingham, North Carolina were also in attendance. Friends from all over North Carolina and other states lined the pews. My family and friends from South Carolina, my mother, Lula Mae McCrea, and others, including my parents' pastor, sat in attendance. Uncle James, Aunt Bernice and relatives from New Jersey, Aunt Pauline and her family, relatives and friends from Greensboro and my co-workers from Winston-Salem State University were there. My cousin Sonya of Lane, South Carolina, served as flower girl, and my cousin Lionel McCray served as ring bearer. My sister Felesha came from Jersey City to serve as my maid of honor. My bridesmaids were Lue Belle, Janet, Jean (Chick) and Marian from Wells Temple and my cousin Miriam from Conway, South Carolina. Robert from Wells Temple in Greensboro served as Elder Turner's best man. The groomsmen were John and William of Wells Temple, Willie and TC of Rockingham, Elder Turner's cousin Lacy of Southern Pines and my brother TJ. Deola Wells Johnson was my wedding and reception coordinator. During the ceremony, Lacy almost fell and Marian fainted. But I didn't see any of it. Elder Turner had my undivided attention.

The joy and excitement that filled my heart were indescribable. It seemed as though I floated down the aisle. When Bishop Wells said, "Do you take this man to be your lawfully wedded husband…?" I looked into Elder Turner's eyes and said "I will" with all the love and respect I had in my heart.

Oh, what a wonderful day! The reception was held immediately following the ceremony in the fellowship hall. My new husband was ready to leave for the honeymoon. We stayed only long enough to pose for pictures and cut the wedding cake. I threw the bouquet on the way out the door. The flowers landed in the hands of Evelyn, a young woman from the Temple Church of Rockingham. We were off!

We stopped to pick up my luggage. I had a lovely, pale-yellow suit laid out for the honeymoon trip, but my husband told me to bring it with me. When we got back in the car, he said that we would be honeymooning in the beautiful mountains of Asheville, North Carolina. But we were spending our wedding night in town. He drove to a Holiday Inn Hotel. With him still in his tuxedo and me in my gown, he carried me over the threshold into the bridal suite. Everyone's eyes were on us. Oh, I couldn't have dreamed anything as romantic!

Standing: Bishop Wyoming Wells
Standing on stage (left to right): William (Dead Eye) Royster, Chick and Lue Belle Lawson.
At the altar: Felesha, Belle, Bride and Groom, Robert Lawson and Lionel McCray
Seated: James and Lula Mae McCrea, Odell and Aunt Betty Turner, Rev. Jenkins and Rev. Days.

The Wedding Party
Seated: Bishop Wyoming Wells
Back row (left to right): Catherine, TC, Janet, Robert,
Lue Belle, Chick, Lacy, Marion, James, Willa, Willie,
Felesha, John, Miriam, William and James
Second row (left to right): Lionel and Sonya.

Family
Back row: Aunt Betty, Odell, Lula Belle (Parent), Bride and Groom, Lula Mae, James (Parent), Felesha, Miriam, Clara, William, Aunt Pauline, Annie Mae, Clayton
Front row: Lionel, Sonya, Jimmy, Cheryl and Gary

Power to Overcome

Bride and Groom Cutting the Cake

Willa D. Turner

Bride and Groom Serving Each Other

Power to Overcome

Elder and Mrs. James H. Turner about to
Take Their "Just Married" Ride

Honey got dressed for bed quickly. "Aren't you going to change?" he said. I was still in my wedding dress. I had thought about what my friends told me the first time would be like until I was afraid. I said, "I'm hungry." He ordered a turkey club sandwich, but he ended up eating it. Without me telling him, he knew what was wrong. He said I didn't have to be afraid because he was prepared. He showed me a tube of K-Y Jelly. Bishop Wells had a long talk with him about marriage and how to treat his bride. I took courage and went to the bathroom to change into my short, see-through, white-lace frilled, nylon negligee. After about thirty minutes, I came out and got into bed with my love. He was so gentle, until all my fears vanished away. I can't say how glad I was that I'd waited.

When I was a teenager, my friends would come to school and tell me about their weekend of sexual escapades. Listening to them made me want to try, if just to have something to brag about on Monday mornings. But my mother's love, teaching and trust along with my fear of my father helped to keep me. After I received Christ as my Lord and Savior, Jesus kept me. It was easier to abstain with Him on board when those times of anxieties came.

We left for Asheville that Sunday morning glowing with happiness. James had reserved the bridal suite at the Sandman Motel. He carried me over the threshold there too. The room was lovely, decorated in lavender and white, from the white French-provincial furniture, to the lavender and white curtains framing the windows. The first two days we went riding, sightseeing and motorcycle driving. I must have been crazy in love because when I rode with him, it was his first time on a motorcycle. We visited Superintendent Johnson's church that Tuesday night and ended up conducting revival services for the rest of the week. We churched by night and honeymooned the remainder of the night and all day long. On Friday night the church gave us a surprise wedding shower. Needless to say, our honeymoon was beautiful.

I didn't know how poor we were until Honey began praising the Lord on the way back from our honeymoon. He thanked God for using him in a mighty way and for blessing us. Then he shared with me that he was almost broke when the superintendent asked him to conduct the revival. He said, "I am glad that I paid for the bridal suite in advance." It was then that I recognized what a man of faith I had married. I had asked my father for help when I found out how much the wedding would cost, but he said he didn't have any money. My mother gave me One Hundred Dollars to help me finalize everything. I had paid for my wedding gown, my husband's ring, the decorations, the reception and everything. After the wedding, I only had about seventy dollars. The Lord knew what Honey needed, and He supplied.

We made it to Greensboro that Saturday evening and picked up the wedding gifts Lue Belle and Robert had kept for us. We said good-bye to our friends, and then we were on our way to begin our new life together as husband and wife with the saints at Temple Church of God in Christ in Rockingham.

CHAPTER 8

Wife–Pastor's Wife

My dream had always been to have a husband and children and a brick home–in that order. Well, the day was here. I was a wife! And not only a wife, but a pastor's wife. I had said I would never marry a preacher. When I was younger, story after story came out of one of the preachers in my hometown being caught in the cow pasture. I didn't want any part of that kind of life. But I had never met anyone like James H. Turner. Even with the blessing of my pastor, I sought the Lord about my marriage. The Lord gave me the go ahead, and I knew in my heart that I would never have to experience betrayal.

About six weeks before our wedding, Elder Turner had me visit Temple Church's Sunday service. The church was a small, wooden structure on Church Street with about fifteen-twenty adult members. At the age of twenty-five, about a year before our marriage, Elder Turner had been sent to hold the church together. The former pastor had walked off, leaving the pulpit vacant and taking most of the younger members with him to Winston-Salem, where he started a new church. That morning Elder Turner stood in the pulpit and introduced me to the congregation as his bride to be. Everyone stared in shock. They said they didn't know he was seeing anyone. One of the young ladies told me that she and others thought something was wrong with him because he didn't talk to any of the girls.

Elder Turner was supposed to be the pastor at Temple Church until Bishop Wells sent a permanent pastor. Our plans were to move to Raleigh and begin a Church of God in Christ there. We had gone to Raleigh and put in applications for jobs and a place to live. Three weeks before the wedding, Bishop Wells asked Elder Turner to stay at Temple Church a little longer. When Elder Turner told me, I thought, no way am I going to live in Rockingham. But I told him wherever he went was the place I wanted to be.

Honey lived in Southern Pines and drove thirty miles for each service. Just before our wedding, he rented a room from an elderly gentleman who lived near the church. We had a bedroom and access to the kitchen and the bathroom. Before we were married, Elder Turner and some of the men from the church tried to find another place for us to live. They couldn't, so that was home.

When I went to cook for the first time, I discovered I would have to contend with roaches for the kitchen. I had to get dressed to go from our bedroom, through the living room, to the bathroom–not in a bathrobe, but fully dressed. I knew my husband was a little jealous, but I didn't know to what extent until then. Our landlord was handsome and a widower. I guess my husband thought the old man would be looking at me.

The first storm after we moved in, we discovered leaks in the roof–two to be exact, both in our room. We tried moving the bed to one side, but that didn't work. We moved it to the other side, but that didn't work either. No matter what we did, at least one leak hit it. The bed ended up where it had been in the first place, with pots on it catching the water. We were so in love we could have lived almost anywhere together, but we both knew it was time to go before it rained again. It wasn't long before we found a place–an old, well-preserved house on Stewart Street. The owner moved her things into the third bedroom, locked the door and moved to New York, giving us access to the kitchen, bathroom, two bedrooms, the living room and the dining room. We finally had a place of our own!

When we moved to our own place, it seemed we carried the roaches with us. We shook our clothes and double checked everything as we packed. The only piece of furniture we bought with us was a Hi Fi, and we were sure that's how they got transported. They were everywhere–the drawers, the Hi Fi, the kitchen…everywhere. We got tired of sharing the house with those bad boys, so one evening we got together and prayed. Honey told the Lord, "Let them come out of the drawers and whatever hiding place they are in." And the Lord heard our cry. The next morning we swept up dustpans full of dead roaches. They had come out and died on the living room floor, in the hallway and on the kitchen floor. We never had trouble with roaches again. Thank You, Jesus! We realized that God is able to perform whatever kind of miracle you need.

As Thanksgiving approached, Sis. Leak and I decided to cook dinner together at my place. The turkey turned out all right, but the dressing was another story. I cut up all the ingredients, mixed them in the meal and put the mixture in the oven like I was cooking corn bread. It had a strange look when I took it out of the oven. Our husbands would not eat it, and as we were washing dishes, I gave the dressing to Paps, Elder Turner's big German Shepherd. That dog got one sniff and took off running. I left the dressing there for a few days, and Paps wouldn't touch it. We had a big laugh about that. With practice, I learned to make some of the best dressing.

Our first winter in the old house was a cold one. There was a heater in the living room and a smaller heater in the bathroom down the hall. We closed off the dining room and the kitchen and left our bedroom door open at night, hoping the heater along with our bodies would keep us warm. I usually went in the kitchen in the mornings, cooked breakfast and took it to the bedroom for my husband to eat before he left for work. Some mornings I found frozen water in a glass on the kitchen counter. One day I woke up sick. After Honey went to work, I grew worse. The right side of my torso throbbed with such pain, until I didn't think I could take it. We didn't have a telephone for me to call my husband. But then out of nowhere, he drove into the driveway. He said he felt like something was wrong, so he came home around noon. By the time he got in the house, I was crying so hard he could barely understand me. He took me to the doctor and carried me into the office. The receptionist beckoned him to take me in the waiting room, but he said, "My wife is sick, and I want someone to see her now!" She took my information and promised the doctor would see us shortly.

There were two waiting rooms across from each other, one for colored people and one for whites. He took me in the waiting room for whites, and we sat there until called. Eyebrows were raised and a lot of whispering was done in both rooms. We saw the doctor, who diagnosed me with pneumonia pleurisy and prescribed medication. About a week later I was all right again. From then on I got up earlier to turn the oven on and let the kitchen warm up before I went back to cook breakfast. We found out later that, after our visit, all the blacks started going in the whites' waiting room. The office eventually made the colored section a storage room.

Elder Turner worked at Homeway Furniture Store in downtown Rockingham to make ends meet. He made about seventy dollars a week on the job. His pastoral offering on Friday nights was around eight dollars and on pastoral Sundays around sixteen dollars. When the Lord told him to come off the job and go full time into the gospel, he was reluctant. He talked to me about it, and I told him he'd better obey the Lord. He didn't say anything else about it for a while. One day he said, "The Lord is calling me into full-time ministry." I told him again, you'd better obey the voice of the Lord. He said that he wanted to pay off some bills he had brought into the marriage first. I also had one bill from my single days, and I was not working yet. "As soon as I pay off these bills, I am going full time in the gospel." Some time passed when all of a sudden, Honey took sick. A severe pain came in his chest. He couldn't even stand to put on his T-shirt. I prayed for him, but he was still hurting. I called Deacon Cameron to come and pray for him, and he did. But the pain wouldn't leave. I took my husband to the Emergency Room later that night. They examined him but could not find anything. They gave him a shot to put him to sleep. The nurse said to me, "Hurry and get him home because the shot will put him out for the rest of the night. You can't handle that big man if the shot takes effect before you get him home." At home, he paced the floor all night long. I took him to Greensboro the next day for Bishop Wells to pray for him, but Honey was still in excruciating pain.

It was time to go to the Holy Convocation in Memphis, Tennessee. Honey said he was going, pain or no pain. I took him to the doctor and got a prescription for some pain pills to send with him. I packed his suitcase and took him to the airport. I tried to get him to stay home, but he insisted on going to the meeting. All that week he was in pain. The pain pills that he took with him didn't work. The night before the convocation closed, he said he threw the pills in the trash can and went to his room. The pain racked him all night. On his way back to the service the next morning, he saw the pills lying in the trash can. He said that he started to pick up the bottle of pills, but he decided to leave them there. At the close of the service, he raised his hand for the benediction. When he was telling me about it, he said, "Baby, I saw pain." The pain left his body through his right middle finger and sailed up to the top of Mason Temple. And it didn't return. I picked him up from the airport in Charlotte, and we drove home rejoicing.

As soon as we got to downtown Rockingham, he said, "Stop the car. Stop the car." I stopped, and he got out and started talking to a man. When he got back in the car, he told me the man was his boss. He had told his boss he could not work another day for him. I asked if he was going to work out a notice. He said no. He had promised the Lord that as soon as he saw his boss, he would tell the man that he had to quit. Honey didn't get healed until he promised the Lord that he would do what He said. From then on Elder Turner went full time in the gospel for Jesus Christ.

When I first arrived at our church, some people treated me nicely. But many acted as if I didn't belong. I was a new bride in a new place with no family or friends. It did not take long before I missed Wells Temple and all my friends. After a while we finally got a telephone so I could at least call them. That helped a lot. But with that phone came disturbing things. Every time Honey left the house, the telephone rang. No one would say anything on the other line; only heavy breathing and sometimes music playing in the background came though. I would lay the phone down and then pick it up in intervals and speak, but no one said a word. Sometimes I waited thirty minutes to an hour. After a while the person hung up the phone.

One day my husband left to conduct revival services in Wilmington, North Carolina for Elder Peterson. Honey took most of what little money we had, and I had a little for food. Shortly after he left, the phone rang and again the heavy breathing started. As in times past, no one said anything. Night came and soon it began raining. Seemed as though every drop of rain was coming through the roof. I was not a fearful person, but panic gripped me. I began crying. I don't know how I made it through the night.

At daybreak a thought entered my mind: if I wanted to live saved, I had better get out of Rockingham. I grabbed a suitcase. I was saying, "Yes, Lord, I am getting out of here." I was going to leave my husband a note. Then another thought, as soft and calming as a whisper or a still small voice in my ear, assured me that if I could live saved in Greensboro, I could live saved anywhere. I stopped packing and stood straight up, tears flowing down my cheeks. Tears of joy this time, for I knew that the

Lord had spoken to me. I apologized to the Lord for saying yes to the first voice, which came from the devil. I asked the Lord to help me and He did. My husband had told me not to let people see me cry because they would keep me crying. Well, after that experience he didn't have to be concerned because I was a different person. I was delivered and had peace.

Honey came home from the revival beaming and bubbling over with joy. He said, "Tell me your good news, and I will tell you mine." I shared with him how the Lord had delivered and blessed me spiritually. I also told him that while he was away, Mother Harris' daughter Mamie who lived in New York wrote a letter containing her tithes. Mamie said that from then on, she would be sending her tithes to her home church. He then shared with me that the revival was a great success. The Lord had saved, healed, delivered and worked miracles. Elder Peterson was such a financial blessing to him through the revival. That was a week of change for us. The Lord used the revival and Mamie's letter to show Elder Turner that He was with him and He would provide.

We wanted to build a house of our own, but Honey said, "I will not build me a house until I build the Lord a house." We had been talking about building a new church for the Lord. When it rained outside, it poured inside that old church building. One wall was called the "crying wall" because of the water stains. Whenever one of our homemade pews fell, the others tumbled like dominoes. And when the Spirit of the Lord moved and we began to go forth in the dance, the floor moved with us. The membership was small and money was short, but no matter the challenges, we knew the time was right to build. Elder Turner met with the members, and we started to work towards a new edifice. It was only the beginning of a life where we learned to put the Lord first. The check from New York was the kickoff for the building fund.

One Saturday evening Honey and I had a disagreement. We didn't get it right before going to church the next morning. The Spirit of the Lord fell mightily in that old building, and when the shout broke out, we both wanted to get in the dance. But we couldn't. He looked at me and beckoned me to the office. We apologized to each other and got things right. Then we went back in the service and glorified the Lord in the dance. From that day on we lived by Ephesians 4:26: "Be ye angry, and sin not:

let not the sun go down upon your wrath…" Don't let night or death come before getting it right.

I had a surprise visit from a daughter of one of the missionaries one day. She stopped by my house on her way from school. We talked. She told me some of the members treated me badly because some mothers in the church had Elder Turner picked out for their daughters. She kept stopping by on her way home, and others started visiting with her. I treated all of them nicely, and they kept coming. After a while mothers started calling my house to see if their daughters were there. Most of the time they were. Though the young people asked to stay longer, I told them to go home so that they would be allowed to come again. I had all the latest gospel records, and they liked listening. It wasn't long before the telephone calls with the heavy breathing stopped and members began treating me better at church.

I began working with a lovely missionary, Missionary Spencer, at a convalescence home on Leak Street. The Lord met us in the services there. We had to kind of contain ourselves in the home because some of the people had retired for the evening. But the anointing would be so strong on us that we would shout and praise God in the middle of Leak Street after coming outside. When the anointing lifted, we went home rejoicing.

Honey had gone to Southern Pines. I was in the back room ironing. The Spirit told me to turn off the iron. I said to myself, "Turn the iron off? But I am not through yet." Elder Turner had been teaching on the Holy Ghost, and I had been praying for a refilling of the Spirit. I obeyed and the Holy Ghost got a hold on me that afternoon and would not let go. I ran and jumped through the house, praising and magnifying the Lord. I lay on the floor and rolled around for a while. I sat up speaking in tongues and glorifying God. When I was able, I looked at the clock. It had been about three hours since the Spirit told me to turn off the iron. Honey came home, and I was standing in the hallway, still drunk in the Spirit. He looked at me and said, "What's wrong? You look a little weak around the eyes." I told him the Lord had visited me and stayed for about three hours. He said, "You can have that Visitor anytime." Then he began praising the Lord.

Elder Turner was a member of a group called BAN–Black Action Now–which consisted of preachers in the Rockingham area. They were trying to get businesses to hire blacks. Many times they had found jobs for blacks, only to have the businesses say that the people were not qualified. BAN asked me to help. The first place BAN sent me hired me, and I worked there for three months. The business started hiring other blacks there, so BAN came to me again. They wanted me to apply at a bank. I was the first black person hired at Southern National Bank in Rockingham. I wanted to work as a teller, but they refused to put me in that position; however, they did make me a bookkeeper.

The employees treated me roughly, and the only task I was given at first was to balance savings books that had lain in a drawer unbalanced for years. But I didn't care. I balanced the books to perfection within a few days. They couldn't believe it. The Lord was with me. All the things I had learned in accounting at A&T kicked in; all those calculations, which had seemed hard in school, were easy on the job. Finishing those books helped me make friends with people who had tried to balance them and couldn't. One of my friends had a sister who refused to work with a black person and had herself transferred to the bank in Hamlet.

Like most couples, Honey and I had a joint account. We were pooling our monies so that we could build a new church. I got paid once a month, and I took twenty dollars a month from my check to cover everything personal. Our focus was on building the Lord a house. Mamie was sending her tithes to the church each month, and we raised money through special building fund programs. Bro. Kendall, Mother Kendall's husband, wasn't a member of the Temple church. But when he heard we were going to build a new church, Bro. Kendall stopped Elder Turner downtown to pledge his tithes for the building project.

In the meantime, Bishop Wells was stepping down from the church in Southern Pines. He wanted to appoint Elder Turner as pastor. Elder Turner had set his mind on Raleigh, so he didn't want to take on the responsibility. But Bishop told Elder Turner the work was too much now that he was older. It meant a lot to Bishop that Elder Turner have Wells Tabernacle. Elder Turner thought the people in his hometown church would see him as "James Henry." But he respected the bishop's wishes and was appointed pastor.

When he took over Wells Tabernacle, the members had been used to having Sunday morning service on fourth Sundays, having Sunday school on the other Sundays. Elder Turner set up morning services on second and fourth Sundays and evening services on Wednesday and Friday nights. When he first started going to the Wednesday night services, the only lights on were in the front of the sanctuary. Only a few people sat ready for Bible study. He told them they had to expect God to send the people by turning on all the lights, outside and inside. Sure enough, the service began growing.

It was a second Sunday morning at Wells Tabernacle. Elder Turner was in high gear preaching. Then, all of a sudden, he closed his Bible and said, "You all didn't come to have church." And he sat down. Silence fell over the whole church, and everyone looked at each other. I was looking at him, trying to figure out what had happened. Our choir director had the choir to stand. Only their song broke the silence. They took up the offering, and we were dismissed.

After service I told him the Lord, not the people, had called him to preach. He had to preach the gospel no matter how they responded. The congregation still looked at him as Bro. Turner. Some even called him "Bro." But that day things changed. Wells Tabernacle began to respect Elder Turner as pastor, not just as a big brother from their home church. The Lord began to save, sanctify and fill with the Holy Ghost, and the church continued growing.

CHAPTER 9

A New Edifice

Construction began for our new house of worship. Deacon Marvin Cameron knew a lot about building. With him and the contractor, things began to move. Elder Turner and the church brothers did a lot of the work with their own hands.

Deacon Cameron and I were talking one day when he told me that the "monkey" almost got Elder Turner. He meant Elder Turner wasn't used to working out in the hot sun and got overheated. Elder Turner, Deacon Cameron, Elder William Cromer, Minister Curtis Morman and others labored day after day. The women were glad when the church was finished and we got our husbands back.

Inside the Old Building
Back row (left to right): T.C. Covington and Elder T. C. Leak
Front row (left to right): District Missionary Josie
Jackson and Mother Lugenia Baldwin

Power to Overcome

When we finished the new Temple Church of God in Christ, we were overjoyed. In October of 1970, we marched from the old building on Church Street to the new edifice at 105 Stewart Street. Our Bishop of Greater North Carolina Jurisdiction, Bishop Wyoming Wells, was guest speaker and dedicated the church. Many former members traveled from other states and cities in North Carolina for the dedication and celebration. Well-wishers from the surrounding areas also came for the grand occasion. Together we packed out the church.

The March

Elder T. C. Leak, Elder J. H. Turner and
Deacon Marvin Cameron

Mother Hattie Williams, Mother Lugenia Baldwin, Mother Nannie Mae Terry, Mother Lou Mattie Kendall, Missionary Louise Cameron, Missionary Rosa Morman, Elder Cromer (holding Billy) and others.

The New Edifice: Temple Church of God in Christ
Organized Approximately 1913 A.D. – Erected 1970 A.D.
Theme: "I can do all things through Christ
which strengtheneth me." (Phil. 4:13)
Elder James H. Turner, Pastor

The church would seat about three hundred. But it kept on growing, and soon members filled the sanctuary. We had to set up chairs in the fellowship hall and open the door to the sanctuary. The Lord poured out of His Spirit. Revival had broken out, and the Lord blessed at church and in the homes. Some Tuesday and Friday nights after having "knockdown, drag out" services, we got home and the telephone rang. Someone would say, "Come over here. The Holy Ghost is falling." Then someone else would call, saying, "Come over here, the Holy Ghost is falling." Elder Turner and the saints left one house and went to the next place where God was moving. This all went on for some time. As we lifted up the name of Jesus, the Lord continued to add to the church. The Lord blessed us with a radio broadcast and a choir who sang beautifully under the anointing of the Holy Ghost. Some people came to hear the choir. Then Elder Turner preached the Word of God until it seemed heaven opened up. The Word would prick hearts, and people came to the altar to give their lives to the Lord. It was Pentecost all over again. God drew people from miles and cities around, and a church that had been left with about fifteen to twenty members was growing by leaps and bounds.

Elder Turner preached under the anointing of the Holy Ghost. When he preached, it seemed as though the words came alive off the page, lifting you up in the Spirit. Whenever the anointing came upon Elder Turner, there was a glow about his face and his voice changed. It was something to witness. He never closed a service without giving the invitation for those who wanted to give their lives to Christ. Sometimes the prayer line reached all the way to the door, curving around the walls. But he took time to pray for everyone who came. He laid hands on people, and they fell out under the power of God. Some got up speaking in tongues as the Spirit gave utterance, and others sat up rejoicing and proclaiming that Jesus had saved their souls. The sick were healed, delivered and set free. Alcoholics lost the taste for alcohol, got saved, sanctified, Holy Ghost filled and became servants of the Lord and the church.

Those who were demon possessed were delivered. Elder Turner laid hands and cast the devil out. Those devils came out screaming. Some talked back, saying, "I will not come out." Elder Turner would say, "You are coming out of here." By the power of God and in the name of Jesus, they had to go. When the devil was gone, it was like there was a different person sitting in front of Elder Turner, so calm and peaceful was that person's countenance.

Children and teenagers were also being touched. Many times little Rosa Gilchrist got in the prayer line, tears in her eyes. When asked what she wanted the Lord to do for her, she said, save me and my mom. The Lord eventually saved her mom, Marthel. Cynthia and Denise were young teens who stood for prayer, that the Lord would send their mothers home. Cynthia had lived with her grandmother, Mother Baldwin, since her mom left for New York when Cynthia was about five years old. Denise's mom lived in Pennsylvania. Denise lived in Rockingham with her dad, Bro. Everett. Those girls held on to the Lord, and He heard their prayers. The Lord sent Sis. Everett home, and she became a servant of the church on the usher board. Sis. Baldwin came home, and after the Lord saved her, she served on the Pastor's Aide and as church secretary.

Mother Williams often got into the prayer line. She said, "Please pray for my wicked daughter, that the Lord would save her." One day Mary came to the church and gave her life to Christ. She began working with the Home and Foreign Missions. After Mary got saved, the young children said they thought all that time Mother Williams' daughter was named Wicked.

Elder Turner knew the Bible. When people asked him about a certain scripture, without opening a Bible, he told them right where to find it. He could quote whole chapters at a time. Strange, because his memory wasn't too good in other things. I kept a record of all his appointments and remembered other things for him so that he wouldn't overlook something. It was amazing how he could remember the Scriptures and forget so many other things.

Sis. Nellie Gaines visited the Temple and gave her life to Christ. She lived a saved life before her husband, and eventually Bro. Flake came, gave his life to Christ, stopped his bootlegging and joined the church. He, his wife and their children were members at the Temple and served there.

One day Sis. Nellie said the Lord told her to feed her pastor. She organized some of the women, and they faithfully fed us scrumptious meals on first and third Sunday afternoons. They brought covered dishes to the house, set the table, served us, washed the dishes and put everything away. She wouldn't let me wash a dish. Most of the time we had afternoon services, and she and the ladies would also attend those. Before she organized the Sunday dinners for us, I would begin cooking my Sunday dinner on Saturday evenings so that I could finish after church. She was a great blessing to me.

One Saturday some of the ladies decided they were not going to bring covered dishes anymore. They said they had paid their tithes and offerings and that was all they were going to do. When Bro. Flake noticed Sis. Gaines was not busy getting things ready for that Sunday, he asked why she was not preparing to feed the pastor. She told him what the ladies had said. He then gave her some money and said to her, "Go ahead and feed your pastor." That family was truly blessed for being a blessing. Bro. Flake has since gone on to be with the Lord, and Sis. Nellie has moved to another state. But she is still a blessed person and in the feeding business. She works with her current pastor in feeding the hungry.

One Sunday Elder Turner was preaching a funeral at the Temple Church. When it was time for the flower girls to carry the flowers, everyone got up except Mother Ingram. We discovered she had died in the midst of the service. Riga mortis had already started. Elder Turner sent another preacher to the cemetery to commit the body, while he stayed at the church and prayed for the mother. The family cried and someone called the ambulance. Elder Turner and Elder Cromer called on the name of Jesus and rebuked death off that mother. When Elder Turner laid hands on her, she came back to life. When she came to herself, she asked, "Why did you bring me back here?" She said the last thing she remembered was flying out of that window, to which she pointed. She lived many years afterwards and gave her testimony many times in churches and on the radio broadcasts.

CHAPTER 10

Mother Through Prayer

Before we were married, we decided we would not have children for at least three years. We wanted time to get to know each other and to get on our feet financially. We were not using any kind of contraceptives because Honey did not believe in them. We believed God would give us our hearts' desire.

We had gone through many things within a year and a half of our marriage: the roach epidemic, the pneumonia pleurisy my first winter at our Stewart Street residence, the resentment I faced as the pastor's wife, the opposition towards my husband because the people didn't want a young pastor and his sickness when he did not heed the voice of the Lord. And we had come out victoriously. After the Lord had brought us through many things, we were mindful that nothing was too hard for Him. So we decided that we didn't want to wait to have children. We had our hearts set on having a child and had fun trying to make it happen. When I didn't conceive, I decided to go to the doctor.

I made an appointment with a specialist. After he examined me, he said I would never have children because of the position of my womb. The doctor said my womb was ten degrees retroverted, and in the event that I somehow happened to conceive, the pregnancy would abort itself at about three months. He asked me if I experienced a hard fall as a child. I told him no, but my daddy had kicked me in the pelvic region when I was a young girl, and I couldn't walk for a while because of the resulting infection. He said that was probably the reason why my womb was tilted backwards. I left the doctor's office in tears. We began to pray. Not only

Honey and I, but Bishop Wells, Mother Hallman, all of our friends and the saints were praying. We were believing God for a miracle. Months went by with nothing. I cried each month when it was apparent I wasn't pregnant. Honey tried to comfort me. "Don't worry about it. The Lord will do it when He gets ready," he said. Then one day he told me that the Lord promised him four boys. I said, "Four boys! I only want four children, two girls and two boys."

It was during this time that we survived a car accident. Honey, three or four girls from the Temple and I were traveling down Highway 1 South on our way back from a church event. We had stopped at the traffic light. While waiting to make a left turn, a drunk driver hit us from behind. The policeman deemed the accident as the other driver's fault, and we were taken to the Emergency Room. I had been driving and suffered whiplash from the impact. I had to wear a collar for a while, and one girl had some ongoing problems. But Honey, Cynthia and the others were ok.

We pressed charges. Even though it was not the drunk driver's first offense, nothing was done. When we sought for damages, we found out he did not have insurance. Our collision policy paid for care for my injuries and the other girl's ongoing problems, and a settlement was paid to the parents of all the other girls who rode with us.

At the time of the accident, my monthly period was three weeks late. My period came every twenty-eight days. We had decided to wait another week before going to the doctor to confirm my pregnancy. The inner joy that we shared with each other was special—we knew our prayers had been answered. But we wanted confirmation before we told anyone. The day after the accident, my period came. I still believe I was pregnant and the accident caused the death of a new life. I wondered again and again, if the drunk driver had been a black man who had rear-ended a white woman, would he have gone to jail and been in a world of trouble. But it was a white man who had rear-ended a black woman and nothing was done. That was the day in which we were living. I pray that times have changed enough that people can expect equal justice.

Not long after the accident, Mother Hallman joined hands with us and prayed. The next month God blessed me to conceive. I waited another month before going to the doctor, but I already knew in my heart. We were ecstatic when the doctor confirmed I was two months pregnant.

I was about three months pregnant. We had gone to the convocation in Greensboro. While there, it seemed as though something dropped in my abdomen. I started spotting blood. My first thought was what the doctor had said about the baby aborting itself at three months. Honey prayed for me, and we went to Bishop Wells and told him what was happening. He prayed for me. After his prayer, there was a flutter in my stomach, and I knew the fetus had moved back in place. The Lord Himself had worked a miracle in my body. Thank You, Jesus!

We returned home on Sunday afternoon, and I went to the doctor on Monday morning. When I told him what happened, he directed me to stay in bed for a week and to avoid Coca Cola and pork for the duration of the pregnancy. And I did. I was working at Southern National Bank at the time and went back to work after a week without further problems.

I drank Coke all the time, but I didn't know I was addicted until I was told not to drink it. We had a small Coke machine at work, and I went and stared at that machine every day. Sometimes the only thing stopping me was my husband. I knew when I got home, he'd ask if I'd had one. After my pregnancy, I did not drink Cokes because I wanted to break the addiction. Coke has never tasted the same after being off of it for years.

The one thing I craved while I was pregnant was lemon meringue pie. Sometimes it was near ten o'clock at night when I had to have some pie. The only store that was opened that time of night was across town on Airport Road. Honey would go out and get it for me.

It's a Girl! – Therese Lynn Turner

My first child weighed six pounds, four ounces, was twenty-one and a half inches long. She was one of the sweetest gifts I had ever received. We named our beautiful miracle from the Lord Therese Lynn. Honey named her Therese after Napoleon Bonaparte's wife. My husband was in college at the time, studying the life of Napoleon. I named her Lynn after my paternal grandmother, Lynorean. Since we did not have insurance or money for care, we paid the bill with our Master Card. We called her our Master Card baby.

Therese woke up every two hours to drink two ounces of milk before she went back to sleep. Even though her father was driving to Sandhills

Community College every weekday, he got up for her night feedings. She only cried when she needed to be changed or wanted milk. The first time Honey changed her dirty diaper, he almost vomited. That was funny to me.

She was perfect medically, except for the fact that her feet and ankles were straight and pointed. Whenever we stood her up, she stood on her toes like a ballerina. We didn't give much thought to it, believing her feet would normalize as she grew. We put soft shoes on her until she was about seven months old.

When we bought her first pair of walking shoes, she was still standing on her toes. Her heels would not go down in her shoes. We prayed for her and took her to church. After a Tuesday night service, Honey took off her shoes and stood her on the offering table. Her heels went down flat for the first time. She never stood on her toes again.

Willa D. Turner

Therese and Grandma Lula Mae
(Maternal grandmother)

Therese and Grandma Lula Belle
(Paternal grandmother)

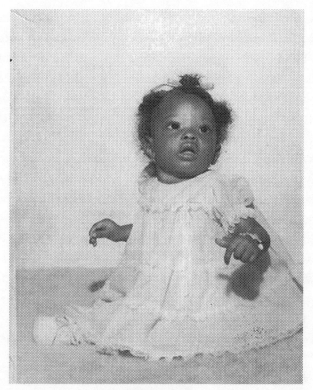

Therese at Six Months

I still thank God for giving me Therese. There were days when we had given our last in church, and we had to shake her piggy bank for change to get her some milk. But we never complained, for it was a joy to have her. When I think of her, I remember chapter one of Second Samuel where God blessed barren Hannah with her first child. God still works miracles! God is an awesome God!

I stayed at home for a while after Therese was born. We wanted to enjoy our beautiful blessing from God. I had prayed to the Lord not to send me another child for two years. After a few months, it seemed I was often sick in the mornings. I made excuses for the nausea. It persisted, so Honey said, "You are pregnant." I told him, "No, I'm not because I have already prayed." We made an appointment with the doctor. He examined me and said I was pregnant. The first words out of my mouth were, "No, I'm not. I have a tumor." Well, I had a baby, not a tumor. That was my first experience where God did not answer my prayers the way I thought He would. I wanted more children, but I also wanted them two years apart. I thought the Lord had stopped hearing me. I got upset and didn't pray for a while. When I finally came to my senses, I begged God to forgive me for being foolish in thinking I could dictate to Him on spacing my children. Fear came over me when I thought of how I could have died in that state and been lost. Thank God for His mercy! From then on, I learned more about praying in His will.

Honey had said if the baby were a boy, we weren't going to make him James Jr. When Elder Turner was born, his father's sister had asked to name him. She chose James after his father and Henry after his mother's doctor. Honey liked his father's name, but not Henry.

One Sunday we were in Southern Pines for service. Mother Harrington invited us to dinner after church. I was sitting at the table next to a visiting minister, when my bottom grew wet. Water started seeping out from under me, and I couldn't hold it. I can't say how embarrassed I was to have to go past our guest on my way to the bathroom. With each step, water leaked down on my stockings. I had never had that experience before, and I was afraid. I had asked Missionary Banks to go with me to the bathroom. When I told her what was happening, she explained how my water had broken. The baby was on its way. My water did not break with Therese until I was on the delivery table, and I didn't understand why it would happen earlier than that. I told her the baby was not due for three more weeks.

Elder Turner had an afternoon appointment that day, so he sent me back to Rockingham with Mother Thomas and Missionary Banks. I sat in the back, a folded towel under me, while Sis. Thomas flew down the road. The hospital admitted me, but I still didn't think I was going to have that baby.

It's a Boy! – James Henry Turner, Jr.

After midnight a hard pain hit me. I said, "Oh, I guess I am going to have this baby." Around eight o'clock on a Monday morning, I gave birth to my first son. He weighed five pounds, fourteen ounces and was nineteen and a half inches long. Honey took one look at him and said, "I guess we are going to have a junior." We called him James Henry Turner Jr.–June for short. He was born three weeks premature, but he was fine. We selected Percy and Syretha Lawson as his godparents.

Mother David worked at the hospital, and she came to see me shortly after James Jr. was born. I told her about how I had asked God for a two-year period. She looked at me, laughed and said, "How are you going to tell the Lord not to send you a baby for two years when you are doing the thing that causes you to have a baby? You were enjoying yourself to get the baby, so enjoy your baby."

June was so small, I was afraid to hold him except when he was on a pillow. He cried constantly for about six weeks. I tried nursing, bottle feeding, rocking, singing, walking and caressing, but nothing worked. He was quiet for Mother Harris and for Lois when we went to church, though. Mother Hallman said he had colic and gave me a home remedy for him. Someone else told me that because he was born premature, he needed a lot of swaddling. He finally outgrew that stage, but he came through sucking his thumb. We tried everything to keep his finger from his mouth, but to no avail.

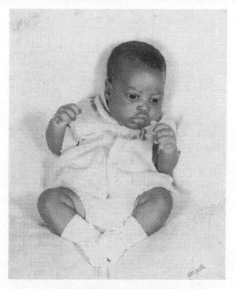

June (First Picture)

June sucked his thumb till he was about to turn thirteen, and his front teeth suffered the consequences. He told us he wanted a moped for his birthday. We told him that if he stopped sucking his thumb, we would get it for him. After all those years, we didn't think he would stop for anything. Well, June stopped sucking his thumb three weeks before his thirteenth birthday. We had to give him a moped. Sometime afterward he and his dad went to play basketball. His dad jumped. When Honey came down, his elbow crashed into June's mouth. When the blood was gone, June's teeth were as straight as we could wish, so we didn't have to get braces for him.

James H. Turner, Sr. & James H. Turner, Jr. (June)

June on His Moped

When June was about six months old, Rev. Henry of Black Action Now asked me to go to work at Rockingham Housing Authority as a secretary. There had never been a black person as a secretary there. The projects for the blacks were on one side of town, and the projects for the whites on the other side. Once a month I went to the office in the white neighborhood to collect rent. Some did not want to give me their money. But I kept being nice and doing my job.

When I went to work, I enrolled Therese and June in Lollipop Nursery. It was a job, getting two babies ready, taking them to the nursery and getting to work by eight every morning. When it got to be too much of a hassle, we got Sis. Leak's mother, Mother Allie Mae Smith, to keep the children. She was a loving, kind and considerate saint who enjoyed children and people in general. We took turns picking her up in the mornings and taking her back home in the afternoons. The arrangement worked out fine.

Honey was riding my brother T. J.'s motorcycle down Armistead and Steward Streets when the brakes failed. To keep from running into someone's house, he threw the bike down. He broke his big toes. He also tore a hole in the pants of his new, navy suit–the one we had scrimped to buy. After he assured me that he was all right, we got ready for church. After the long day his toes throbbed, and I took him to the Emergency Room. The doctors said they couldn't do anything because the broken bones were too small. They would have to heal on their own.

Honey never missed church. He put on his shoes and preached as if nothing was wrong. But as soon as we got home, I had to get him a pan of warm water with some Epsom salt so he could soak his foot. It took a long time for his toes to heal. Afterwards, we had a big laugh about how the preacher was riding a motorcycle wearing a helmet and a suit. He never rode a small motorcycle again. Instead, he went to Hamlet for his uncle Jay's Harley Davidson. He used to ride it as far as Wilmington. I would be afraid for him, but I couldn't keep him off his uncle's motorcycle.

CHAPTER 11

House of Our Own

Our family was growing. A crib and a cot sat in the hall, where Therese and June slept. And we had a third child on the way. Now that the house of God was finished and thriving, we could think about one of our own.

A contractor came to see us one day. He was new to town and had heard we wanted to build a house. Honey told him we didn't have the money then. The contractor said, "I will build you a house, even if I have to build it myself." We only had to have five hundred dollars at closing. Well, in the early '70s, five hundred dollars was a lot of money. But we agreed to the terms. The contractor found us a corner lot a few minutes from our current home. Soon the building process began. God is an awesome God! When the structure was up, I looked around, and the contractor allowed me to change the floor plan. I had fun picking out the bathroom furnishings and wall colors and making other homeowner's decisions.

Our noon-day prayer group met at the church then. Every day construction stopped as Elder Turner took the contractor and the builders to prayer. That contractor got saved and went on to become a gospel preacher.

We moved into our new, brick, three-bedrooms, two-baths home in 1973, just before our third child's birth.

It's a Boy! – Christopher Emmanuel Wyoming Turner

We were on our way home from evening service when I began having contractions. Honey said he was going up the street to see his friend, Elder Sawyer. I told him not to go because I thought I would need to go to the hospital that night. He thought I was wrong. He left, promising he'd be right back. I went in the house and began cleaning the kitchen when a contraction hit me again. I waited a while. Another one, stronger this time, hit me. I called my brother TJ, who had moved across the street from us, and asked him to take me to the hospital. My sister-in-law Yvonne kept our children. I got to the hospital near midnight. They told me I wasn't ready and tried to send me back home. I told them if I was not ready, I would never be ready. They admitted me but didn't pay me much attention. No one started prepping me for delivery until it was evident the baby was coming. By then it was too late. He was here.

Our third child weighed ten pounds, one ounce and was twenty-one and a half inches long. We named him Christopher Emmanuel Wyoming Turner. Christopher was my choice, and Emmanuel was his dad's choice. We named him Wyoming after Bishop Wyoming Wells. We asked Missionary Mary Ruth Turner and her son Emmett and Joyce and Cynthia to be his godparents.

With the size I swelled to while carrying Chris, I thought I was pregnant with twins. The doctor said he only heard one heartbeat. But I wanted twins. I already had twin names picked out: Christopher and Christina. But instead of two babies, I met one big boy. My labor was shorter with Chris– three hours as opposed to the eight it took to deliver his siblings. Despite a safe delivery, diabetes had showed up during the pregnancy. The doctor advised that I not have any more children. But I felt too good to pay the doctor any attention.

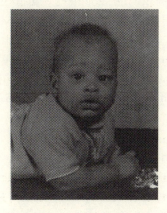

Chris (Four Months Old)   Chris at Three and Half Years Old

I had been working for the housing authority for two years before Chris was born. I was scheduled to go back to work when he was six weeks. But my husband told me to go down to the office and resign. He wanted me at home so that I could rear the children. I told him that I wanted a career and I was going back to work.

The morning I was supposed to go back, I woke up with a terrible headache. I got out of bed and headed to the bathroom, where I fell on the floor. I didn't know how long I was unconscious. Before I could open my eyes, my husband kept saying, "Fight, Baby, fight in the name of Jesus." When I got up, everything was fine. But Honey told me that I was a sick woman. If he had tried to get me to the hospital, he felt they would have pronounced me dead on arrival. Then he said, "Now will you go to the office and tell your boss you cannot work anymore?" I got dressed, went in to work and resigned. After that incident I was glad to give up a career and focus on being a good wife and mother.

Since the moment he opened his eyes, Chris never saw a stranger. He smiled all the time. His hair was red, and his looks were more like a Barnes, his dad's mother's side. When he was full and dry, he was okay. I nursed him, gave him a bottle and then as soon as I could, I put cereal in his bottle to satisfy him.

My husband wanted twelve children. Except for having Annie Pearl, his first cousin who lived with his family, he grew up an only child. He and Pearl lived next door to his cousins. Oh! The stories he told about growing up with his Aunt Betty, Uncle Ariah and their children, Perlee, Liz, Geraldine, Lacy and Odell. He loved his cousins like they were his brothers and sisters. He wanted lots of children, and he wanted them to grow up as close as or closer than he and his cousins had been.

After each birth, I went to the spa and worked out. But as soon as I got a waistline again, it got me into trouble. Christopher was seven months old when I found out I was pregnant. It seemed I would fulfill my husband's dreams.

It's a Boy! – Ithiel Timotheus William Turner

My fourth child was a month late. He weighed ten pounds, eight ounces and was twenty-two and a half inches long. The name Ithiel was my choice. I took it from Proverbs 30:1 and from Bishop Ithiel Clemmons. His dad gave him the name Timotheus from Acts 16:1 and William for his godfather. Elder and Missionary Cromer were his godparents.

Ithiel was a handsome boy with a head full of nice, black hair. Unlike our other children, he was quiet. He didn't cry much. Usually he'd stare at you with a flat expression. He liked to kick, coo and play by himself. He paid a lot of attention to the mobile unit hovering over his crib. Talking to and playing with it satisfied him. After a warm bath and feeding, I laid him in his crib or on my bed, and he played until he drifted off to sleep.

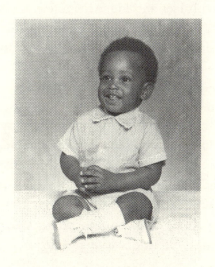

Ithiel at Eleven Months   Ithiel at Two Years, Five Months

One Monday I had just finished feeding, bathing and dressing Ithiel in a pretty, little blue suite. I laid him on my bed while I packed his dad's suitcase. Honey was going to minister in an out-of-town revival. Ithiel stared as I left the room. I got Elder Turner out the door and saw him off. As soon as he left, I went to check on Chris. Chris easily caught colds or bugs and had been running a temperature. Since his dad was going to be out of town all week, I had asked him to pray for Chris before he left. When I went to check, I said, "Oh, he forgot to pray for Chris." Well, then I went to check on Ithiel, who was still lying on my bed. There was some kind of grease on his forehead. I couldn't figure out where it had come from, so I went over and sniffed. It was healing oil. I said, "He prayed for the wrong baby!" I couldn't help but laugh. I anointed and prayed for Chris, and he was fine. Honey and I had a good laugh about it later.

Five months after Ithiel was born, I experienced morning sickness. I knew that I was with child for the fifth time. This pregnancy was rougher than the others. I had little energy to take care of my ten-plus-pounds baby boy. My doctor said my iron was low. Until I could get my strength up, my husband made arrangements for Ithiel and me to stay with Felesha in D.C. He got Aunt Betty to help him care for the other children.

My sister's daughter Ieisha and Ithiel were only three weeks apart. Felesha had a time taking care of two babies and me. After a few weeks of eating liver and spinach and resting, I was ready to return home. After Honey came for us, I did not experience any more problems for the last few months of my pregnancy.

It's a girl – Willa Emell Turner

My fifth child weighed in at nine pounds, eleven ounces and was twenty and a half inches long. Before she was born, I dreamed I would name her Andreka Emell. Honey did not like Andreka. He said it was a German name, so he named her Willa after me. I gave her the name Emell. After three boys in a row, I was excited to have another girl. We prayed before each birth that the Lord would let our baby be normal and healthy. Praise God, she was as normal and healthy as the others had been, and she was pretty. I thought it was vain to ask for beauty, so I only asked for health. But God gave us an added blessing. We selected Elder and Sis. Clegg for her godparents.

Emell stayed healthy as she grew. She didn't cry much and was the first of my babies I was able to satisfy with nursing. Always seeming to have a mind of her own, she could turn over, sit alone and crawl early. Her godparents had one child, a son named Jonathan. They saw Emell as a daughter. They, along with Sis. Betty Quick and us, spoiled her. Sis. Quick loved her two children Zavier and Lisa, but she loved Emell also. She and the Minister's Wives Circle gave me my first airplane trip. She kept Emell while I joined my husband at a revival in Harrisburg, Pennsylvania. I had always been afraid to fly. But as soon as we were in the air, I was enjoying how the sunlight hit the clouds, turning them into what appeared to be cotton. I fell asleep as we glided through the clouds

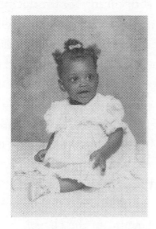

Emell at Six Months

Emell
(At Eighteen and a Half months)

Morning sickness started. Yes, I was expecting my sixth child. I asked my husband not to announce it. I would show up in a maternity dress when I couldn't hide it any longer. Well, he was too proud to care what people said. He had to tell or burst.

By this time many of the saints were saying, "Again? Are you pregnant again?" Some of them acted as if I had done something wrong. One missionary treated me badly with each pregnancy. I couldn't understand why. She and I were good friends until I started having children. Then one of the members told me she couldn't have children. She had adopted her son. I began praying every day for the Lord to let her conceive.

My pregnancy went pretty well. I retained excess fluid during some of my pregnancies, so the doctor put me on fluid pills. He had expressed some concerns after my third child, but I had been all right so far. This time there was more swelling, but I received good reports on most of my check-ups.

It's a Girl – Aprille LaNise Turner

I went to the hospital in throbbing pain. With the boys, I hurt in the front. But with the girls, the pain started in the middle of my lower back, eventually circling around to the front. It was like my upper body went one way while my lower body went another. But the pain was more intense this time. I had been there a few hours, and I kept asking for my doctor. But the nurse wouldn't call him. She kept telling me I was crazy for having so many babies. The things she did hurt me enough that I stopped making noises when the pains hit. Only when my doctor finally came did I feel free to moan and groan. Shortly after he got there, the head came out, but then the birth process stopped. He had to pull my baby out with the help of forceps. She could not breathe well on her own. At nine pounds, thirteen and a half ounces and twenty-two inches long, she was rushed out of the room and placed in an incubator. I was asleep for a long time, but when I woke up, I found out neither she nor I had been expected to live.

The next day the nurse came into my room and said, "Your husband sure loves you." She and the staff could hear him in the chapel, praying, all the way down the hall. She said, "He promised the Lord all kind of things if He would just spare your life." The Lord heard his cry for me, and he tried to prepare himself to lose the baby. The nurse also told me that my baby was born dying. I found out later that the forceps had damaged the nerves in her right shoulder, leaving her right arm paralyzed. And she would not drink any milk. They said if they couldn't get her to eat, she would die. I couldn't nurse her because they had given me a shot that dried up my milk. During the pregnancy, they found a lump in my breast, and the doctor thought it best for me not to breastfeed until they found out what caused it.

I went to the Lord for my baby. Missionary Banks and some of the other saints from Southern Pines came in to see me right after the nurse left. I told them everything and asked Missionary Banks if she had any healing oil in her purse. She did and gave it to me. After visiting hours were over, they brought the baby to me. I tried to get her to take the bottle, but she would not. I anointed her with oil and prayed for her before the nurse came back to get her. About thirty minutes after they had taken her back to the nursery, the nurses came running through the door. "Mrs. Turner, we got her to drink two ounces of milk!" they said.

When the doctor told us she was due in April, we decided to name her April. But we didn't want to spell her name like the month. We came up with Aprille. I gave her the middle name LaNise after Aunt Carnise, her dad's aunt. We stayed in the hospital nine days before going home. That was the longest I had remained in the hospital after a birth. Her godparents were Aunt Betty, Deacon and Missionary McMillan and Sis. Mae Frances Adamson.

While I was in the hospital, they told me that, except for Aprille, all of my babies' collarbones had broken at their births. Hers locked in place, which was why they had to use the forceps. I had had two doctors, and apparently each thought the other had told me about the broken collarbones. I was upset when I found out, and told them that if I had known, I could have handled the babies differently. They told me that when their collarbones broke, the babies were able to slip right out of the womb. Since babies heal quickly and didn't feel any pain from the injury, it was nothing to worry about.

Aprille was still sick when we took her home. We had to be standing right over her when she cried because she was too weak to cry loud. The doctor said she would never use her arm. It would fall out of socket, leaning backwards like a rag doll and it turned dark and rubbery. They showed me how to put it back in place. When I took her back for her check-up, she was stronger and could cry louder. They showed me how to make a sling for her arm out of a cloth diaper. There was still no feeling, though. But I would not accept her paralysis as the final word.

The doctor in Rockingham made an appointment for Aprille at Chapel Hill. We took her there. The doctors stuck pins up and down her right arm, but she didn't show any response. After that session they told us there was no life in the arm. I would not accept it and kept praying. They arranged for a nurse to come to the house each week to work with her. Weeks went by, and the nurse could not get a response from her.

Aprille was six months old. The nurse had left, when Aprille moved her right arm. I could not hold my excitement. I ran to the door to tell Honey, but he had already backed out of the driveway. When he came back, I told him Aprille had moved her right arm. He said, no, she didn't. Then he saw her arm move, and he began rejoicing.

 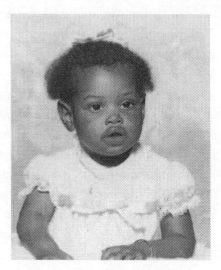

Aprille at Four Months   Aprille at Six Months

We believed God for a miracle on her behalf. She is still using her arm to this day. Thank You, Jesus!

Aprille at Age Five

Therese was around three years old. We were driving to Southern Pines for church when she started reading the road signs out loud. We didn't know she could read! It turned out she could also read some sentences in the little books at home.

Power to Overcome

When Therese was about three and a half, she began waking up at night, screaming. She had nightmares. I would go to her room and talk to her until she settled down and fell asleep. One night, again, she woke up screaming. Her dad said, "Let me go. It's a demon, and you have to cast a demon out while he is acting up." He took the oil and went to her room and I followed. He anointed her and prayed, but she got worse. He began to say, "Come out! Come out you demon spirit in the name of Jesus! Get out of this house!"

That demon said, "I ain't coming out! I will kill you!" That little girl pushed her two-hundred-and-some-pounds dad around like he was the three year old. I stood in disbelief. Finally, I began to plead the blood of Jesus. We prayed and pleaded the blood of Jesus until the demon came out of her. She went limp. Then she looked up at her dad and said in her normal voice, "Daddy, may I have a glass of water?" The demon never came back. Thank You, Jesus!

People came to our house for prayer at all times of night. Elder Turner cast the devil out of them in the living room with the door closed. But he said one of those demons made its way down into Therese's room. After that he started praying for people at the church only. Years later when the *Gremlins* movie came out, Therese came running to me. She said the gremlins were what she saw in her dreams. I told her someone else had experienced those same demons and was able to convey what he saw on screen. She also told me that she used to see snakes all over her floor and hanging from her canopy bed. Everything disappeared when I turned on the light. Thank God, those things never plagued her again.

June was little but strong. He walked and learned to go "potty" early. June was about four and was playing outside under the carport. When we looked, he had climbed up to the roof of the carport. We all held our breath until his dad got him. But June thought it was funny.

June loved to ride his bike. It was late one afternoon when June was six. He had been riding when his dad told him to put the bike up. Honey walked in the house, but by the time he made it through the kitchen and den and into our bedroom, he heard, "Someone just ran over Elder Turner's son!" Honey looked out of the bedroom window and saw a car stopped in the street. He ran back through the house and outside, jumping the high fence to get to June, who came crawling from under the car. The bike was pinned underneath in the middle between the wheels of the car. His dad had to make June lie still. June wanted to prove he was all right because his dad had told him to stop riding for the day before the accident. Our neighbor who was driving the car was shook up and kept apologizing. The sun was setting and the glare blinded her. The other passenger said that she had hit someone. The ambulance came and took June to the hospital, where he stayed for three days. He had a fractured foot but otherwise was okay. We had trouble keeping him on the crutches.

When Chris was about four years old, he had another bad bout of fever. His temperature rose in the middle of the night. Around three in the morning, I went to check on him. His skin was burning. When I touched him, he jumped out of the bed, got on his knees and started praying. He said, "God bless Mommy and Daddy, all my brothers and sisters and God bless Sabbie," then got back in the bed. I picked him up and took him to his dad. Elder Turner put on his bathrobe and laid Chris on his chest, tying Chris and himself in his bathrobe. And he prayed. He asked the Lord to take whatever sickness Chris had and give it to him. Chris was healed immediately. I didn't know how bad that sickness was until months later. Elder Turner gave the testimony of how he asked God to take the sickness off his son and give it to him because he felt he could take it. Honey said when God did as he requested, he nearly died from that sickness. But God!

A few days after his illness, Chris was playing in the hall. I kept telling him to stop doing whatever he was doing, but he didn't pay me any attention. Thinking he was being disobedient, I got my belt and got ready to spank him. But then the Spirit dropped in my heart that Chris couldn't hear me. Chris' back was turned to me, so I took him by the shoulders and turned him around to face me. I asked him if he'd heard me say stop. He said, "Mama, I didn't hear you." I prayed for his ears, and he didn't have any more trouble hearing. I gave God thanks for speaking to me.

It was clear early that our little children loved to worship the Lord. Therese and June were always asking to go to Vincent's church. Vincent was our next-door neighbor's son. He loved the Lord from a small child. He grew up coming to the Temple to hear Elder Turner whenever he could. Vincent loved to preach. He would go across the street to our insurance agent's backyard and set up his church. Other neighborhood children, some younger than Vincent, joined mine to be his audience. I glanced out of the window one day; Vincent was standing on something and had on what looked like his mother's choir robe. Every time he made gestures with his arms, the big sleeves flapped in the wind. I couldn't help but laugh. But this little preacher's congregation was absorbed in the sermon. After he finished high school and college, God called Vincent to the ministry. He is now a real preacher with a large congregation in Raleigh, North Carolina. And he can preach!

I was fussing at my husband about something one day. But he wasn't saying anything. I followed him into the bedroom, fussing. He walked out, but I stayed in the bedroom doing something, still fussing about whatever had made me upset. I thought he was in the den. I walked to the den, still fussing, when I discovered I was fussing all by myself. I was furious! But after I cooled off, I laughed and laughed at myself. When he walked in about an hour later, I still tried to act mad. I asked him why he walked out on me while I was talking to him. He told me that he had already said all that he was going to say about the matter, so he wasn't going to argue anymore. He left until I calmed down. I told him how I came out of the room and found him gone, and we had a real good laugh about it. I learned from then on to express my feelings and then leave it alone.

One day when Ithiel was around three and a half, he asked his dad for something to eat. Honey was cooking and talking at the same time, so he couldn't pay attention. His dad said ok but continued talking on the phone. Ithiel waited for a while. Then he went to the silverware drawer to get a knife and a fork and climbed up on the chair at the table. When his dad saw Ithiel with a knife and fork, patiently waiting for something to eat, Honey dropped what he was doing and fed Ithiel. Many times afterwards Honey used that story to teach a lesson on faith.

On nights when I left the children with a babysitter, I anointed them with oil and prayed for them. Usually they had long fallen asleep when I returned, but I would anoint them anyway. Ithiel was the only one to sit straight up when the oil hit his forehead. His eyes were as wide seemingly as an owl's, but he didn't say anything. After I was through, he went back to bed.

We had planned an outing to the park one day. I had told Therese and June to clean their rooms, but like children they didn't. So I packed a lunch and took the others to the park, leaving them home with their dad. He had closed himself up in his room, studying. Therese and June decided to run away. They got the brown suitcase out of the closet, packed their favorite toys and left. They were going to Sis. Gaines' house, which was about a block away. They drug that big, heavy suitcase down the street until they had to rest. While they sat on the suitcase, they talked it over and decided to give us another chance. They came home, but their dad didn't know they had gone. It was a long time before they told us what happened. We had a good laugh when they did.

CHAPTER 12

Loss of My Child

It was the around April of 1978 when I began having morning sickness. My husband made an appointment with a new the doctor. On the day of my appointment, I was too sick to drive, so Honey took me. The doctor confirmed that I was pregnant and gave us a due date of December fifth. I told my husband, "This is that fourth boy, and he will be born on December eighth. And this will be my last child." As we sat in the doctor's office, I told the doctor of my concerns because my last child had been born with a paralyzed arm. I wanted a cesarean this time. The doctor assured me that everything would be all right.

During the course of that pregnancy, as with others, I continued to swell. I would report it to the doctor, but he seemed to think I was okay. My skin became several shades darker, and I was much larger than ever before. I could barely get around and had trouble breathing. Near the end of my pregnancy, I couldn't wear any shoes. I wore bedroom slippers to church service. Besides that I seemed fine.

Shortly before I was due to deliver, my brothers Willie and Franklin came from Washington, D.C. and stayed for a while. They cooked and cleaned for me, and we really had a good visit. Then they left and went to South Carolina to visit Mom and Dad. A few days later Momma came and stayed with me for a while. It was strange for her to come that close to my due date because, except for when Therese was born, she always came to help out after the birth. Momma came down with the flu, and my sister-in-law Helen came when Therese was born. I found out later that my brothers had told Momma that she needed to come see about me. Shortly after my mother arrived, my cousin Annie Mae called to check on me.

I didn't understand everyone's concern because I was doing okay. I didn't know how sick I looked. And I didn't have any idea anything was wrong until that dreadful day.

On Tuesday, December 5, 1978, I went to the doctor for a routine check-up. I was hoping he would send me to the hospital for a cesarean section. Thinking back, nothing had happened out of the ordinary except for on the Saturday night before my appointment. My husband had gone to preach in Winston-Salem, and I was waiting for him to come home. I became restless. What I thought were violent contractions started. I began timing them and was going to call the doctor as they grew closer with some consistency. They only occurred three different times and didn't last long. After the last time I didn't notice any movements. I thought the baby was so big that it didn't have room to move. I didn't worry and was going to mention what happened to the doctor when I went for my check-up on Tuesday.

When I went for my appointment, the doctor examined me and examined me. He went out of the room several times, leaving me with the nurse. Each time he returned, he used one apparatus, then another, to check my stomach. I had been lying flat on my back till I was miserable. No one said anything, but they wore strange looks on their faces. Something was wrong, but I was afraid to ask. Finally, I said, "Is something wrong?" The doctor threw the stethoscope across the room and blurted out, "This baby is too good to be dead." He had been searching for a heartbeat but couldn't find one. All the time he spent out of the office, he was trying to reach my husband and get him to come before telling me.

I was numb. The nurse helped me get dressed. I sat in the waiting room until closing time while they still tried to locate my husband. I wanted to get out of there, but they wouldn't let me drive. The doctor asked one of the nurses to take me home.

My husband had just gotten home when we got there. He'd conducted a funeral that day. Afterwards, he and one of his preacher friends, Elder McClurkin from Winston-Salem, sat in the car talking, so they didn't hear the church's phone ring. Except to tell the nurse how to get to my house, I had been silent from the time the doctor said the baby was too good to be dead until I walked in the door. My husband was standing in the kitchen. When he saw me, I began crying and said, "The baby is dead."

The doctor told me to go to the hospital the next day for more tests. We went early. The tests confirmed what we dreaded. They said the baby weighed about nine pounds. We asked for the unborn to be taken, but the doctor said it would be too dangerous to induce labor or give me a cesarean section. All I wanted was for everything to be over and done. I didn't understand how nothing could be wrong during the whole nine months, only to have this doctor tell me that my body was in bad shape. They sent me home to wait.

Two days later, on December 8, as I got my children ready for school, I went into labor. My husband took me to the hospital, where the nightmare continued. I was in hard labor for a while. Then the pains stopped. As I lay there praying, I thought Jesus was leaning against the wall opposite me. I thought, *why doesn't He come to my rescue?* I looked at the doctor and the nurses. They were bewildered. The doctor looked at me and said, "Villa, if the Lord don't help us," and sighed.

I had more pains. I pushed with all the strength I had left. Eventually, the head came through, when the birth process stopped. In the course of my pushing and pushing, the nurse said, "What's that?"

The doctor's said, "It looks like her bladder." He pushed it back in around the baby's head. We waited for something to happen. The doctor called for help, and someone told the nurse to give me more anesthesia. Even though they had already given me the max dosage, the nurse gave me another needle. I didn't know if I would wake up again.

My eyes popped open as Elder Williams walked through the door. I was alive! The Lord had brought me out! I had been asleep for hours by then. Elder Williams worked for a funeral home, and I knew in an instant that he had come to get my child. I asked him to let me see my baby. He started to unwrap the white shrouded bundle, but the nurse stopped him. My doctor and husband felt the trauma would be too much for my heart. Elder Williams took my fourth son, my seventh child whom I had wanted as much as I wanted the first, without me seeing his face. The baby weighed fourteen pounds one ounce at birth, but the doctor said he probably weighed about fifteen pounds at his death. We had planned to name our fourth son Cornelius Bennett Turner—Cornelius from Acts 10 and Bennett for my father. I didn't find out until much later that Elder Turner had named our son George, after a deceased uncle. I called him Neal, and I still do when I think or talk about him. Elder Williams said he'd try to bring the child back before the burial. I never saw my baby. Years later, tears still come to my eyes.

The next morning, I asked the nurse how they finally got the baby delivered. The baby had broad shoulders, which locked in place, halting the birthing process. The doctor had to break his shoulder bones. I asked the doctor why he didn't perform a C-section after he saw that I couldn't give birth. He told me the head had already come; there was no way of reversing the process without decapitating the baby and then cutting my stomach to get the rest of his body. "I knew you wouldn't have wanted that," he said. The doctor also said that my uterus was in such a terrible condition that I would have bled to death as soon as the knife cut the womb. When he told me that, I thought, *that's why the Lord took the child before I had a chance to have a cesarean, to spare my life, to keep me from dying in child birth.* Thinking about God's hand in all of it lifted me for a while.

I never had such confusion as in the days following. Voices spoke, but I wasn't able to open my eyes. When I finally got my eyes to stay open, I noticed my daddy sitting in the corner of my hospital room. *My daddy came to see me.* I was happy he came. But then I thought, *if my daddy came to see me, I must really be sick.* I blinked, and it was my husband sitting in a chair in the corner.

Another time I remember Elder Leak's voice saying everything was going to be all right. I managed to open my eyes as he leaned over me. He was dressed in his black shirt with the white piece in the collar. I shut my eyes again because I knew he was there to bury my child.

I thought there were bugs on my bed, and I kept brushing them away. They seemed to crawl along the walls too. But my husband said there was nothing there. People had brought me flowers until the arrangements filled my room—there were so many, the nurse brought in extra tables to display them. I constantly thought my room was a cemetery. When visitors left, I mustered whatever strength I had and put all the flowers on the floor so that I couldn't see them while lying in the bed. Every time people came, they would say, "I wonder why all these flowers are on the floor?" and put them back on the tables. But as soon as everyone had gone, I put them down again.

No one knew yet, but a great fear had come over me. Later in the week as my strength grew, I tried to read the Bible. Psalms 27:1 came to me in the midst of my tormenting fear: "The Lord is my light and my salvation; whom shall I fear …" I knew there was more to that scripture, but I couldn't remember what. I found it in the Bible, but it wouldn't stick in my mind. I had to read it over and over again. Before I went to the hospital, I could quote scripture verse after verse. But then I couldn't remember much of anything.

My blood pressure was too high for the doctor to release me. I wanted out of there. I thought my fear had to do with the hospital and what went on upstairs. Whenever I closed my eyes, the delivery room and the big lights over the operating table appeared. After all that I had been through, I still had to have surgery. I couldn't help believing that I would die on the operating table. My body shook as they prepped me. A nurse said, "She's going into shock," and someone gave me another shot. Soon I lost consciousness. The cold blade of the surgeon's knife touched my skin as I was falling asleep. It reminded me of experiences I'd had when I was a little girl. Once I had grabbed for an open can and sliced my thumb wide open. Another time I jumped on an opened hash can while playing outside. My bare right foot was almost severed in two. I still have the scars from both accidents. The pain came back as the doctor's blade cut into me. When I opened my eyes, I knew Jesus had brought me through. Thank You, Jesus!

I persuaded the doctor to let me go home on the seventh day. Six other times I had gone home with a new life. This time I had nothing but a frail, half-crazy, sick body. My discharge day was a hard one. I thought being at home would help me, but things were worse. Again, bugs crawled everywhere. Cynthia kept saying, "Momma, there is nothing there." There were days when a lady dressed in a white chiffon dress walked down my hallway. No one could see her but me. I prayed but kept seeing things that weren't there. I was too tired to do much of anything, and I didn't remember much for the next seven months. It was like I was in and out of reality.

About three weeks after I had come home, one of our friends, Elder Moore from Virginia, called. He'd had a dream about the baby and me and was calling to see if everything was all right. After I told him what had happened, he told me he would be on his way as soon as he hung up the phone. He was there in a matter of hours.

Elder Moore gave me his testimony. He had lost an infant child long ago, when he lived in the Virgin Islands. As I listened to how the Lord brought him through, I started to feel hope for the first time since the ordeal began. For many nights I had struggled with fear and hopelessness. I prayed and tried to read my Bible, but the depression persisted. When I got on my knees the night Elder Moore talked with me, my eyes closed, a light appeared, no bigger than a pin's head. It was shining bright in the midst of the darkness. To me it was the ray of hope I needed. The fear left, and from then on I stopped hallucinating.

My recovery finally seemed to start. My body slowly gained strength. But when I was strong enough to go back to church, I was startled that I didn't know who the people were, people I had worshipped with for eleven years. I didn't want anyone to know that I couldn't remember names, so I smiled and tried not to say much. But worse than that, I couldn't remember anything from the time Elder Turner got up to preach until after he sat down. I would be sitting there when a ball of smoke shaped like a Frisbee, turning and turning, came towards the left side of my head. When it got to my head, I wouldn't be able to remember anything else until it came out the left side of my head, spinning as it went away. I thought people would laugh if they knew what was happening, so I didn't tell anyone, not even my husband. I thought I was going crazy.

I battled and battled this thing for months. I knew it was the devil because it only happened when it was time for the preached Word of God. One day as I sat in service, it started coming. I said to myself, *Oh no, not this time.* I got up and praised the Lord, even though my husband had just got up to preach. You could say I took the service for a while. But I got my deliverance that day, and, thank God, it has never happened again. When I gave my testimony, people had the reaction I expected. Some laughed and some were skeptical. I think my husband was embarrassed. Sis. Cohens, who was a nurse, smiled and said, "You didn't see that. You just thought you did." I didn't say much about it afterwards. But whether others believe or not, I know how the Lord delivered me through prayer and praise.

It was July, seven months after the death of my child, when I found out I had to re-live the whole event. My husband sat me down for a serious talk. The reason I couldn't remember anything, he said, was because I didn't actually go through the experience. It was so painful that I had blocked it out of my mind. If I wanted my memory back, I would have to go through the ordeal again, only this time I had to go through it the right way. He said I had to face what happened and accept it, even though I didn't understand why. I had to turn from disappointment because God didn't work things out the way I had planned and praise Him for all things and in all things, completely trusting that it worked together for my good.

I can't put into words how difficult all of this was for me. But I wanted the power to overcome. And gradually the Lord granted it. When I went to the State Ministers and Workers Conference, I couldn't remember how to get down to Greenville, though I had driven down there many, many times during the years. Cynthia drove for me that day. I was telling her what I thought was the right way, but in reality it was all wrong. At the conference many people stopped to tell me how they had prayed for me during the time I was sick and that they were glad to see me. I would thank them and smile. After they left, I asked Cynthia about them. She would tell me who each person was, and it would come back to me.

Shortly after that talk with my husband, I began to go back through the experience. It was like it had just happened. But through faith, prayer and fasting, I made it through each stage. Most of my memory returned. There were some things I didn't remember about my childhood, but my mother was able to fill in the gaps. There were other things friends have helped me remember. I still cannot remember where to find scriptures the way I used to do. But I thank God for remembering the scriptures themselves, and I can always look them up in the Word.

Even though I knew I was in terrible condition, my mind had been too foggy for me to comprehend my body's dangerous state. One evening, about four months after I left the hospital, my husband and I were talking. He began sniffing me all over my body. I asked him why. He told me that I had carried the smell of death from the time before I went to the hospital until that day. He told me about the times when, though he knew I wanted him there with me, he couldn't stand the smell and had to leave the house. Death had a grip on me but had loosed its hold. He looked at me and said,

"You're going to live." It was the power of God that broke that grip in April of 1979. Praise the Lord!

It was during our talk that he began to tell me the interpretation of my dreams. I would always have dreams, but I couldn't interpret them. My husband interpreted, and things would work out exactly as he'd said. But he hadn't said anything about the three dreams I had during the last stages of my pregnancy. In the first dream I was all dressed in white, marching down the aisle to get married. As I was going down the aisle, I looked down at my stomach, which swelled with child, and then up to the front of the church, where this handsome man waited for me. As I got closer to him, his whole countenance changed. A big, greasy-looking face, darker than charcoal, appeared. I looked up and said, "I can't marry him," and started back down the aisle towards the door. Then I woke up.

Another night I dreamed I was in a place near a beautiful garden, which was enclosed with a white fence. I had seen that garden before in a vision after Aprille was born and made the choice not to go inside the gate. As I approached the garden, I noticed "Granny," Mother Allie Mae Smith, who had been dead for some time. She stood among the beautiful flowers and beckoned for me to come on in the garden. But I kept shaking my head, no, because I knew in my dream that she was dead. She reached across the fence and tried to pull me. Her grip was tight, and we struggled before I knocked her down and got away.

I was disturbed by that dream because Granny was such a loving, God-fearing church mother. When I told my husband how sorry I was for hitting Granny in my dream, he said, "You were supposed to hit her because in your dream she represented death."

In the last dream I was in trouble, and a foreigner was praying for me. My doctor was a foreigner, but I didn't make the connection. Elder Turner reminded me about the dreams and told me what each meant. One dream dealt with my child and me facing death. One dealt with my conquering death and the other dealt with the foreigner, my doctor, praying for help. My husband said, "Now do you see why I wouldn't interpret your dreams?"

The same morning we were talking about my dreams, I asked my husband to take me to see Sis. Allred. The Lord had given me a message for her when I first got pregnant. When He gave the message to me, I was having terrible morning sickness and kept missing noon-day prayer. One day, even though I still had morning sickness, I got off the couch and went to prayer. I was surprised that she wasn't there that day. You could always count on Sis. Allred showing up for prayer. When Sis. Allred wasn't at church that Friday night or that Sunday, I asked Elder Turner about her. He informed me that she no longer went to the Temple. She had gone with her son-in-law, Elder Legrand, who had started a new Church of God in Christ in Hamlet, North Carolina. I didn't call her or say anything to her because I didn't want her to think that I was trying to get her to come back. I forgot about the message for months, until that morning when Honey and I were talking. It came back to me with an urgency to tell her. So we went to her house, and I gave her the message. We had always been good friends, but she was upset with me that day. She said, "You should have told me!" She had said to someone, "Sis. Turner shouldn't be suffering like that. I don't understand it." Then she told me I suffered the way I did because I didn't obey the Lord. I apologized for not telling her before then. We talked for a while, and before we left Elder Turner laid hands on her as we prayed.

When I went home, I pondered in my heart what Sis. Allred had said. I repented to God for not telling her what He said when He said it. Afterwards, I did not hesitate when the Lord gave me a message for someone. If the nature of the message required, I would get permission from the pastor. There was one occasion when the pastor said the person would not accept it coming from me. I didn't want to get in trouble with God, so I asked him what to do. He said he would release me, take any consequences that may occur and deliver the message.

After I was able to travel again, I went with my husband to Wells Tabernacle in Southern Pines every other Sunday morning. During service, I slipped off and went to the cemetery where my son was buried. I cried and talked to that dead baby. Maybe my burden would have been lighter if I had been able to see my child. My husband told me to stop going or else I would end up in the cemetery myself. Shortly after he told me that, the Lord let me see my son. We were staying at a motel in Southern Pines during the District Meeting, and I had a dream about him. I knew he was mine because he looked just like Chris. He was playing with other children in a beautiful, peaceful place. I was standing there looking at him from a distance, trying to get his attention, but he was too busy playing to look at me. After that my burden lifted. God is loving, merciful and kind!

My surgery left me with a hernia, which caused me excruciating pain from time to time for about two years. I couldn't do much of anything. No lifting, no sweeping, no vacuuming, nothing strenuous at all, or it would trigger the pain. After vacuuming one night, the pain was so severe that I crawled on the floor, crying and praying that the Lord would heal me. Well, He did that night, over thirty-eight years ago. That hard spot in my stomach is still there, but it doesn't bother me at all. Thank You, Jesus!

I was on eight pills a day for various ailments. As I took each of them, I prayed for healing so that I would not have to depend on them for my health. In 1980, I began to get sick. I couldn't figure out why, so I went to the doctor. He told me it was the medication. I couldn't take any more of those pills because I didn't need them. I was healed. Thank You, Jesus!

Years later I thought about how my husband had begged God for my life after Aprille was born, and how I begged God for Aprille's life. The Lord turned things around then. It came to me that God took little Neal "George" before I had the chance to beg for him. Surely I would have, and He had other plans. Besides the six children with whom the Lord blessed us, there were others who spent time in our home and whose lives we touched.

Cynthia was around nine years old when I met her. When Elder Turner went to Rockingham to pastor, she stole his heart. He would come to visit and tell me about her, saying, "There is this pretty, little, big-eyed girl in the church that I want you to meet. You will love her. She looks like you." After we got married and settled in Rockingham, I got the chance to meet Cynthia. Just as he said, I loved her. Cynthia lived with her grandmother, Mother Lugenia Baldwin, whom she loved very much. Mother Baldwin was a church mother at the Temple. The widow of Deacon Baldwin, she was a sweet, saved woman who was rearing Cynthia and her three siblings. Cynthia was a timid little girl who was looking for a mother's and father's love. We didn't have children yet, so we had all the love to give. Mother Baldwin allowed us to share Cynthia. She grew up in the church, and when she was old enough, Cynthia drove Elder Turner to appointments. He did a lot of "read on" preaching and teaching, and she would read for him. She also helped me out around the house and with the children. When I couldn't get out, she was my legs, running errands until I got back on my feet. When our children came along, Cynthia became big sister to them. "Sabbie," now Evangelist Little, is still Big Sis to them.

We taught our children not to fight, and sometimes other children took advantage of them. One day when Therese was in elementary school, she came home with dried tears on her face. I asked her why she had been crying. At first she wasn't going to tell me that one of her classmates was pushing her down about every day. Her dad taught her a lesson on love. He also showed her how to position her legs so that if someone tried to push her down, he wouldn't. She came home, all excited, the next day. She told us that when her classmate tried, he couldn't get her down.

June came home several days with either a bloody nose or a bloody mouth. He was being bullied on the bus. The bus stop was right in front of our house, and I met it one day. June got off with a bloody face; I didn't know whether it was coming from his nose or mouth. I jumped on the bus and asked the bus driver who did it. He didn't know. I asked the students. They sat there with wide eyes. Then someone pointed to the student who did it. I asked where the child lived. No one said a word, so I took the child off the bus, telling them to tell the child's mother to come to my house.

I took the child in the house and fixed a snack. The child and my children all ate together. After the fact, I knew I was wrong for taking that child off the bus. Later, the mother came to our house along with Sis. Lelia B., one of the members of our church, who knew her. I apologized and we talked about the continuous bullying. We parted on good terms, but it was not over with me. Even though I had asked God to forgive me, it took me a long time to forgive myself. I overreacted that day.

Honey came home with a new bicycle he had bought for exercise. One day I noticed he came home pushing the bike. But he didn't say anything. A few days later, Sis. Legrand called, asking if Elder Turner got hurt when the bike threw him. She had been at the beauty shop on Leak Street and had seen it all. My husband wasn't about to tell me that. When I asked him about it, he said he wasn't hurt and that it threw him when he was changing gears. Honey never rode that bike again. He gave it to Bro. Cameron.

CHAPTER 13

Parenting Others

Joyce came to live with us in 1973. She had graduated from high school and was living with friends in another city. She had not found a job yet. When we were preparing to go to the National Holy Convocation in Memphis, Tennessee, we asked her to keep the children for us. She did, and after we returned home, she continued to live with us. She found a job and began taking classes at the community college. We helped her get a car so she would have transportation from school and work. She became part of our family and stayed until she met a fine young man and decided to marry.

Elder Best, who was from Greenville, North Carolina, came to live with us also. Not only did he love Elder Turner's preaching and teaching, he enjoyed being around Elder Turner. He took in Elder Turner's every word, whether he was teaching spiritual or natural things. Elder Turner used any chance to teach all that he could. He was like a father to Elder Best.

Joe, who was from Connecticut, came to live with us in 1976. He had met Jackie, one of the members from the Temple Church, when she moved to Connecticut to live with relatives. He met her at church and fell in love with her. When she moved back to Rockingham, he followed her. He lived with us until he and Jackie got married in 1977. Elder Turner was getting a lot of practice at having a teenager or young adult in the house. We really didn't have any problems out of them. Elder Turner always gave the young people a curfew and, for the most part, they kept it. When it got close to his wedding day, Joe bought a trailer in Hamlet,

North Carolina, in preparation for his bride. Joe didn't make his curfew one night, so Elder Turner got upset. He was pacing the floor, belching. When Elder Turner got upset about something, he belched repeatedly. I told him not to worry about Joe because Joe was a grown man. He paced a little while longer. Then he decided to go out and find him. When they came in, I asked where he had found Joe. Elder Turner said Joe was at the trailer. He had already told Joe that he couldn't live in the trailer until he got married. Elder Turner was not going to give the devil the opportunity to tempt the young couple.

Victor was stationed at Fort Bragg, and he came to stay on weekends. He liked Jeanie, one of the young ladies from our church. One night he had walked Jeanie home and was almost late getting back. His feet were hitting the pavement loud enough for us to hear them as he ran up the street to the house. He had about two minutes to spare, but he made his curfew that night and all the other times that he came.

Superintendent and Mrs. James H. Turner

Left to right (front row): Aprille, Ithiel & Chris
Left to right (center): Willa Dean, Emell & James Jr.
Left to right (back row): James Sr. & Therese

CHAPTER 14

Founder of Churches

The Lord continually blessed the churches. We were at the Temple on first and third Sunday mornings, second and fourth Sunday nights and on Tuesday and Friday nights for services. We were at Wells Tabernacle for service on second and fourth Sunday mornings, first and third Sunday nights and on Wednesday nights. Elder Turner preached under the anointing of the Holy Ghost, and the Lord was saving souls, filling with the Holy Ghost, healing the sick, setting those who were bound free and adding to the church.

Bishop Wells appointed Elder Turner Superintendent of the Asheboro District. At that time there was only one small church in the district. It was in Biscoe, North Carolina, and the pastor and first lady were Elder and Missionary David. Elder Turner had preached for Elder David before and was looking forward to building up the district. In our last service in that little building, the Spirit of the Lord filled the place. Sometime later Elder Turner went by to check on the church, only to find it had been closed, the pastor having left to start a new church in Wallace, North Carolina.

Elder Turner wanted to establish a Church of God in Christ in Asheboro, North Carolina. His uncle James, his aunt and their two children, as well as his cousin Margaret and her husband and their children, lived in Asheboro. He went up one weekend to look around for a building to hold services. He was supposed to be back for Sunday morning service at the Temple. But he called Saturday evening to let me know that the Lord had laid it on his heart to stay with his uncle James and go to church with them the next day. He called me collect so that the cost would be charged to our phone and not to his uncle's phone. He wanted me to tell his assistant to go to the radio station in the morning and do the broadcast. When I told Elder Cromer, he told me that he didn't do broadcasts. I called Elder Turner back and gave him Elder Cromer's response. He told me to do the broadcast. I was to take a record with me to the station and give it to the DJ. The DJ would give me cues as to when to come in with the announcements, the second song and the message. I wasn't a missionary at that time, and I was nervous about doing it. But I brought the Word on a live broadcast that Sunday morning.

Six months later, Uncle James died of an erupted appendix at the age of thirty-five. Elder Turner was very saddened by his uncle's death but was grateful that he had followed the Lord's leading. He witnessed to his uncle and family while he was there and took them to church.

A few months later, the Lord led Elder Turner back to Asheboro for a revival. The Lord saved souls, filled with the Holy Ghost and poured out His blessing on the people. At the closing of the revival, Elder Turner established the Asheboro Church of God in Christ. He got permission for the Temple Church and Wells Tabernacle to be part of the Asheboro District, and he chose Mother Mary Hallman to be his District Missionary. He was pastor of the church until Elder Best got married. Then Elder Turner turned the church over to him. Elder Best later relocated the church to Randleman, North Carolina and renamed it Acts Temple. It grew for a while then folded. Elder Best and his wife moved to Connecticut, and now he is Bishop Best.

The Lord led Elder Turner to Troy to establish a church in 1976. Sis. Costella Marshall had just moved into her new home, and she let him use her old house for services. The Lord sent revival. Elder Turner preached under the anointing of the Holy Ghost, and people were saved, blessed and set free. He was up teaching one night when suddenly he stopped. He told everyone to call on the name of Jesus. The saints began saying, "Jesus! Jesus! Jesus!" All of a sudden the door flew open. People who had been outside the door fell on the floor and crawled to the altar. When they got up, they said they had been sent there to shut down the revival. Some of the people in Troy did not want a Church of God in Christ in their town. But the church was organized in the home of Bro. and Sis. Joseph Jones that same year. Elder Turner named the church Revival Temple Church of God in Christ. The church was established, and the Lord continued to bless it. Sis. Doris Martin was the first member. Now, years later, she is the Asheboro District Missionary. Sis. Flora Horne, now Sis. Moses, followed her along, with many other wonderful people, including Bro. Jones, Sis. Jones, their daughter and grandchildren. Sis Flora became church secretary and still serves in that capacity. Minister Clegg was a member of the church in Southern Pines, and he served as assistant pastor in Troy. Those were some of the sweetest people that I had ever met. After Minister Clegg was ordained, Elder Turner turned the church over to him as pastor. Elder Clegg served the church until his death. From its infancy till today, Revival Temple has lived up to its name, for its services are like a revival every time. And the people are still sweet. Elder Paul Whitley has been the pastor for the past twenty years.

The Lord sent Elder Turner to Hoffman to establish a Church of God in Christ. So he pitched his gospel tent and preached the Word of God with power and authority. There he met opposition again. The authorities of that town said there had never been a holiness church in Hoffman, and there never would be one. Elder Turner told them, "Yes there will be." He conducted revival services under the "Big Top," where the Lord blessed in great ways. When it got too cold to hold service under the tent, Mother Hart opened up her home. The Spirit of the Lord met us and continued to save and move on the people. Elder Turner named the church Hoffman Church of God in Christ. After acquiring land to build a house of God, he turned the church over to Elder Quick. I still have those land papers filed away in a folder labeled "The Hoffman Papers." Elder Quick built a church from the ground up and renamed it Full Gospel Church of God in Christ. Shortly after Elder Turner's death, the marquis listed Elder Quick as the founder.

Elder Turner felt led to go to Candor, North Carolina to establish a Church of God in Christ. He began a Bible study class there in the home of Sis. Martha Cooper, which met once a week for a long while. The Holy Ghost was falling and the Lord was blessing in the Cooper's home, but because of Elder Turner's workload, he had to give up the class for the time being. He didn't have anyone to put there at that time, so three families from the Bible study class joined Wells Tabernacle in Southern Pines. The others went different places.

Elder Turner later went back to Candor with the Big Top for a tent revival, determined not to leave until a Church of God in Christ was established in Candor. The revival began. Elder William Everett preached a week, Elder Patrick Wooden preached a week, Elder Mitchel Little preached a week, Elder Garcia Morman preached a week and Elder Wooden preached the last week closing out the revival.

. Many of the people who were in that Bible class came to the revival. When it was about to close, some of them came to the house and asked Elder Turner if he was going to stay as their pastor. He told them he wouldn't be able to be their pastor because he already had too much work and couldn't give a new church the time it needed. Instead, he was going to leave Elder Wooden there as pastor. They told him that out of the preachers from the revival, Elder Wooden was their choice, and they would stand with the church. After they left, Elder Turner told me that he was going to send Elder Wooden to Candor. And instead of naming the church Gospel Light Church of God in Christ, he would let Elder Wooden name it. Bible study was then held in the home of Bro. and Sis. Cagle. Elder Wooden continued to teach and preach the Gospel of Jesus Christ under the anointing of the Holy Ghost. The Church of God in Christ was established in Candor, N. C. under the leadership of Elder Patrick L. Wooden, Sr. He named it Lighthouse Church of God in Christ and the church soared.

Elder Turner also worked with Elder Canty in ministering the Word of God and praying for the people in Cheraw, South Carolina. Elder Turner was instrumental in helping to establish Canty's Temple Church of God in Christ in there. Later, Elder Turner went to Raeford, North Carolina and preached the Word of God. The House of Prayer Church of God in Christ was birthed there. Elder Turner left Elder Herbert Bullock as pastor.

Many times Elder Turner met with oppositions as he worked in the kingdom of God. But it seemed as though he thrived more during those times. He would go through many things, but he would take and take and still keep on loving and treating people right.

Earlier in our marriage there were times when I wanted to take on these people. I saw myself with my left hand holding one missionary by the collar, my right fist boxed up, about to sock her for being disrespectful to my husband. I wouldn't dare talk to the man of God the way she used to when she couldn't have her way. When I told my husband about it, he said never to let the devil cause me to do it because I would never live it down. I began to fast and pray that the Lord would take those kinds of feelings. During the process of fasting and praying, the Spirit assured me that not only would God deal with those who bothered my husband, He would deal with those who bothered me. After that I would follow my husband's example, taking and taking while I continued smiling, praying and praising God. Sis. Lois walked up to me after church one day and said, "How do you take it?" I said to her, "It's the Lord, not me." I realized we have to let the Lord fix us on the inside in such a way that we will not be moved by Satan's attacks, from either without or within. Just know that whenever the Lord is blessing, the devil is messing in one way or another. But you can be assured that God will take care of His own.

Bro. Price, a member who faithfully ministered music with his guitar during service at the Temple Church, suddenly started coming to church only now and then. After a while he got sick and sent for the pastor. We went out and had prayer with him. He confessed to the pastor that he had stopped coming regularly because Sis Lois told him that Elder Turner said he couldn't really play the guitar. Bro Price said, "I had a vision. I saw you and I picking fruit off a big, beautiful fruit tree. The tree was full of fruit." Elder Turner said that the fruit being picked off the tree represented souls that they were winning together. Brother Price said, "I was supposed to work with you, and I am sorry I didn't."

One of the ministers at the Temple would verbally rebut almost everything Elder Turner said while preaching. Elder Turner wouldn't turn around and set him in order. Instead, he continued preaching under the anointing of the Holy Ghost. People got saved in spite of the adversity. God is a powerful God! That minister wouldn't pay his tithes either. He said he gave his tithes to the poor. When he went to the Bishop behind Elder Turner's back to try to get ordained, the Bishop sent for Pastor Turner. During the meeting, the minister promised to pay his tithes. The Bishop ordained him. The minister paid his tithes for a few months before quitting and going back to his old way of trying to be a distraction.

One Sunday night one of the young ministers who had been ill came up for prayer. The pastor prayed for him and told him to walk to the front door, touch it and come back. The minister began taking little steps when the assistant told him he could run. So he began to run—he fell before he got to the door. That minister could have gotten his deliverance that night if he had followed the instructions of his pastor.

Elder Turner was a great man of God, whom the Lord was using, and I was his number one fan. He would preach a "God spell" on me almost every time he stepped to the pulpit. I didn't want to hinder the ministry in any way, so I endeavored to be nice and kind to all of the members. However, I would tell them the truth.

One Sunday evening the leader of the Pastor's Aide was talking to some of the young people outside of the church. One of the young ministers heard her say, "I told you all about that black Willa Turner." The choir had gotten new robes, so they went off to sing that Sunday afternoon, without the pastor's permission. They returned a few minutes before Y.P.W.W. I said the pastor was going to get them because he had publicly said that the choir would not be going out to sing unless they were on an appointment when he was preaching. So they reported me to the Pastor's Aide leader.

That same evening before dismissing the service, Elder Turner stepped down out of the pulpit and called me to him. He said to the congregation, "You see this woman here? The Lord gave her to me, and I am going to live with her with or without the Temple Church of God in Christ." I was shocked, but I tried not to show it. I hadn't talked to him about what happened before service. I hadn't complained to him about anything. After service the missionary who gave me the most trouble came up to me and said, "I was wondering when he was going to say something." When we got home, I told him that I was surprised by what he did. He told me he hadn't done anything before because he felt I could handle it. But things had gotten to where it was time to say something. Someone asked me later what I said about being called "that black Willa Turner." I simply told the person, "I am black, and my name is Willa Turner." There was no need in me getting angry at the truth. Besides, the Lord had already fixed me on the inside.

The Lord began to speak to Elder Turner again about going to Raleigh to establish a Church of God in Christ. He talked with me about it, the finances it would take and the time that he would be away from us. I told him to do what the Lord said and we would be ok. We prayed and believed God for the way He would make for the new church and for us.

I wanted very much for the church to be established. It was Raleigh where the Lord had sent him to establish a church thirteen years prior, but he went to Rockingham at the request of Bishop Wells instead. I knew the church would be a success.

Instead of taking his shirts to the cleaners, I began ironing them like I did in the beginning of our marriage. By then he used between ten and fifteen shirts every week. I also decided that while he was away, eating hotdogs, hamburgers or sandwiches, buying store brands instead of the brands we really liked and, except on special occasions, not going out to eat or buying those aged steaks would be no sacrifice. I wanted to save as much money as I could for the new work.

Elder Turner was not going to be spending as much time with us. He wanted us to keep up the family prayer and talk sessions. We were all on our knees in the living room one night, using the couch and the two extra chairs as altars. All of the children had prayed except Ithiel. It was silent for a few seconds when Elder Turner said, "Ithiel." Ithiel said, "I don't know what to say." Ithiel knew how to pray because we had taught him. But for some reason, he wasn't going to pray that day. His dad responded in a dad's tone of voice, "You better say something." Ithiel prayed, and we didn't have any more trouble out of him about praying.

Elder Turner told the church at Rockingham and the church at Southern Pines what he was about to do. They had worked with him in the establishing of the other churches, and they seemed eager to help him get this church started. His District Missionary, Mother Hallman, worked with him wholeheartedly in everything he did. She always encouraged the people to do so also.

July of 1980

We came to Raleigh for a soul-stirring revival held at the YMCA on Bloodworth Street. It seemed like heaven touched earth. Elder Turner preached under the anointing of the Holy Ghost, and the Lord did bless. The DeVeaux family from Greenville, North Carolina rendered the music. They would bring their own equipment each evening. Sis. DeVeaux sang while Bro. DeVeaux played the keyboard. Their son Chad played the drums, and JT and Chris played the bongos. I, along with others who had tambourines, beat the tambourines to the glory of God. Talking about church–we were having church!

We were on our way to the YMCA one evening for service and had stopped at a red light. A young man crossed the street in front of us. Elder Turner looked at him and then at me. He said the Lord told him that the young man would be a member of Elder Turner's church one day.

After a few weeks of revival, the church was established. The Lord had given Elder Turner the name for the new church. We had not discussed it before when he asked me, did the Lord speak to you about a name for the church? I told him, yes, Upper Room. He said, "That's the same name He gave me." The dedication service for the newly established Upper Room Church of God in Christ was held on Saturday, August 16, 1980 at noon in a renovated building: 411 East Martin Street in Raleigh. The Asheboro District choir along with the DeVeaux family rendered the music. Supt. C. E. Anderson preached the message of dedication. Elder Patrick Wooden preached the first message in our first permanent place of worship on Sunday morning, August 17, 1980.

The Upper Room Church of God in Christ began with Supt. James H. Turner, Founder/Pastor, Mother Willa D. Turner and their children, Therese, James Jr., Chris, Ithiel, Emell and Aprille; Bro. Odell and Missionary Beverly Turner and their children, Tara, Michelle, Stephanie and Otissa; Bro. Theodore and Sis. Alfleta DeVeaux and their children, Chad and Shawn.

During the time when the Upper Room was being established, Elder Turner's oldest daughter came to live with us. He had gone to California for her high school graduation in June of 1980. I told him when he left that she would probably want to come back with him because he was such a loving person. When he got out there, he found her living with her stepfather. He told her to go back home to live with her mother. She didn't come back with Elder Turner, but she called in August and asked to come to us. He asked me if it was all right, and I said yes. He talked to the children about her and then to the churches. Until then, Therese thought she was the oldest. When she found out she wasn't, she was devastated. She was only ten years old and felt betrayed. I wanted to tell the children long before that they had an older sister, but their father thought it best for them not to know. Some of the members of the Temple Church were not taking it well either. She came to us in August.

When we became serious in our courtship, Elder Turner told me about his past life. He was brought up in a Christian home and in Wells Tabernacle COGIC. At age sixteen he graduated from high school and moved to Washington, D.C. He lived with his sister and brother-in-law, James and Annie Pearl Bellamy, and their children Larry, Carolyn and Cheryl. He said his uncle Dave and his cousin Tom introduced him to the nightlife, drinking, smoking and dancing, after he went to live with Annie Pearl.

He later joined the Air Force and served in Massachusetts, California and Okinawa and then found himself back in California. He said by the time he got out of the Air Force, he was an alcoholic and smoked a pack and a half to two packs of cigarettes a day. He was living a ragged life. He met a girl who had two little boys and moved in with her. Although he saw a man's clothes and shoes in the closet, he said he didn't ask any questions. He found out later the man was in prison. Out of that relationship his little girl was born. Her name was Gail, and he loved her very much.

He told me he had gotten so disgusted with his life that he had planned to drive his car off a bridge. As he approached the bridge that night, the car cut off; he tried to start it, but it wouldn't start. He left it where it was and caught a ride home. When he went back the next day to have it towed, he got in, and it cranked right up. He sold the car that day for enough money to get home and left California. He didn't have quite enough to get to Southern Pines, but he was able to buy a bus ticket to Fayetteville and had enough money left for a few nabs. He said he made the three day trip on nabs.

When he got to Fayetteville, he called his father and asked him to pick him up at the bus station. His father came and took him home. Elder Turner said when he saw his mother, her head was white. Her hair was black when he left, and he felt guilt-ridden, thinking he was the cause of her hair turning white. He had been gone for seven years without contacting his parents. His mother told him that she and Mother Hallman had prayed at noon-day prayer all that time that the Lord would bring him home safely.

Even though he was home, he was still drinking, smoking and being disruptive. One night he was thrown in jail. He woke up the next morning to the birds singing outside, and he said to himself that the birds were freer than he was. The Lord began to work on him at that moment.

Shortly afterwards, Bishop Wells had Elder A. Jones conduct revival services at Wells Tabernacle. Elder Turner's father asked him to go to the revival, and he went. He said seemed as though Elder Jones was preaching just to him. When Elder Jones made the altar call, he slumped down in his seat. Elder Jones came to where he was and asked him to give his life to Christ. He did and that night was saved, sanctified and filled with the Holy Ghost. It wasn't too long there afterwards when the Lord called him to preach the gospel.

By the James returned home, his father, Elder James Turner, was pastor of Anderson Temple Church of God in Christ in Fayetteville and Bolten Church of God in Christ in Bolten, North Carolina. His mother, Missionary Lula Belle Turner, worked with her husband in his churches. Wells Tabernacle was their home church, and it was in his parents' home church where Minister Turner preached his initial message. His father had the proud honor of introducing Minister James H. Turner to the congregation. Minister Turner drove for his father and worked with Wells Tabernacle. It was about six months after Minister Turner got saved when his father took sick and died.

After we were married, we called and talked to Gail from time to time. She was around four years old then and would get confused about to whom she was talking. One day she called him by her stepfather's name. Honey was hurt and decided not to call anymore so that she would grow up with one father. He started calling again when she got older and could understand. I sent a check to her mother for her every month until she came to live with us in 1980.

Before Gail came, I made up in my mind that I would be the best stepmother I could. I had heard much about wicked stepmothers, and I didn't want that reputation attached to me. It was a great adjustment, especially among the children, and it seemed as though I couldn't do anything right. I was refereeing and trying to keep the peace a lot of the time. Noon-day prayer was my time for myself, and I went there looking for strength. The assistant pastor was using the occasion to promote himself.

The day he said, "I don't have any skeletons falling out of my closet," among other things, I planned not to go back. But I found myself going back and praying fervently to God for help.

Gail decided to get married a little over a year later in 1981. There was a friend of hers in California who seemed to love her very much. He called asking her to come back, but she decided to marry Albert, a young man from the church. They were having some problems, so I went to check on her one day. While we were talking, she told me she had resented me from the time she got off the plane. She apologized, and we became closer than we had ever been.

Elder Turner was at Upper Room on Monday nights, Thursday nights and every fifth Sunday morning. Many times he would send Elder Wooden to preach on Sundays. Other times Elder Turner would send preachers, until he got an assistant and preachers on staff in the church. Sis. Beverly and her girls were always there, carrying on the Sunday school and conducting the devotional services. One Saturday evening the children and I drove up from Rockingham so we would be at Upper Room for Sunday school and service the next day. As we pulled up on the church grounds, gun shots were fired. I told the children to hit the floor. We all crouched down in that brown Lincoln, praying no one would come and shoot in the car. We stayed down for about thirty minutes; then I took the keys out, and we made a B line for the door. After I got them in safely, I went back to the car for our things. We didn't turn on any lights that night because we didn't want anyone to know we were in there. We were glad when Sis. Beverly and the girls came the next morning. The Martin Street building was in a rough neighborhood, but we worshipped there until we had to move because of a city ordinance. Afterwards, we worshipped in Bro. Odell's and Missionary Beverly Turner's home for a while and then for a short time in a renovated house on Hills Street. A few services were held at the Safety Club on Branch Street and then at the Central Trailer Park in the Community Center on Rush Street.

Everywhere we moved the Lord blessed and added to the membership. Some of those who joined the ministry during that time included: Wanda Carmon, Darlene and Donnell Murden, Janice, Mycenia and Demetrius Moore, Clarence and Edna Morgan and family, Dortry and Lillie Miller and family, James Smith, Carolyn Bell, Geneieve Petty and family, Elder

Willa D. Turner

Donald and Missionary Myrtle Foster and family, Shirley Bryant and family, Minister Kent McNeil, Minister Darnell Bryant, Gwen and Jeremy Everett, Kim David, Robbie and Trevia Shade, Joyce Wicker, Elder Jesse and Mother Ella Taylor and others. The Lord blessed us to buy a church building on Lake Wheeler Road. Mr. Stanley Green, the banker, asked Elder Turner, what was he going to do with that big church? Elder Turner's response was that he was going to fill it up.

We had a motorcade from the trailer park to the church on Lake Wheeler Road in August of 1983. The Asheboro District was there in big numbers. People from the Raleigh area were there along with the members of the Upper Room for the dedication service in our first church building. Even Mr. Stanley Green was in attendance. It was a glorious day. The Lord had blessed us with a choir that was second to none, and they were singing the songs of Zion under the anointing of the Holy Ghost.

Elder Turner continued to preach under the anointing of the Holy Ghost and with the power and authority of Jesus Christ. The Lord began to fill up the church.

Superintendent James H. Turner

The Motorcade to Lake Wheeler Road

The Motorcade to Lake Wheeler Road

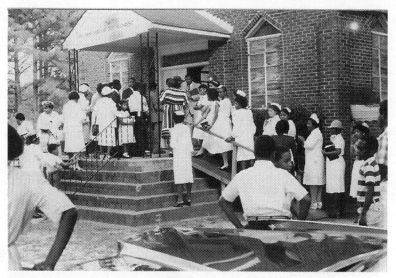

From the Trailer Park to Lake Wheeler Road

Elder Turner organized the financial part of the church in the way that the Lord instructed him–according to Malachi 3:6-12. He didn't have pastoral Sundays and church Sundays. The church was blessed through tithes and offerings. For years he did not take any finances from the Upper Room Church, but the Lord continued to bless in every way. Elder Turner was a happy man. This was "his baby," and he was glorifying the Lord for it. He told us that the church was going to be a soul-saving station–many people would come because they knew they could get delivered in the Upper Room, but all of them wouldn't stay. The young man whom we saw crossing the street that night on our way to the revival at the YMCA had come and joined the church. His name was Moses Daye. The Lord saved, sanctified, filled him with the Holy Ghost and called him into the gospel ministry. Another man, Elder Burt, gave up being the pastor at a Baptist church and joined the Upper Room.

The Lord continued to add to the church: Deacon Joseph and Missionary Patti Morgan and family, Evangelist Margaret Mose and family, Early and Evangelist Daisy Burgess and family, Deacon Carl and Sis. Annett Clark and family, Sis. Dorothy Cooke, Missionary Evelyn Teasley and family, The Cozart family, Gwen Bronson and family, Missionary Geraldine Capers and family, Evangelist Mary A. Mayo and family, Renita Whidbee, Charles (CC), Pam and Michelle (Cookie) Chrisp, and so many others. Talking about church, we were having church, and the Lord was continuously saving, sanctifying and filling with the Holy Ghost. We had a couple who were shacking when they came. After salvation they came to the church and got married without the pomp and circumstances. They just wanted to do right.

When I came to Raleigh, I told the people that I didn't come looking for love but to show love. As we grew, though, you could feel the love from heart to heart and from breast to breast. We became like one big family. When we were commuting, the distance didn't seem long because we knew the feast of the Lord was waiting for us. Our picnics at Pullen Park with all the saints seemed like family reunions. Everybody was somebody.

I told the saints what the Lord had told me one day. If life dealt a sour lemon, take it and roll it until it got soft. Prayer will soften life's sour lemons. Then draw water out of your own well of salvation—the Holy Ghost is the pitcher; squeeze the lemon's juice in that water by fasting and praying and put some sugar in it. Love is the sweetener. Then stir it up with faith as your ladle. You can enjoy your lemonade you made out of the sour lemon the world dealt you by praising and worshipping the Lord while the devil watches. What the devil meant for evil will turn out for your good.

Elder Turner was continually concerned about lost souls. The Lord led him to Benson, North Carolina, and he pitched the Big Top and had revival. By that time he had a tractor trailer to haul all of his equipment—the tent, sound system, keyboard, drum set, microphones, chairs, etc. From that revival he established the Upper Room Outreach Ministry Church of God in Christ. After taking down the tent, he located a place to have services and continued to work in Benson. He later turned the Upper Room Outreach Ministry over to Elder Michael Ferrell.

Elder Turner, God's man on the move, not only founded several churches. He was also the founder of Power for Every Hour Ministry, Inc. and also the Movement to Save Raleigh Crusade, Inc. He had a telecast and was broadcasting on five different radio stations.

One Sunday morning he went to the radio station to do a live broadcast. The station manager handed him a wire that had just come in from California. The wire was entitled "Shot-Gun Wedding." Elder Turner had just performed a wedding that Saturday and could not believe that the incidents of the wedding had already reached California.

The wedding processional had already begun, and it was time for the father to take the bride in the sanctuary. The wedding march was being played, but they weren't moving. I beckoned for the father to start moving. He shook his head, no, so I went to him to find out why he wasn't taking his daughter down the aisle. He said that he was disrespected because the groom did not ask for his daughter's hand in marriage. He was not going to take her in the sanctuary. I kept reasoning with him not to destroy his daughter's wedding. Finally, I persuaded him. He took her to the altar, and when asked, "Who giveth this woman to be married to this man?" He shook his head, no. He was asked a second time and again he shook his head, no, and walked out of the church.

Elder Turner began to rush through the ceremony. He finished in record speed and told the groom to salute the bride. The bride and groom rushed out of the church and went straight to the limousine and left. They had just pulled away when the father returned with a gun. The wedding party and the guests were exiting the church. I had just stepped down off the side of the vestibule and was standing on the ground. Everyone started running. I looked down—there were people on the ground as others jumped over them in panic. Someone said, he has a gun. I still hadn't seen him, but I started looking around for my children. Thankfully, some of the saints had them.

About that time Elder Turner was coming out of the side door of the church, in the process of taking off his robe. The father of the bride was walking up the side with the gun aimed at him. One of the guest tried to stop him. The gun was knocked up in the air and it fired. The father came down on the man's head with the butt of the rifle. Another guest grabbed the rifle, picked the father off the ground and subdued him until the police arrived. Those men saved Elder Turner's life that day.

The guest who got hurt was later taken to the hospital because of his injury, treated and released. Later that evening the father was also taken to the hospital and placed in the psychiatric ward for a time. He said he was going to kill the groom and Elder Turner for not seeing to it that the groom asked him for his daughter's hand. No one knew he was upset until that day.

On the way home from the wedding, my husband told me that he knew the father was going to do something crazy. That's why he rushed through the wedding. He had also whispered to the groom not to tarry but to go straight to the limousine and leave.

CHAPTER 15

The Move to Raleigh

When we decided to move to Raleigh, my hope was that the children would not have to go through the prejudice they had faced in Rockingham. Therese was a smart little girl. By the time she was in the third grade, they couldn't keep enough work for her to do in class. They would send her to the library to read. Later, she was placed in the academically gifted class, where she was the only student of color. She did not have any friends year after year. When she went on trips with her class, she had to sleep in the room with her teacher because none of the students chose her as a partner. And when they stopped to eat on their trips, she had to eat with the teacher. She would put her tray on the table where the other girls sat, and the girls moved it as soon as she went to get her drink. Not only were the students prejudiced, but some of the teachers were also.

June looked up to his big sister and wanted to excel as Therese did. He worked hard and continuously made good grades. Therese did not have to study as much. He didn't care how hard he had to study if he made good grades like she did. If it was something that I couldn't help him with, which was math most of the time, he would wait up till all hours for his dad to get home and could help him. His dad only had to help him once or twice. Once June got it, he had it.

June experienced the same prejudices as his sister. The teachers couldn't believe blacks could be smart. One year, a teacher talked about failing him in one of his subjects. Thankfully, I had saved all of his papers. In the meeting, I presented the papers to them with all the A's and B's, and they had to give him his grade. Ithiel did not experience prejudice. But he went through difficult times in the Rockingham School System. We were praying that the move to Raleigh would be a helpful change for him.

In August of 1984, we decided to move to Raleigh. We tried to find an apartment, but no one would rent to us because we had six children. We couldn't believe it. After trying for about a month or two but to no avail, Honey said we were going to move if we had to move into the basement of the church. School was about to start, and we still didn't have a place to live. So we moved into the church basement. We continued to look for a place to live, but now we were looking for a house. After a few weeks, the basement began to flood. They found out a tree root was growing into a water pipe, so we moved to a motel. It was during our stay at the motel that I accepted my call to the gospel ministry. After I finally said yes to the Lord, a great peace came in my soul. It was about two months until we closed on the house at 412 Plaza Drive in Garner. We were all relieved to have a place of our own again.

Many of the saints from the Temple church were angry when we moved from Rockingham. Several of them stopped paying tithes. Elder Turner had changed the financial set-up for Temple Church and Wells Tabernacle, putting into place a tithing account. The church as well as the pastor was blessed out of the tithing account. When the account decreased, that meant his portion decreased. He never believed all the tithes should go to the pastor. During that time I would write the checks for the bills, put them in envelops with stamps and hold them until there was enough money to cover the checks. I never told my husband exactly what shape we were in because I didn't want him to be concerned about the finances. His mind needed to be free to preach. My husband always said God would send a miracle each month. I knew the Lord would make things better. And He did. In the last two or three years of his life, he accepted a salary from Upper Room Church. The church received sixty percent, and he received forty percent. That's the only way he would accept it. He allowed Upper Room to give him one pastoral anniversary in his lifetime. They raised twenty-one hundred dollars, but Elder Turner took eleven hundred and gave the church one thousand. He was never promised any certain amount, and he never charged to conduct a revival. But the Lord would bless him abundantly in revivals. Elder Turner always returned with more than enough.

When we lived in Rockingham, I would get up about thirty minutes earlier than everyone else. I would go into the laundry room and pray before cooking breakfast. Then I went into each of the children's rooms and woke them up with words from a song: "Rise, Shine, Give God the Glory!" At the Plaza Drive home, the laundry room was in the basement. So, I would go in the living room to pray, using the antique, black-leather chair as my altar. After we had been at the new residence for a while, my husband told me he really missed hearing me pray in the mornings. I looked at him with a puzzled face. For eleven years I had prayed in the laundry room to keep from awaking him. He told me he could hear me pray through the vent in the bedroom. It sounded like music to his ears. The bedroom was at the back of the house–pass the closet, a bathroom, hallway, the den and the kitchen. But he still heard me. It was good to know that he enjoyed hearing me pray.

My mother was hospitalized about nine months after we moved to Raleigh. She had open-heart surgery five years prior and had seemed to be doing well. Then one day she fell out of her back door with a stroke. She was in a coma at a hospital in Charleston, South Carolina. We got one of our long-time babysitters, Ogretis from Rockingham, to come stay with the children while we went to Charleston. Shortly after we arrived in Charleston, we received a call saying that Aprille had cut her arms and was at the hospital. Elder Turner came back to Raleigh and found out how serious it was.

Ogretis and Therese had done all the right things and got Aprille to the emergency room just in time. If Aprille had arrived a few minutes later or if Emell had not suggested that they wrap her arms in a towel, she would have bled to death. Aprille had knocked on the front storm door, trying to get in to get money for the ice cream truck. The glass shattered, cutting her wrists and barely missing her arteries on both arms. One arm was also cut on the upper arm. She was eight at the time and Emell was nine. Ogretis sped through all the lights while Therese held Aprille's arms in the towel. The towel was soaked when they got to the hospital. I'm told the nurse gasped when she saw how much blood Aprille had lost. When the hospital discharged her, Sis. Beverly took Aprille to her home and took care of her until Elder Turner arrived. This was Aprille's second miracle, the second time God had spared her life.

Willa D. Turner

My mother stayed in a coma for a month. She died at the age of sixty-five without regaining consciousness. That was a hard time for me. I loved my mom dearly, the sweetest person I knew. A truly saved person, she taught me about Christ in her words and example throughout her life. Thank God for my husband. He kept comforting me, even while he suffered the loss for he loved her also. I kept calling on the Lord, for I knew He was the only One who could lift such a heavy burden and give me the strength I needed. And He did.

The church grew by leaps and bounds after we moved to Raleigh. The Lord continued to bless, save and add to the church many other families: Sarah Stover, Maria Waddell, James and Clara Robinson and family, Lannie Robinson and family, Floyd and Joanie Chavis and family, Minister Wayne Williams and family, Elder Michael and Missionary Celestine Ferrell and family, Minister Andrew and Edith Roberson and family, Elder Donnie Parker and family, Ministers Arnold and Donald Broady, Brenda Beaushane, Michael Bland, Elder Dale Jones, Bro. Vernon Ratliff, Deacon Jimmy Springs, Bruce Miller, Minister Steve and Anita Burch, Michael Bland, Beverly Willis, Gerald Gause, Sis. Annie Larious Estes, Mother Leomie Sanders, Ronnie, Cynthia, and Nicole Sawyer, Sharon Pinkney and family, Missionary Barbara Carter and family, the Land family, Bro. Hall, Jenine, Terry Carter, Cathy Covington, William Peacock, the Sanders family, Minister Jay and Lucinda Moore and their son Jael and others. Vocalist "T" Lett was a friend and constant visitor of the ministry. She would come and sing the songs of Zion to the glory of God. Among others who were visitors and joined later were Deacon Leon Smith, Minister Wiley and Della Aultman, Sharon Leach, Vicky Jenkins, Patricia Lester, Yvonne Smith, Myron Henderson, Shelly Williams, Bro. Arline and Sis. Arline and others.

The church had a seating capacity of around two hundred and fifty. The sanctuary was filled to the walls, and we had to fill up downstairs as well. With the use of a Beta Camera, Elder Turner and Bro. Vernon installed monitors downstairs to accommodate the overflow. They set up one monitor in the largest classroom and the other in the fellowship hall. They also installed a serving window in one of the kitchen walls so that Missionary Patti Morgan, Sis. Edna Morgan and Sis. Lillie Miller along with others could watch the service while preparing dinner for the college students, the pastor and family and the saints. They also mounted a wire under one of the pews upstairs, near the center aisle, so that Bro. Bland could videotape the services. Michael Bland had given his life to the Lord and was working in the ministry, using his own equipment and tapes to record the services. He did that service for the church out of his own pocket. Elder Turner and Bro. Vernon also built a sound room opposite the pulpit so that Bro. Ratliff could make tapes for the broadcasts and help monitor the tone of the microphones.

Sundays were overflowing and Thursdays were full to capacity. People were standing around the walls upstairs. Chairs were in the aisles, and people were standing on the steps that led downstairs. Downstairs was also full to capacity. At times, people were outside listening to the service. Monday nights were the smallest crowd, but the anointing seemed greater. When the sanctuary was full, Pastor Turner asked some of the grown-ups to go downstairs and watch the service on the monitors while the children stayed upstairs. He always showed concern about the children. He never called any child a "kid." When our children were small, he told me that we would never call our children kids because a kid was a goat and we didn't want them to act like goats. There was the Sunshine Band and the Purity Class for the children, as well as Sunday School and Y.P.W.W. classes for each age group. But he never had children's church because he wanted the children in the sanctuary when he preached. Some fell asleep, acted up or chewed gum during service. No matter whose child it was, he called him or her out, correcting the child before going back to preaching.

The Lord began to add to the church through natural births. The Ferrells added to their family; Charles and Wanda got married and then came Shakinah and Princess Chrisp; Jimmy and Darlene Springs and then came Candice; and Steve and Anita Burch decided to add to their family. Other members that decided to marry were Bruce and Trevia Miller, Moses and Janice Daye, Kent and Renita McNeil and James and Carolyn Smith.

We would always have family rap sessions with our children. These discussions were mostly on Saturdays. Their dad had told them they could ask any questions or tell him anything that was on their hearts without getting into trouble. The children asked or spoke what was on their minds, one by one, and their dad took time with each. He answered their questions biblically while connecting the answers with their everyday lives.

We were all seated around the dining table during a family session, and it was Chris' time to speak. He asked his dad, what was wrong with going to a Christian club? Some of his classmates were going to a Christian club that had opened up in town, and he wanted to go too. His dad told him that there was no such thing as a "Christian" club. He gave Chris scriptures to back up his answer. It was styled after the world, and we were not to conform to this world, so he couldn't go.

Then Chris asked him what was wrong with a little wine every now and then. Yet again, Elder Turner gave him a biblical answer as to why it was wrong to drink at any time. Chris' reply was, well, in the Bible, Timothy drank wine. His dad told him that Paul allowed Timothy to have a little wine for his stomach's sake because he had a stomach condition. He said, "Your name is not Timothy, and you don't have a stomach condition, and you are not drinking wine." Elder Turner then went on to explain the effect that strong drink would have on a person's life.

After the session was over, I took Chris into the bedroom. I asked, "Son, how long have you been thinking those kinds of thoughts?" He said since he started Junior High. Then he began telling me about his classmates smoking in the bathroom. I asked him, where were the teachers when all this was happening? He said they were in the classroom. I didn't want to send him back to that school. We continued to teach him and the others what was right and what was wrong. The older children may have had problems in Rockingham, but not the kind of problems the younger ones were facing in Garner.

There were times when you'd think our neighborhood in Garner was a war zone. The Stewards lived on one side of us, and they were great neighbors. But I didn't know what was wrong with some of the others. Emell was always getting into trouble trying to keep the neighborhood children off Aprille and Mycenia. Mycenia would come to our house to catch the bus with Aprille and Emell. Aprille had a lot of mouth, and when our neighbors' children came after her and Mycenia, Emell would take on all of them. June and Chris were being bullied by some of the girls and boys of the same family as those harassing our girls.

My children told me about a time when they got tired of a particular family jumping them every day. They decided to do something about it. They came home, put their books down, got their baseball bats and went back up the street to take care of the matter. June said he knew there were at least three children, and he felt they could handle them. But when they got to the house, the other children kept coming out, one by one, until it looked like there were about ten of them. A woman from inside the house said, "Get them." June said he didn't know whether it was the mother or grandmother. They decided it was best to get away from there, so he and his siblings ran as fast as they could till they were out of sight.

We had a fenced-in backyard. All the children were outside one day, playing. Then out of nowhere, a boy from up the street jumped over the fence and slapped Therese in the face, jumping back over the fence and running before someone caught him. It was a blessing that Elder Turner was in New York in revival at that time—no one messes with a man's daughter. I went to the house of the boy to talk with his parents. During the conversation I found out they were my husband's cousins. Uncle Dave and Tom knew them well. They were apologetic and had their son apologize. Afterwards, I went to our other neighbors' houses to meet with them. When we bought the house, the downstairs was unfinished except for one bedroom, a small laundry room and a large open area with a fireplace. We had the downstairs finished with a second bedroom, a sound-proof room that Elder Turner used for making his broadcast tapes and a large family room in the area of the fireplace. I found out from our neighbors that the man whose house we'd bought had a big game room set up downstairs, where the young people from the neighborhood went for recreation. The neighborhood children were upset with us for interrupting their play place.

My family's appetites had changed, and I didn't know it until the day I cooked dinner as usual for the family of eight. We were doing different things and had not eaten when JT came home from football practice. He ate the whole dinner. When we got ready to eat, I said, where's the food? JT said he thought everybody had already eaten. I thought he was going to get sick. But he didn't, and I realized his appetite was working in overdrive. His appetite got bigger and bigger. As I prepared more and more, I found out that they all had bigger appetites.

Elder Turner felt burdened about our children, as well as the saints' children, going to secular schools. He spoke often about a Christian school where we could send our children. But not only did we need a bigger church, we also needed a building for the school. The search was on. The brothers from the church found some property that had a school and a chapel on the campus. We went to see it. When we went to the chapel, Elder Turner said it would be the place where the students would begin their day with prayer. Negotiations for that property began.

My husband was first assistant to Bishop Davenport of Greater North Carolina Jurisdiction, the Superintendent of the Asheboro District, pastor at Upper Room, Wells Tabernacle and Temple Church, an evangelist, husband and father. He also had a live TV broadcast in Raleigh and radio broadcasts in Raleigh, Southern Pines, Rockingham and the Fayetteville area. He made his broadcast tapes in the sound room at home and then sent them to the various stations, usually via Vernon. With all the work that my husband was doing, he went into business with two friends. They were running a convenience store. Well, I told him I didn't agree with him being involved with the store because I thought it was too much for him with all the work he was already doing. I tried to talk him out of it.

Instead of praying in the living room, one morning I knelt down by the side of my bed. While praying for my husband, I reached up on the bed and laid my hand on his leg. His flesh quivered, which concerned me. When he woke up that morning, I told him what happened while I was praying for him. I also told him that he was more tired than he thought. He told me that his flesh wasn't quivering. He also explained that he wanted some kind of business to generate cash. That way he wouldn't have to depend solely on the churches. Later, I did talk him into taking a vacation. We planned to go to the Virgin Islands as soon as the children got out of school for the summer. I had been with him in a revival in St. Thomas a few years before. We both wanted to go back to such a beautiful place for relaxation.

Superintendent Turner's last District Conference was the best financially he had ever had. The members of the district blessed him with a little over six thousand dollars. It was also the first meeting where I was able to keep what they presented me with on First Lady's Night. All the years before the gift was what we used in the meeting for offerings and other expenses, but I never complained. I also received the largest offering that night than I had in any previous meeting.

My husband would always lend our cars. Sometimes I knew it and sometimes I didn't. I was going to buy groceries one day so that I could be through cooking when he and the children got home. But there was no car in the yard. When he came home, I told him that I needed a car of my own. I wanted a Volvo. That following Sunday afternoon, I went to Weaver Bros. Volvo. I found a car on the lot I wanted, so I put my handkerchief on it and asked the Lord to make it possible. I went back on Monday, and the salesman said the one on the lot had already been promised to someone else. But he would order me one out of Atlanta. It would be there by that weekend. When he told me how much money I would need to drive it off the lot, it turned out to be the exact amount I had received during the district meeting after paying my tithes. I purchased my 1987 Volvo in March of 1987. Elder Turner took me to pick up the car, and I drove it home.

One night around three in the morning, Therese woke up crying. She came in my room and told me that she had to talk to her daddy. I told her he was probably asleep. But she insisted on talking to him then, so I called her dad in Rockingham and gave her the phone. They talked for a while, and she calmed down a great deal. When she hung up the phone, she told me that she had had a dream. In it, she could see a casket and the person in it, but she couldn't see the person's face. She said someone important was going to die. After talking to her dad, she went back to her room. I knew some people who were sick, so I laid in the bed and prayed before finally drifted back to sleep. When Elder Turner came home, we talked briefly about Therese's dream. He didn't have much to say about it.

Sometime earlier I had had a dream. In it, Elder Turner and I were in a body of raging, cloudy water. Near us and on the edge of the water, there stood a fence with a tall pole midway between each end of the fence. Elder Turner was holding on to the pole, and I was holding on to him. I was afraid of the water, but I was sure I was safe holding on to him.

I didn't understand the dream, and it began to trouble me. When I couldn't get it off my mind, I talked to Elder Turner about it. He told me that clear running water in a dream meant peace and muddy or cloudy water meant trouble. He also said that I should have been holding on to the pole instead of holding on to him because the pole represented Jesus. I began to fast and pray that my grip would be on Jesus, the only One who would bring us through whatever trouble we would face.

In April of that year, he went to the call meeting in Memphis. He came home and was telling me about the meeting when he said, "I don't ever want to be a bishop because they have to compromise too much." He was a member of the appeals committee and chairman of the election committee for the national church. He witnessed something that he didn't like, but I didn't know what. He never wanted to be a bishop afterwards.

May 3, 1987

On Sunday Elder Turner went to Rockingham. The children and I drove up later, and we had a great service at the Temple. Therese and JT went with him to Wells Tabernacle for the evening service, and Chris, Ithiel, Emell, Aprille and I came back to Raleigh. When he came in that night, he talked about the service in Southern Pines and how the Lord had blessed.

When he got up Monday morning, I knew that he had something on his mind. But he wouldn't say what it was. He began getting dressed and told me he was going to Durham to see his friend, Bro. Powell. As we were talking, he looked at me and said, "You are a strong woman. Anything you set your mind to do, you can do it." We talked about other things, and then we began to talk about Neal "George." Suddenly he began to sob and sob. He had never behaved like that in front of me over the baby we'd lost, not even when the baby died. I consoled him as much as I could. Then he went to Durham.

When he got back in town, he called to ask me to meet him at a Chinese restaurant. I did, and as we were eating, I asked him if he felt any better. He said somewhat so. Then I asked him if he was ready to tell me what was on his mind. He said, "No. Maybe Bro. Powell will tell you sometime."

The house next door to the church on Lake Wheeler Road had become available. We were scheduled to move on Wednesday morning. I was busy packing and didn't go to service on Monday night. When Elder Turner came home, he laid the tape from the service on the nightstand and told me that he wanted me to listen to it. He went to Rockingham Tuesday night for service and to the Consecration Union in Southern Pines on Wednesday night. I wasn't through packing yet, but on Wednesday morning the movers came and moved most of our things to Lake Wheeler Road. We still didn't have a telephone connection at the new residence. Elder Turner came home after the Wednesday night service, and on Thursday I drove us to Wells Tabernacle for the last night of the Consecration Union.

On Friday morning Elder Turner went to Plaza Drive and picked up more of our things. After we had dinner that evening, I left for a service at Mrs. Stewart's, our neighbor from Plaza Drive, church. When Emell, Aprille and I finally found the church, the service was over. I came home to find Elder Turner in bed resting.

CHAPTER 16

The Beginning of the End

May 9, 1987

It seemed like any other day. We had just moved into a six-bedroom house. On the top floor there were three bedrooms, along with a kitchen, kitchenette, dining room, a large living room with a raised ceiling and a fireplace, and a bath and a half. On the bottom floor were the other three bedrooms, a spacious kitchen, large family room, a full bath and a half, laundry room and two bomb shelters. One shelter was being used as a study and the other as a storage room and closet. All of the closets downstairs were walk-in closets. We were going to entertain guests upstairs, while the bottom floor was the children's domain. The interior decorator still had to make and hang the curtains, and we had other small things to do. It seemed as though life was set. We had almost everything we could ever want. My husband had dreamed of having a Mercedes, and he had purchased it eleven months prior. I wanted a Volvo and had purchased it two months before. Yes, everything was great.

On Saturday mornings I usually slept a little later before getting up to pray and meditate before getting started with the day. But I will never forget this morning before Mother's Day. The Lord woke me up at dawn. I slipped out of bed, knelt down beside it and began to pray. I prayed for some time before opening my Bible to I Corinthians 6:19 and 20. After I finished praying, reading and studying, I made breakfast. I woke my husband to serve him. It was during our meal when he said to me, "I want you and June to settle your differences." June was about to turn fifteen.

He listened to his dad, but it seemed as though he didn't want to hear anything I had to say.

After breakfast we began to get dressed for NC State University's graduation exercises. Two of the members from our church, Minister Dale Jones and Thelina Brown, were graduating. My husband very seldom, if ever, complained. That day he complained about being tired and having some swelling in his legs. I suggested he stay home and rest. But he wanted to go, so we did. On our way home we stopped by the store and by the Ferrells.' He stayed in the car while I went up to the Ferrells' apartment, which was unusual because he always enjoyed talking preacher talk with Elder Ferrell. We didn't stay long. But when we got home and as soon as he could change, he got on the riding lawn mower and finished cutting the lawn. It was a huge yard, and it was hot that day. Afterwards, he came in and laid down for a while.

Deacon Miller was having a picnic in honor of the graduates at his house that afternoon. As I was getting ready to go to the picnic, Elder Turner said he didn't think he would go. Again, that was unusual. He was the one who was always non-stop. I told him I wasn't going to stay long because I wanted to be refreshed for church the next day. We both went on, and as I was preparing to leave the picnic, he told me he was going down the street with the men of the church. I said, "I thought you were tired." He said he wouldn't stay long. I told him ok, but I was going on home. I stayed a little longer, talking, and was about to go to my car when someone told me, "Elder Turner fell." When someone said, "I'll take you to him," I thought he had stumbled. No one told me he was ill.

As I came near to him, he was sitting on the ground with Moses Daye supporting him, back to back. There was dirt in my husband's hair, and big balls of sweat rolled off his face. His eyes had a strange look to them. I realized it was serious. I must have been visibly shaken because he said to me, "I'm all right. don't worry about me. I'm all right." Then he called me by my pet name, "Baby," which he had not used since Therese was little. She started calling me "Baby," so he started calling me Mama. That day he said, "Baby, I died. I was in a peaceful place when I heard Jimmy Springs and someone else's voice I didn't recognize praying for me, and something snatched me back from where I was and brought me back here. You will have to see it to believe it. The Bible doesn't even describe it like it really is."

He kept telling me he wanted to go home. I was going to take him home when the paramedics arrived. They had difficulty getting a pulse reading. A few minutes later the ambulance arrived, and the attendants took over. It was still hard to get a pulse reading. Elder Turner asked them what the reading was. When they told him, he said, "If that's what it is, I'm supposed to be dead." He didn't want to get on the stretcher, but they laid him on it. They took him to the ambulance where they worked on him for what seemed like eternity. Then we left for the hospital.

While at the picnic, my husband had witnessed to Deacon Morgan's daughter, Dee-Dee, about being saved. As they were unloading him at the hospital, he was still witnessing. He wanted to know if the attendants were saved. Minister Kent McNeil had come up as we were going in, and on the way from the ambulance to the ER, Elder Turner was witnessing to him. Elder Turner told Kent that even though Kent felt like people didn't love him, he was loved.

They worked on Elder Turner in the Emergency Room for a while. Then they let me see him. He gave me instructions about some things and then asked to see the children. He said to June, "Your mama is not your enemy." I didn't catch what else he said. When he talked to Therese, she ran out of the room crying. I found out later that he told her that he was the person in her dream. He had already seen two of the children when the nurse asked how many more had to come. I said four more and she said, "Let them all come in at one time because we have got to get him upstairs." After the children, many of the members who were there came. He gave what would become last words and testaments to many.

He kept quoting Philippians 1:21-23. Every time he said, "I don't know whether I want to live or die, for me to live is Christ but to die is gain," I would tell him how much the children and I needed him. How much the members needed him. How Paul decided in that same scripture to live for the people's sake. I was not getting anywhere at changing his mind when I noticed Deacon Morgan and Deacon Miller standing at the door. I said to them, "You'd better talk to your pastor. He is talking crazy." They tried, but he kept saying the same thing. I found out years later from Deacon Morgan that my husband told the deacons to look out for his family.

A few minutes later the doctor told me that my husband had suffered a heart attack. They were going to move him to the intensive care unit. By the time they got him moved and settled, Elder Wooden and Elder Garcia Morman had arrived from Rockingham. Elder Morman went to the men's room while Elder Wooden came straight to Elder Turner's room. Elder Wooden got the chance to talk with Elder Turner briefly.

Evangelist Mose and I went in to see Elder Turner; as we were talking with him, he had another heart attack. The medical unit sent us out while they worked on him. Before day break, the doctor came to the waiting room to talk with me. My husband had had another heart attack in his sleep. The doctor said they wanted to move him by helicopter to NC Memorial Hospital at Chapel Hill early the next morning. NC Memorial had the equipment needed to handle a tachycardia, a type of heart attack where the heart was pumping too fast for the blood to travel to all parts of the body. Of course, Elder Turner did not want to go to Chapel Hill. He said his father had died there. He just wanted to go home.

Before we left Wake Medical Center in Raleigh, Elder Turner kept asking for water. But they would not give him any. They didn't feel he could handle water and wanted him to wait until he had a series of tests at Chapel Hill.

Early Sunday morning the helicopter arrived for the transport. They would not let me ride with him, so I went by car. I stopped by home long enough to shower, change, throw some clothes in a bag and give instructions to the children. Therese, James Jr. and a good friend, Beverly Turner, rode with me to Chapel Hill. By the time we got there, Elder Turner had already been moved to ICU. He was sitting up in bed when we came in his room. His eyes had a strange look, but otherwise he seemed okay. Much to my surprise, they had fed him lunch. He had eaten everything but a roll, which was left on the plate near him. Not only had he been given water but solid food as well. His name could not have been on the lunch list because he had just arrived and had a heart problem. I couldn't understand, and it made me uneasy. They wouldn't give him water at the hospital in Raleigh, yet they had given him solid food in Chapel Hill before he had the series of tests.

I visited with him for a while. Then I left so June and Sis. Beverly could go see him. A few moments after they went in the room, they came out saying something had happened. The doctor had told them to leave. A doctor came to the door shortly afterwards and told us that Honey had another heart attack. They were working on him, and we were asked to go to the waiting room.

What seemed like hours was actually less than an hour. The doctor came to the waiting room and said they had done everything possible–medication, shock treatments–to bring him around speedily. But they were not able. Elder Turner had stayed out about eight minutes and was now in a coma. The doctor said his brain stem was dead. He said my husband was actually dead. I could not believe it. I couldn't accept that as final. In the midst of my praying and the saints praying all over the state, I had another doctor to come in from Greenville, North Carolina. He said the same thing as the doctors at Chapel Hill. Still, I kept holding on for my husband. Tubes, wires and leads poked out everywhere from him, it seemed. His body was cold and pale and remained in this state from Sunday until Tuesday. Then his body temperature began rising. And his color came back. In spite of what the doctors had said, this change in him gave me more hope. I knew he would recover, especially when so many saints began telling me that he would.

My husband told me two years prior when he saw my mother on life support that if he ever came to that point, he didn't want to be on life support. The doctor wanted to take him off life support, but I could not consent to do it. I felt I had to do everything I could to get him back. The children loved their father very much. I loved him deeply and couldn't imagine life for any of us without him. His mother was praying and holding on to the Lord for her son, and so were his cousin Annie Pear who was reared as his sister and other family members. Nothing else changed. Yet we kept praying for his recovery.

The doctor wanted the other four children, who had not seen their father since the day he fell, to see him. Then the doctor wanted us to make a decision. I had the children brought over to the hospital that Tuesday of the second week of his confinement. Their reactions were heart-breaking. When they saw him with tubes and wires and leads, agony was all over their faces, especially Chris.' He kept talking to his dad, wiping back tears as they rolled down his face. He said, "Daddy, you've got to get well." Chris and Elder Turner were born in the same month on the same day. Chris told his dad that he wanted to celebrate their birthdays together; his father would be celebrating his forty-seventh birthday and Chris his fourteenth.

"I've got some plans. Please, Daddy, get well." I thought the babysitter had kept them abreast. I found out from Chris about two years later that no one had told the younger children their father was in a coma.

When I decided to write this book, this was the first chapter I wrote. It took me five years. The tears ran down like water from a fountain every time I tried to write, and I would have to stop. It still seems like yesterday when Chris had that conversation with his dad who could not answer. The pain that was on his face, and on Ithiel, Emell and Aprille when they saw their dad for the first time in that condition, still brings tears to my eyes, as it did on that dreadful day. I wanted to reach out and do something that would ease their pain. No matter how much I wanted to help them, nothing could be said or done. So I asked God to help my children. Therese and June were at the hospital with me most of the time, so they knew what was happening. They were looking for that miracle that many were telling me was coming.

We met with the doctors. They told us the only thing they could do was insert a feeding tube and discharge him. When the doctors left, we talked among ourselves. We decided to let them insert the tube and then take him home. I sent Therese and June home that day so that they could go back to school. They had been there the entire time, almost two weeks. The doctors were to insert the tube Friday morning, and then he would be discharged.

On Wednesday morning I went by the hospital chapel before going to see my husband. I began agonizing before the Lord. I asked God as I had done many times to heal my husband. I fell prostrate on the chapel floor, crying out of the depth of my soul, when suddenly my tears dried up. I said out loud, "Nevertheless, whatever you do, I will not charge you foolishly." I left the chapel cheerful and peaceful and went to the ICU to visit with Honey.

When I got to his room, it was as if he were sleeping quietly. I prayed for him, massaged him with oil and lotion, read to him and played one of his preaching tapes. The doctor came in and said they were going to move him to a room. I thought that was a good sign. Later in the day they moved him to his new room. It was bright and cheerful, with a striped curtain at the window. He was off life support and was breathing on his own. Even though he remained in a coma, he seemed able to move his leg off the bed.

Every time I put his leg back, he would hang it off again. The nurses said the leg movements were only reflexes, but I was hopeful. Mother Hallman and Elder Kelly came to visit him that night. Mother Hallman saw me put his leg back on the bed. She told me to leave his leg alone because he knew what he wanted to do with it. She said there would be a miracle by the next morning. A church mother from Washington, North Carolina, sent me word that Elder Turner would get up on Friday morning.

After the visitors left, I decided to go to the room that the hospital had given me and rest. I wanted to be refreshed and at Honey's room early Thursday morning, looking for a miracle. I said my goodbyes and told him I would see him early in the morning. Sis. Beverly and I left his room about midnight.

The telephone awakened Sis. Beverly and I just before dawn. The doctor asked me to go to the waiting room close to my husband's room, and he would meet me there. I knew my husband had either died or awakened. Even though my heart was saying he was dead, my mind was saying he's awake. Almost as soon as we arrived, the doctor came. He said they did all they could, but my husband's heart had slowed down and stopped. Even though the kind of heart attacks he had before caused his heart to pump too fast, now they were telling me his heart had slowed down and quit. They called the heart attack that caused his death ventricular tachycardia.

We went to the room. He seemed to be asleep and was as handsome as the first time I met him. Even though the doctor said he was dead, I was still looking for a miracle. I held his hand, still praying for him to get up, until he began to get cold. I panicked. I was in disbelief. I begged him not to get cold. My husband of twenty wonderful years, whom I called "Honey" was dead.

CHAPTER 17

Darkest Day

A beautiful day which had started with prayer, meditation and love on May 9, 1987 had ended in gloom on May 21, 1987. The man I loved, the man who loved me and treated me like his queen, was gone. My husband, my lover, my best friend, the father of all my children, my covering, my provider, my pastor and my superintendent was gone.

People had come from all over North Carolina and other states to see him—family, friends, church members, pastors, preachers, missionaries… so many people. The information desk said they had never seen so many visitors for one person before. Everybody could not come to his room, so, per the doctor's advice, I visited with them for a while in the waiting room. Now it was over, and it was time to go home.

I dreaded leaving the hospital without my husband. My heart felt like it would burst wide open at the thought of facing life alone. I had been there with him ten days, and I knew I needed to get to the children. I took courage and left the hospital. That week Elder Wooden was in revival at the Upper Room. He was staying at Vernon's, and I called him there. I asked him to go down to the house with Aunt Betty and tell the children. I didn't want anyone to call and say something before they were told.

It seemed as though I was in a fog. I don't remember much about the days that immediately followed. Somehow God helped me function. The children were pitiful. It was a dark day for all of us. Thank God for Aunt Betty and the saints who were at the house to help us.

Oh, how could it be? This was no ordinary man, but a man whom God Himself had chosen and called and used in the furtherance of His gospel. This man was indeed a special person who was saved, sanctified and filled with the Holy Ghost. The anointing of the Lord rested upon him because God was always first in every way in Elder Turner's life. He was a great gospel preacher and soul winner. He prayed under the power and anointing of the Holy Ghost until he prayed out of himself. It seemed as though you could envision God granting his request. A man who loved people and treated everybody right, despite color or nationality, whether rich or poor, sick or well, young or old, whether smart or needing help or whatever stage of life in which they found themselves.

I was talking to him once about someone I couldn't seem to understand. He said to me, "That young man has a grown man's body but has a fifteen-year-old mentality, and he is not going to get any better. The Bible said comfort the feeble minded." Since that conversation, I have had a soft place in my heart for those who are not as mature in mind as they are in body, for we all belong to God. When he went to the hospital, my husband was still training that young man. He and Bro. Powell were also counseling other young men whom the Lord had sent from others ministries. These young men were some of the many my husband ministered to so that they could be delivered from homosexuality.

He became a father to fatherless children, bringing them into his home many times. He took young people with him as he ministered from church to church. He made sure the young people were fed spiritual food as well as natural food and had the things that they needed. The needs of widows were not forgotten by him either. He had a degree in electronics, and he could fix about any appliance, televisions, radios, washers and dryers. Many times he went into the homes of our church mothers and fixed things.

Prisoners came to church with him. He saw to it that they had spiritual and natural food. Our van was not too good for them. Sometimes people asked me if I was afraid for my children and myself to be in the van with prisoners. I told them that as long as we were with my husband, I was not afraid. He also went to the prisons and preached the gospel of hope. Many prisoners received salvation.

College students held a special interest for him. He helped them from his own pocket and saw to it through the church that they were fed a good, home-cooked meal. He started the Food for the Needy Program at the Upper Room Church. It fed the hungry, whether they were members or not. A room was set aside at the church to hold food. He turned an old gas station on Washington Street in Rockingham into an outreach center. Through the donations of many people, he was able to pass out food, shoes and clothing to those who were in need.

Groceries for people who had no food, house notes and light bills for people when they couldn't do for themselves were paid for from his own funds. Every time we built up a good savings account, he would give it away to people who couldn't get loans at the banks. He also gave to other preachers who needed help at their churches. Elder Turner had a reserve in his home; people could come and get funds for a short period of time. All they had to do was promise to put the money back into the fund so that when someone else in need came, it would be there. He did not touch this fund for any personal use. Not only would his family miss this great man of compassion, but I was sure many other people would miss him.

The revival at Upper Room was already scheduled before Elder Turner had the heart attack. When Elder Wooden asked if he should still come for the revival, I said yes. Elder Turner didn't cancel church for anything. So even though Honey was in a coma, the revival was in progress. As the saints came to the hospital to see their pastor, they would talk about how well the revival was going. I told some I would be with them in revival that Friday night. I was looking forward to taking my husband home that morning and going to the revival that night for a while. I didn't get to bring him home. He wanted to come home the day he fell sick. He wanted to come home instead of going to the hospital in Chapel Hill. I didn't get to bring him home. Oh, my God have mercy on me!

The day of my husband's death was the darkest day of my life, and many, many dark days followed. I guess I was in shock. There were funeral arrangements to be made, along with other things. Although I was functioning, I was numb. I don't remember anything about that Thursday night, whether I went to bed or slept. I found myself walking in the church that Friday night to be in the revival. When I looked up in the pulpit, my husband's chair was draped in black. Then it hit me that the chair was draped in black because my husband was dead. I lost it. Seemed as though my insides dropped out, and I thought my heart would burst.

Willa D. Turner

Trying to console my children and arrange for the funeral was the hardest thing that I had ever done. When my baby died nine years prior and when my beloved mother died two years prior, Honey was there to help me through it. How was I to get through a thing like this loss? Oh, it was Jesus. He was my only hope.

Bishop Davenport and his daughter Odessa came every day to help get things ready. My brother Willie was a mortician by trade. He told me not to worry about picking out a casket. He made arrangements for the casket to be shipped from D. C. For some reason they couldn't ship it to Raleigh, so they shipped it to Winston-Salem. Deacon Joe Morgan and Deacon Dortry Miller went to Winston-Salem to pick it up in Deacon Clarence Morgan's van. Willie said that it was the best–the Rolls Royce of coffins.

We had a service for my husband at Upper Room on Sunday afternoon, May 24th and a service at Temple Church in Rockingham that Sunday evening. We had a viewing at Wells Tabernacle on Memorial Day morning, May 25, 1987 and the home going service that afternoon at Days Inn in Southern Pines, North Carolina.

CHAPTER 18

Life as a Widow

Please. Someone had to wake me up from this nightmare. The first official duty I did as a widow was burying the man I had loved for over twenty years. My heart was empty as I walked from the burial site, which was right down the street from the elementary school my husband had attended. Oh, my God help me!

The saints rallied around us. They did anything they could to ease our pain, even though they were hurting themselves. My friends Lue Belle Lawson and Pecolia Leak stayed with me until after the funeral. Bishop Davenport told me the churches–Upper Room, Wells Tabernacle and Temple Church–would help me for two years. I had no income at the time and hadn't worked in fifteen years. But my mind was not on finances. I tried to keep my mind focused on Jesus. When I thought about His love and the love of the saints, I found courage and strength. It was like I was not alone.

The saints, Evangelist Mose, Bro. Vernon, Cynthia, Nancy Wilson, Marian Snipes and my brother Willie kept coming for months. Nancy was a great help when she came because she talked to the children. They were angry because their father was gone. They let it all out when Nancy was there. Once, Ithiel told her, "If he loved me, he would not have left me." She consoled and prayed that the Lord would bring comfort to the children and to me.

After seven months, we began to face life on our own. At the time of my husband's death, I was head of the Intercessory Prayer Team, president of the Prayer and Bible Band and president of the Ministers Wives Circle.

When I got ready to go back to prayer, the devil had me thinking, you couldn't even intercede for your own husband, so how are you going to intercede for others? He hindered me for a while. Then I told him that if the Lord didn't hear me, I knew He heard all of those people who'd prayed. Then I got mad at the devil. I told him the Lord did hear me, but His will was done. And I went on back to prayer.

When it seemed I was all alone, the phone would ring. It would be Cynthia. She and her husband, Mitchell, and the children drove up from Rockingham from time to time to check on us. For four years she called every day that she didn't come. She loved Elder Turner as a father and was having a rough time getting through his death. She was called to the gospel ministry under the leadership of Elder Turner. She accepted her calling under the leadership of Elder Wooden a year or so after Elder Turner's death when she and her family became members of Lighthouse Church of God in Christ in Candor, North Carolina.

We had some dark days. If Cathy had not come to stay with us while she attended St. Augustine College, I probably would have died. Cathy was a member from the Rockingham church, and she had made arrangements to live with us while she went to school. I didn't have an appetite. But when Cathy came home, she fixed me something to eat and brought it to my room. I was in the room with the door locked, but she would keep knocking until I opened it. She sat on the bed beside me and waited to make sure I ate. One evening she came home and found Therese sitting on the front porch steps, a towel over her head, wailing. My daughter was trying to keep me from hearing her. We spent a lot of time crying alone, trying to keep our pain from each other. What we should have done was talk, cry and turn it all over to the Lord together because we were all sharing the pain.

When I finally got myself together enough to try to care of business, I discovered we didn't have insurance on the houses. There was an accidental policy on the house in Rockingham. But since my husband didn't die of an accident, it wouldn't pay anything. When I checked on the house in Garner, I found out the insurance had lapsed in January. I was shocked. I know that my husband knew nothing about it. I had already signed the papers for the house we were living in then. My husband was supposed to sign the papers on the Lake Wheeler Road property by May 11th. But by that time he was in a coma.

I was in a predicament and didn't know what I was going to do. Then I remembered that Bishop Davenport said the churches would help me for two years. So I felt like I had time to get things together. I sold the house in Rockingham for what I owed on it to keep from losing it. I had fourteen years of equity in the house but did not realize that until after I sold it. I sold the house in Garner for what we owed on it also.

Elder Turner had an insurance policy on himself. It stated that the Upper Room church would be paid off at his death and what was left would go to me. I took what was left after the church was paid off and what was left from his burial policy and paid fifty thousand dollar as a down payment on the house at Lake Wheeler Road. I had the payments set where I felt I would be able to handle them. Shortly afterwards, I went to work part time with Wake County School System, believing that we were going to be all right.

Therese used to sit in her dad's Mercedes and cry and cry. I decided to sell it. It was hard for her and James to see that car there with their dad gone. Therese had driven him from church to church in it the whole summer before his death. It had many memories. Out of the sale I helped her, James and Gail get a car.

While he was visiting me, I asked Bishop Davenport to give us Elder Wooden as pastor of the Upper Room and as the Asheboro District Superintendent. He promised me he would give Elder Wooden as pastor. Bishop Davenport said Elder Wooden was too young for the District Superintendent position. The deacons and I had to go back to Bishop Davenport about Elder Wooden becoming the pastor because several preachers were trying to get the Upper Room Church.

It surprised me that someone whom Elder Turner had caused to be elevated and who had later turned his back on him was trying to get the church in Raleigh and the one in Southern Pines. Another preacher, who disliked Elder Turner and worked to keep him out of the Temple Church in Rockingham, was also trying to get the Temple Church.

The pastor's wife doesn't have much say in leadership matters. Yet she knows who works with her husband and who doesn't. Elder Wooden worked with Elder Turner and Sis. Wooden worked with me. I wanted him for a pastor and his wife for first lady. As pastor of Upper Room Church, Elder Wooden was a God send. When he came, he set up a trust fund for me. It lasted for four years. He didn't implement any major changes for two years while he helped to mend our broken hearts. Now that's wisdom, and the Lord rewarded him for it. Some told him that he didn't have to help us. But he did. Elder Wooden is still being blessed for the love he demonstrated towards a widow woman and her fatherless children. I am grateful to the Lord that the bishop honored our request. Maybe if my requests had been honored for the other churches, these ministries would not have gone through some of the things they did.

We had lived in the house at Lake Wheeler Road for four months before I got the first light bill. I thought I would pass out when I opened it. It was close to thirteen hundred dollars. I had no idea the light bill would be over four hundred dollars per month. Once I got that paid, I made sure the light company sent a bill each month.

For seven months after his death, my husband came to me in my dreams and took care of my needs. Then in a dream, he said, "You know I don't belong to you anymore." That's when reality hit. Up until then, it was like he was away in revival. I would awaken every night around two in the morning and look towards the door, expecting him to come in the room. That night I sat up on the bed and began to cry and talk to him. "Honey, it's time for the revival to be over. It's time for you to come home." I faced the fact that night that he was never coming back.

It was also in the seventh month when my body turned on me. When I went to the doctor, he diagnosed me with diabetes, high pretension, asthma and allergies. I told the doctor that no one in my family had diabetes. He told me the things I had were brought on by stress.

I was put on four types of medication. I was doing all right. Then suddenly, I started having excruciating pains in my lower back. I went to the doctor again, and this time he said all of my inner organs had collapsed on top of each other. He said I needed major surgery. I told him there was no way I was going in the hospital for surgery or anything else. With the smell of the hospital still in my nostrils from my time there with my husband, I wasn't going back. He insisted that I needed a complete hysterectomy. I said no way and came home.

I would hurt so badly that Emell would have to help me across the yard to the church. We did it before anyone came because I didn't want to call attention to myself. I waited until everyone left before she helped me back home.

When Elder Al Jones came to Upper Room to conduct a revival, I was still down on my back. By that time I couldn't walk even with Emell's help. I had laid in the bed for eleven days. One day during the revival, Elder Wooden and Elder Jones came to see me. They prayed for me, and I have not had that pain in over twenty-three years.

Elder Jesse Williams invited me to a service at Wells Tabernacle. He was sponsoring it in memory of my husband and in honor of me. While he was preaching, the Lord dropped in my heart that His son was tired and He had brought him home. A release and a peace that I had not had during my time of grieving came on me. I had cried every day for two years. I would cry, then I would pray and then praise the Lord each time until the heaviness passed. But the Lord delivered me that day. There were days when I cried afterwards—his birthday, our wedding anniversary, Thanksgiving and Christmas were always hard without my husband.

I had paid every debt that my husband left behind and was feeling good. Then one day some friends of my husband approached me. They told me Elder Turner owed them ten thousand dollars, his portion for a business venture. They told me that they didn't have good credit, but since I did, I could borrow the money. They also told me that by the time my children were ready to go to college, the business would be on its feet and able to provide income to help pay their tuition. Even though I wasn't sure it was a good idea, I refinanced my house and gave them ten thousand dollars. Shortly afterward, I found out they didn't own the business. I thought they were buying, but they were renting for over nine hundred a month. I could have cried. Needless to say, it folded after a time.

One day during the midst of one of my struggles, the doorbell rang. When I opened the door, there stood Dr. Leroy Jackson Woolard—now Bishop Leroy Jackson Woolard—and Bro. Walter Robinson. Oh! What a blessing and joy it was to see them and to have them in my home. Dr. Woolard was a friend of my husband, and for him to come to see about us touched me deeply. He spoke words of encouragement, prayed the prayer of faith and gave me a big brown envelope with smaller envelopes inside containing donations from his churches. He blessed me spiritually, emotionally and financially that day. I will never forget how he left me uplifted and renewed in courage and strength. Thank You, Jesus!

Chris and I were riding down Tryon Road one day when I heard a voice speak to me, saying that the devil had a contract out on me and my children, but God would break the contract. I looked around to see if anyone was in the back seat. I asked Chris who was next to me, did he hear someone? He said no. Many things happened to us over the years, but I always remembered that promise from the Lord. I would pray and tell the devil that he couldn't have my children or me. I'm yet holding onto that promise.

In June of 1991, Elder Wooden came to the house to talk to me. He told me that they were getting ready to build a new church and needed to cut down on expenses. The check he had brought for me would be the last one. He said they were going to try to help me for three more months. I told him it was all right. He didn't have to do that since they were going to build a new church. I didn't want to be a hindrance. The bishop told me that the churches would help me for two years. Temple Church where Elder Turner was the pastor for twenty years did not, and Wells Tabernacle Church where he was the pastor for nineteen years did not. But Pastor Wooden and the Upper Room, where my husband was pastor for only seven years, helped us for not only two years but every month for four years.

We had upward of three hundred members when Elder Turner died, and we were negotiating to get a larger church. Quite a few of the members left during the transition. Yet Elder Wooden had preached the church back to capacity again. When I went to the new church, I looked at it and told someone it was too small. When I went inside, I said, "Oh! It's too small." I would invite some of the teachers I worked with to the service at the Sanderford Road church. They had to stand when they came. They told me they weren't coming back. After they had stood on their feet all week in class, they were not going to stand at church. I would have surely given at least one of them my seat. But with all the people, I didn't know they had come until the Mondays when I went back to work.

We were barely making it when the Upper Room trust fund was cut. A few months later the help I was getting from Social Security stopped also. I was juggling to make ends meet, but all the juggling in the world wouldn't work after that. Things crashed for us. I was working with the Wake County School System as a substitute teacher. But school had closed for the summer, and the four hundred dollars a month I was making with them was gone until it re-opened. Our monthly income decreased over a thousand dollars. I also had no insurance for my medication. God bless Sis. Darlene Springs who more than once made sure I had my medication.

Daddy's mother, Belle, (Granny) died in July of the same year at the age of ninety-five. I had gone to South Carolina to visit her. Before leaving I went to her house to tell her I was on my way back. Auntie Becka was taking care of her and told me to go on in Granny's room. When I went in, I couldn't get any response out of Granny. I called Auntie Becka. She examined her and said, "Dean, she's gone." The coroner came, and they took her away. I left later that day for Raleigh to take care of some business.

The wake was set for Friday night and the funeral for that Saturday. I could go to Kingstree and back to Raleigh on twenty dollars' worth of gas back then. But I didn't have twenty dollars. Friday came and I was still trying to find the money to go to my grandmother's wake. I called Sis. Sharon Pinkney, who told me that she would let me have it. I went by her alteration shop to get it, but she found out the money she thought she had in her purse was not there. She told me to wait and she would be back with it. Sure enough, she came back with the money. I drove as fast as I could to get to Kingstree in time for the wake, but it was over. We had missed it by about thirty minutes. But thank God we made the funeral.

Sis. Washington had told me, "The people said that you are sitting up in that big house looking for them to mind you." Except for Darlene, I didn't say anything to anyone about my needs. I didn't ask Darlene for help for the funeral because she had already done more than enough. I couldn't go back to her again so soon.

It was rough that summer. Without a job, I knew I couldn't keep things going with all of us at home. When I told Aunt Betty and Willie what I needed, they were more than glad to help. They took care of my girls that summer. I sent Aprille to stay with my brother in Washington, D.C. and Emell to Southern Pines to stay with Aunt Betty.

Chris, Ithiel and I were trying to make it. We were all looking for jobs. I had cooked almost all the food we had and was asking the Lord for our next meal. The boys' appetites didn't change because our income did. They felt the food should be there, as it had always been. I knew the boys would be asking me what's to eat before long. I wanted the Lord to provide before I was faced with that question. It had been about a day and a half since we had eaten. There was a little bag of trash in the house, and the trash man was to come the next morning. I asked one of them to take out the bag. Ithiel's said, "I'm too weak to take out the trash." The boy didn't move. I thought he was kidding, but he wasn't.

I was used to going at least three days without food while fasting, so I wasn't too concerned. When I realized they weren't used to fasting and probably couldn't make it as long, I went outside and gathered up some apples that were on the tree. I tried to make applesauce. I had a little sugar and a little allspice left but no butter. There was also some flour, so I made drop biscuits. They didn't notice that there was no butter in the apples.

A lady walked up to me after church one night. I had seen her at church before, but I didn't know her by name. She told me that the Lord told her to go grocery shopping for me. She wanted to know if I wanted anything in particular. I told her whatever she brought would be appreciated. Before we got out of bed the next morning, the doorbell rang. I answered. The lady had backed her car up to the walkway and unloaded bags and bags of groceries at the door. I said, oh, why didn't you ring the bell before taking all these bags out of the car so we could have helped you? She said that it was something she wanted to do.

When we unpacked the bags, I discovered everything I had wanted—sugar, flour, jelly, steaks, butter, bacon and more than I could have hoped for. God will provide! Ithiel and Chris got little jobs near the end of the summer, which were great helps to them. By the end of the summer, I was in trouble with the mortgage and with James' car. The car was in both of our names. He used his car to generate cash for himself and to help pay the monthly payment. Something had happened to it, and I couldn't get it fixed.

It was September of 1991, at the close of the State Women's Convention in High Point, North Carolina. Sis. Lockett told me that her husband wanted to see me and asked me to stop by their house on my way back to Raleigh. Evangelist Mose and I were riding together, and we went by to see Elder Lockett. In our conversation Elder Lockett told me that Elder

Turner had been a great help to him in ministry. Elder Lockett wanted to be a blessing to me. And he was a tremendous blessing to me that day.

I paid my tithes, bought some groceries and called GMAC that Monday. I told them that I had two months payment on the car. I was three months behind, and they wouldn't accept what I had. Trying to reason with the representative, I told him that school had started and I was back at work. But the more we talked, the nastier he got. I told him I had found someone who could repair the car and that it was in the shop. He told me that if I didn't tell him where the car was, he would have me arrested. I gave him the address. They picked up the car, sold it at the auction and sent me the balance that was not covered at the sale.

I had asked for the things that were in the glove compartment and the trunk. The representative said I couldn't have anything in the car. Emell had made me a spotlight in one of her classes. It could be plugged into the cigarette lighter, and with a long enough cord gave enough light to change the tires on the front or back of the car. I wanted that spotlight. Having the car repossessed caused me to mourn as though someone else had died in the family. It was the first thing I had ever lost. After that no one would give me a small term loan.

I had been trying to help the ones in college so that they could get out of school ahead of time. Then they could reach back and help their younger brothers and sisters. I couldn't help anymore, and that was hard on them and me. Therese got her tuition from my dad so that she could go to summer school. She had enough for tuition but not enough to stay on campus. She stayed in one of her friend's room until someone turned her in to the college. Then she slept in her car, going to another friend's room every morning to take a shower before class. When I found out she was sleeping in her car, I persuaded her to go to High Point to stay with her dad's aunt Frances. Then she could drive back to Winston-Salem for class. She did that a few times but did not have money to buy gas. I didn't have anything to give her. But she made it through that summer.

Therese found a place to stay off campus and was working and going to school. Still, she ran short of money. It was time for final exams when she called me for help. I told her that I didn't have anything right then; if she could, get the money from a friend, I would bring some money that weekend. She didn't have a phone, so I couldn't call to see if she got the help she needed. I had told her that I would have the money by faith. The Lord blessed, and I went to Winston-Salem on Sunday night. When I got there, I found out she didn't get the money. She had tried to persuade the professor to let her take the exams, with the promise of paying by the weekend. He refused, and in front of all her classmates, he put her out of the class. It broke my heart to see her that discouraged.

James had to drop out of school for a while also, but he went back. He didn't come home during the summer anymore. Instead, he stayed in Greensboro to work and go to summer school. He sang with the A&T Gospel Choir. One January, the choir chartered a bus and went to New York to sing. I knew he was going on tour with the choir, but I didn't know when. James had called, wanting me to ask Wells Tabernacle to help him go on the trip. I gave him the address for the church and told him to contact them for help. I found out he didn't when he called. He asked me to wire him some money. I had bought him a coat the year before, and Vernon had bought him a coat. James also had his lettered jacket from when he was co-captain of his high school football team. But someone had stolen his things, and he was in New York without a coat or money. I asked him where he wanted me to wire the money. But he didn't have an address. My heart was heavy, thinking of him way up in New York, cold and hungry. All I could do was pray. Someone in the choir lent him a coat. After I had it cleaned, James returned it.

During those years, it seemed as though something bad was always happening. One Friday night–October 9, 1992–I came back from a service in Troy to find out that my brother, Franklin, had had a slight heart attack that evening. He had requested to be transferred from the hospital in Kingstree to the VA hospital. As I prepared to go to Charleston on Saturday, his wife called. He had died. I couldn't believe it. She said that he was bleeding from his nose, mouth and ears that morning. Later, one of the doctors told the family that Franklin was given a blood thinner sometime after arriving at the hospital. When they determined he didn't need a blood thinner, they did everything they could to get the blood to clot. But they couldn't. At the age of forty-five, my brother bled to death, leaving a wife and four children.

I ran out of toilet paper one Sunday. That night after service I asked if there was any toilet paper in the pantry. I knew that from time to time, they received different things besides food. The person who was over the food pantry said no. I expected her to reach in her purse and let me have enough money to get a roll of toilet paper; that's what I would have done. I went on back home, and we did the best we could until I got paid Tuesday. Tissue paper thrown in the trash cans suddenly didn't look as dirty. We made it a priority to use the bathroom at school Monday and Tuesday. I missed some of my good washcloths after those two days. I knew without asking that the boys had used them.

During those days, I often needed encouragement. But I had to encourage myself so I could to be strong enough to encourage my children. There were times when it was like I had been wounded and left for dead. Then in the next instance, the healing power of God came on me. The clouds and rain have blocked out the sun in my life at times. But whenever a star sparkled in the darkness, it gave me hope. Despite all the suffering, the physical and mental pain and many disappointments, I could see the breaking of day.

Emell's godparents, Elder and Sis. Clegg, stood by her with their many visits, encouraging words, telephone calls, prayer and financial support. Elder Clegg was a second dad to her, and she loved him in a special way. When he died six years after her dad, Emell was devastated. She couldn't believe she was without a dad again. I had to do some praying and talking to get her back on tract.

Emell came into my room one night, Thursday, October 19, 1993. As she talked, she began to cry. She said to me, "Mama, what has the Turner family done that was so bad that everything bad happens to us? It seems like we have just been going through and going through."

I said to her, "Nothing, Honey. We are just in a test, and we are going to make it. You have been such an inspiration to me all this time, so keep the faith. Don't let the devil steal your faith. That's what he is trying to do. We will make it, so let's not faint because of our sufferings. For me it's already over. I have the victory already in my spirit, and I'm free. So, don't you worry. It's all right." And with some other words I encouraged her.

I had not seen her that down in a long time. She usually kept going and going. I had noticed that she had been struggling to keep a positive attitude ever since my car broke down. When she came home and discovered the telephone had been turned off, it was the last straw. We talked for a while.

I told her that all things work together for the good to them who love the Lord and are the called according to His purpose (Romans 8:28). Of course, she bounced right back. I've learned that we have to believe the Word of God, even when nothing is going right. It's just a test.

Emell nor Aprille knew I was facing foreclosure on the house. I was trying to save whatever money I could. Even though I thought of the phone as a luxury and not a necessity, I had it turned back on the next day. That way, at least they wouldn't be cut off from their friends. Everybody needs some kind of encouragement now and then to help them hold out in faith when everything seems to be working out wrong. Emell was so happy to have the phone back on that she volunteered to pay the phone bill. She worked on Friday and Saturday nights. But she used most of her money to pay senior fees and buy the things seniors needed for graduation.

Emell had accepted Christ three years earlier, praise the Lord, in a Sunday morning service. I was ministering at Revival Temple Church of God in Christ in Troy. At the close of the message, she and seven other young people came down the aisle and asked for salvation. With tears streaming down her face, she asked the Lord to save her soul. It was a beautiful sight. My daughter, whom I had given birth to naturally, was being reborn as God cleansed her soul. Oh! What a joy. She had been on fire for the Lord. Her sweetly saved life was an inspiration to other young people. Emell was singing on the church and school choirs, a member of the Pre-College Club and on the AB Honor Roll. She had also been accepted into the Medical Seminar Class, where she was receiving EMS training.

I had the car fixed. I let Emell have it some days so she could drive off campus with her friends for lunch. This treat was something special for her because it was a senior privilege. She kept the phone on all summer, bought most of her school clothes and bought food for us, all without seeming to mind. At times I thought of myself as worse than an infidel because that's what the devil told me. I was registered with different temporary services and with the Employment Security Commission, but I had worked only a few days. Aprille had only worked one day that summer.

Summer was always hard. I was out of work until school reopened. I had decided to work for the school system so that I could be home when the children got out of school. I didn't want to lose them to the streets.

When my husband died, three of them were teenagers. I knew I had to be on top of things. One day I stopped at the store and got home just after the bus arrived. Chris came up from around the house to meet the bus. He had his book bag, trying to look as though he had been to school. After that I would call the school to make sure that he and Ithiel were there. And I came straight to the house to make sure they rode the bus home.

Tuesday evening, October 26, 1993 (from my journal)

Emell came to my room tonight and blessed my soul. She said, "Mama, I know it has been hard for you, all the things you had to go through. I don't know how you made it. I know that I would have probably gone out of my mind. But you held up for yourself and for all of us. If you had not been here, I know we would not have made it."

Around the time I wrote the above, my oldest daughter called. I had nicknamed her "Miss Doubting Thomas." Whenever I told her that one day my ship was coming in and I would be able to help her again, she always had a real good laugh. She said that my ship had already sank. Well, this time "Miss Doubting Thomas" was talking positively. God has a way of giving you the lift you need at the time you need it most.

It took Emell and me working together to keep Aprille encouraged. And then sometimes it still didn't work. Emell could always do more with her than I could. Aprille felt that I just didn't understand her. She was a daddy's girl and used to think her dad was the only one who loved her. None of the children could understand their father being gone, but she was the worst, especially when hard times hit. Emell's voice carried as she talked with Aprille, sometimes at two and three in the morning. Although Aprille was sobbing, she would listen to Emell. There were times when I thought I should have been gone instead of their dad since he was the bread winner. But with the next thought, I acknowledged that God knew what He was doing. I had to accept things as they had happened without understanding why.

When James went back to school, he did not have enough funds to stay on campus. He came home for the Christmas of 1993. He was sleeping in his clothes, shoes and hat. When I asked him why, he told me he had moved seven times since September. He was used to sleeping wherever and however he could. I found out that by the end of the academic year, he had moved seventeen times. Through perseverance, he made the year in school and was closer to graduating. I praised the Lord.

That winter we stayed in our big house without proper heat. I couldn't pay the gas bill from the previous winter. I paid about twenty-five dollars a month. But the company still placed a note on my account, saying no gas was to be delivered to my address until the balance was paid in full. I bought wood from whoever would sell it at the best price for the fireplace in the living room. But as the winter wore on, it was like using a bed sheet to keep out a blizzard wind. I had a space heater, but it wouldn't work.

Bro. Bullock called to check on us one day. When I told him that the space heater wasn't working, he came over and fixed it. We used the heater along with the fireplace during the winter of 1993-94. I never turned it off, not even when we were gone. I would turn it down low when we left for school. Even though I knew I should have turned it off while I filled it with oil, I only turned it down low and refilled it every other day. I bought a small electric heater for one of the bathrooms upstairs so everyone could shower and dress in warmth. We closed off downstairs and used upstairs. Ithiel was in the army by this time, but he came home for Christmas. It was good to have them all home. The boys had made sleeping pallets on the floor in the living room. That was the last time Ithiel came home. Sometimes I wondered whether he didn't come back because of the lack of heat.

Bro. Bullock heard the brothers laughing at my house. So he came over with his own ladder and paint and began giving the house a face lift. The house was made of brick, but the wooden trim was in dire need of painting. Bro. Bullock taught the Y.P.W.W. at church, and I loved his teaching. We would have long talks about going to heaven, what a great day of rejoicing it was going to be when we got there. He told me that I reminded him of his mother. He cared about how the children and I were doing.

For the three and a half years he was in the army, Ithiel sent me ninety-nine dollars and fifty cents once. I think he sent it because of the cold winter he had at home. I always felt he tried to send a hundred dollars but had to use the fifty cents to buy the money order and mail it. He and Chris had planned to go in the army and make out an allotment for me to help save the house. Ithiel graduated that year, but Chris didn't, so Chris didn't go. I guessed Ithiel changed his mind about the allotment. I didn't hear anything else about it until I asked years later. He told me that the army didn't do that anymore. Because he wouldn't write or call, several times I found myself calling the Red Cross to see if he was all right. They would have him call me. I soon stopped calling the Red Cross when I got concerned about him and prayed instead.

My lawn was in bad shape. It had grown up until it looked like a little forest. Every time I had that riding lawn mower repaired, it would cut about half the yard and break down again. After having it repaired about four times, I couldn't afford it anymore. And the grass kept on growing. Will Leak came to see us one day and said, "Your yard looks like a forest." He asked me, wasn't I afraid of snakes? I was but couldn't do any better at the time. He said he was going to Fayetteville to get his dad's lawn mower to cut my grass. He didn't come back, but the next week Elder Peterson drove up from Wilmington, North Carolina to see me. He told me he heard someone laughing at my lawn and had come to see about getting it cut. He gave me a one hundred dollar bill and told me to have the grass cut. I took out my tithes, paid a young man thirty dollars to cut the grass and bought some grocery with the rest.

One day shortly after that, I looked out the window. Deacon Leon Smith was outside with his truck and lawn mower. He told me that the Lord told him to take care of my yard. He kept my yard looking good until I moved. Some days he came when it was steaming hot. I would try to give him some cold water or lemonade, but he had always brought his own. I would pray for him and thank God for sending him to help.

Aprille had been begging me to let her go to Saints Academy in Lexington, Mississippi. She wanted to finish her senior year there. I didn't want her to be that far away from me, and I wanted her to finish high school with the classmates she knew. Then we heard that my friend Dr. Wells had accepted the position as president of the academy. Aprille worked on me harder then. I talked with Dr. Wells and then decided to let her go.

We took Aprille to Lexington to finish her last year in school. Emell, Chris and Evangelist Mose did most of the driving. We had a memorable, full-of-fun trip. We spent the night in one of the dorms. The next day before leaving, we visited with Dr. Wells at her office and at the executive house where she lived. We had prayer in the chapel, where the Lord met and blessed us. We toured the campus and saw the baptismal/swimming pool. The campus and the chapel were beautiful sights. I'll never forget them. We left with Aprille settled into the Bishop and Mrs. O. T. Jones Girl's Dormitory. I hadn't seen her that happy in a while.

Chris was impressed with the campus. He told me on the way back to Raleigh that if I would take him back down there, he would finish school. It was a sixteen-hour trip, but nothing could have sounded better. Chris was the only one who had dropped out of school. He didn't have sufficient clothes or enough money to enroll. I knew that I didn't have the money to take him back down there. Some bills needed to be paid, and I did not know how or where I was going to get the money to take care of my needs.

I decided to go to South Carolina and ask my dad for help for the first time in over thirty years. He told me that he didn't have any money. Felesha and her husband, Earl, had just returned from a tour of duty in Japan and were there visiting Daddy. They overheard my conversation. They went in their room and came back with what I needed to see me through. I told my sister that I would pay her back as soon as I received my income tax return. When I received my return, I paid my tithes, and she was the first person that I paid out of what was left.

The day my sister gave me a check, I didn't have money to buy gas to get back to Raleigh. Thank God, my dad had given Emell twenty dollars as a graduation gift. I borrowed her money until I got back to Raleigh and cashed the check. Emell had graduated from high school in June of that year and had been accepted into UNC at Greensboro. When we got back to Raleigh, I cashed the check, paid my tithes, paid Emell back, paid as many bills as I could and then took Emell to Greensboro to begin school.

In the meantime, Chris talked with Elder Wooden about going to school in Lexington. Elder Wooden blessed him with the finances to get back down there. Aprille did not want him to come to the school with her, but I was kind of glad that Dr. Wells and Chris would be there to keep an eye on her.

Aprille enrolled at Saints Academy on August 13th, Emell went to UNCG on August 17th and I took Chris back to Lexington on August 23rd. Evangelist Mose was back at work, so it was Chris and I doing the driving. He drove down, and I spent the night in one of the dorms before starting back the next day.

I was still tired from the first trip down there and the trip to South Carolina, but I didn't know how tired. It took me twenty-six hours to get back to Raleigh. Every time I started driving, I got sleepy. I would drive a while before pulling into a McDonald's parking lot. When I woke up, I'd try it again. When I couldn't find a McDonald's, I would pull into a service station. I was driving the Springs' van, so it was easy to rest without getting out of the car. That trip drained everything out of me.

All the children were gone, and I was alone for the first time in my life. After resting a day or two, I started packing to move. I set up a time for the movers to come get my furniture. They came and took my things to storage, but the storage space I had rented could not hold all of my things. They ended up bringing the living room suit and some other things back to the house. I didn't put anything from downstairs in storage.

I had planned to put the house up and pray for a quick sale. But then I talked with one of the brothers from Upper Room who at the time was at Prime America. He told me not to put the house up for sale because he had a buyer for it. He and a man came over one day, and as they were walking around the outside of house, I went to the door and asked if they wanted to see the inside. The brother said, no, because the buyer wanted the house for tax purposes. Before I left Raleigh, this brother told me that the man would buy the house in November. So I told some of the children that he had a buyer for me. Instead of putting the house up for sale, I decided to leave a family in it to help pay the mortgage until then. I was already behind in mortgage payments, and I didn't know how long it would be before I found a job.

I had tried to talk to Elder Wooden for weeks before leaving. I had always been taught not to make a major decision before talking it over with your pastor. I called the church office several times. Every time the secretary would say that he was either busy or not there and that I needed to make an appointment to see him. I thought to myself, *I'm Mother Turner. I don't need to make an appointment.* It came to me later that I was thinking too highly of myself. That was who I used to be; someone had already told me that I wasn't a minister's wife anymore.

As I was on my way out of town, it seemed as though my husband's voice said, "You should not make a major decision without talking it over with your pastor." I stopped by the Grocery Boy Jr. store up the street from the house and used the pay phone. I called around until I got Elder Wooden's home number. I called him, and he answered the phone. I told him that I was moving to Greensboro and had called to say goodbye. I asked to speak to Sis. Wooden to say goodbye, but she was not there. I hated leaving without at least saying goodbye to the saints. I was grateful for how good they had been to me before and after my husband's death. Only a few saints knew that I was leaving. I didn't want to get up in church and say anything without talking to the pastor first.

I was actually on my way to Colorado, but I only had thirty dollars. I planned to stay in Greensboro long enough to make the money for the Colorado trip. The year before I had a strong urge to go to Colorado but was financially unable.

CHAPTER 19

Starting over at Fifty

I left Raleigh for Greensboro on August 30, 1994 with my clothes and a TV in my car. I was back to stay after twenty-seven years. I had talked to friends in Greensboro before packing to leave. I thought I had a place to live until the afternoon I arrived. Lue Belle had told me that she thought I could stay at a mutual friend's house because the friend had moved elsewhere. By that time my phone was off, so I asked her to check with the friend for me. When I went to Lue Belle's house, I found out that Lue Belle had not talked to her. When I called from Lue Belle's phone, my friend told me that she could not rent me a room. Lue Bell told me to go to see Sis. Keys, who rented rooms. I went to see Sis. Keys, and she said, "I don't know who told you that lie. I never rented rooms." By then it was church time, so I went over to UNCG and picked up Emell, and we went to church.

They had a visiting preacher at Wells that night. He came from Columbia, South Carolina. Elder Hutchinson, I think was his name. When he got up, he said someone should go crazy for Jesus. So I did. I took the man's service for about twenty minutes; the Spirit of the Lord came over me, and I praised and praised God. We had a great service that night.

No one knew I didn't have a place to stay except Emell. I started to take her back to campus when she asked me, where are you going? I told her that I was taking her back to the dorm. She said that she wasn't going to get out of the car. I told her that she had a place to stay and not to worry about me. When she asked me where I was going to stay, I told her I didn't know, but I would sleep in the car if I had to. She refused to go back to her dorm without knowing where I was going to stay.

We were riding up and down the streets when the Lord dropped the name of my goddaughter, Lydia Leak, in my mind. I had forgotten that she lived in Greensboro. I was coming up to a church at that particular time and pulled into the parking lot. There was a phone booth on the edge of the property, and I pulled up to it. I took the phone book and looked up Lydia's number without having to get out of the car. When I told her my situation, she told me that I could come to stay with her. I took Emell back to campus. After about an hour, Lydia found me lost, looking for her house. I followed her home, and that's where I lived for a year and three months.

Sis. Mabel Scott told me to put in an application with the Guilford County School System. I also put in one with Dillard's department store and with the Employment Security Commission. I was offered eight jobs through the Employment Security Commission when I hadn't been able to find a full-time job in Raleigh through them all summer. I had interviews in Raleigh, but the younger people always got the jobs. I turned down the eight jobs and kept the two that I found. The job at Dillard's came through first, and I went to work. After working at Dillard's full time for two months, I was offered a job at the school system. I took the job at Brooks Global Studies Extended Year Magnet School full time and worked Dillard's part time for the next six years. I started over at age fifty, and it was hard working two jobs at that age. But the Lord gave me the strength.

I had insurance through the school system, and it was a blessing. When I went to the doctor in Greensboro, I found out why I stayed sick. I was allergic to some of the medication that I was taking. The doctor put me on the right medication and things got better. I had bronchitis the first winter I was there, but through the help of God, I stayed well those six years.

I was sending one thousand dollars a month back to Raleigh on back mortgage payments and four hundred dollars a month on back taxes. I didn't mind because I thought the house would be sold in November. November came and went, and I didn't hear from the church brother who was selling my house. When I called him in December, he had forgotten about what he had told me. After that I guess I gave up on the house.

It was about time for the children to get out of school for the summer. Emell was about to finish her first year of college, and Aprille and Chris were graduating from high school. I was searching frantically for a place of my own. When I couldn't find an affordable place, Lydia said that we could all stay with her for the summer. Just before leaving for Mississippi, I found an apartment in the place where I wanted to live–Stonesthrow Apartment Complex. I couldn't make the deposit and pay for the trip to Mississippi, so I asked them to hold the apartment for me until I got back. They said they would. There was no way that I was going to miss my children's graduation.

Cathy, Emell and I went down to Saints Academy for the graduation. Aprille and Chris graduated with honors. Chris was valedictorian of the class, and he and Aprille were granted full scholarships to Mississippi Valley State University in Itta Bena, Mississippi.

When I returned and came up with the money for the deposit, I found I could not get the apartment. They had rented it to someone else, so they said. The four of us, along with Lydia and her son, living in her three-bedroom home proved to be too much. By the end of the summer, I knew that I had over stayed my welcome.

I received a call from a young man who had just started a business in Fayetteville, North Carolina. He said that he had a plan to save my house. I didn't know him nor did I tell him that my house was in foreclosure; he probably read about it in the newspapers. I told him that I was interested. He sent a packet through the mail for me. We set up a time to meet.

Shortly afterwards, Sis. Wooden called to tell me that they were having a Founder's Day celebration at Upper Room. She asked me to come. The Lord blessed in that service, and I saw many friends I hadn't seen or heard from in a long time. It was great to be home. Pastor Wooden and Upper Room presented me with enough money to bring myself out of foreclosure that day.

In the meantime, a retired preacher from Raleigh called me, stating he wanted to buy the house. He said he did this kind of deed for people who were in jeopardy of losing their homes. We made an appointment, and Chris and I met with him at the house on Lake Wheeler Road. He promised to buy the house before the foreclosure date and said he would pay ten thousand dollars above what I owed on it so that I would have enough to start over. He was to give me a call to finalize things.

It was the third time I was facing foreclosure on the house. Deacon and Sis. Springs came to my rescue and saved the house once, Pastor Wooden and Upper Room came to my rescue and saved the house at another time. So since I had a buyer for the house, I decided to sell it and use the money that I received from the Founder's Day Service to help the children who were in college. I called the man whom I was supposed to meet about saving the house and told him that I had a buyer and decided to sell.

It was getting near the date of the foreclosure. I hadn't heard from the reverend. I called again and again but could not reach him. I was in a panic. Finally, about a week before the foreclosure date, his wife answered the phone. She said that her husband wasn't there and that he was not going to buy my house.

I called the banker to let him know. He told me to take my things out of the house and drop the key in the drop box at the bank that Sunday night. The auction was set for Monday morning. The Greater North Carolina Convocation was going on at the Convention Center in downtown Raleigh. I arranged to ride to the service with Will Leak in his pick-up truck so that we could get my things out of the house after the convocation closed that day.

We went to the house and got as many things as we could from upstairs. I couldn't get anything from downstairs because we ran out of space on the truck. I had to leave the den set, refrigerator, stove, lamps, the marble-top table that I loved so well, bedroom furniture, my favorite waffle iron and the cooking utensils that were downstairs. After Will got everything that he could out of the house, we pulled out of the driveway. I was trying to hold back the tears, but I couldn't. I stuck my head out of the window and cried and cried. Will didn't say a word, and I didn't say a word. I cried until the pain in my heart lifted a little and I had no more tears for the time being. We took the things that we had on the truck and unloaded them in Lydia's garage.

I started looking for a place of my own again. One of the saints at Wells had a house way out in Plum Nelly; as my mother would say, "Plum out of the city and nelly out of the country." I moved into the four-bedroom, brick home on Thanksgiving Day, 1995. I went to Thanksgiving Day service at Wells Memorial that morning and then to K & S afterwards. I had a quiet Thanksgiving dinner. Then I went to the house and cleaned and cleaned before bringing in my clothes and things I had with me. Later that evening I asked Will Leak to bring my couch over so that I would have something on which to sleep. The couch along with other things had been in Lydia's garage since the foreclosure in August.

The next week I bought a new mattress set in hopes of soon getting my other furniture out of storage in Raleigh. Emell moved in with me. Both of us were gone most of the time. She was going to school and working.

Chris and Aprille came home for Christmas. Chris slept on the couch and Emell, Aprille and I slept on the queen-size mattress set. I had planned to get the furniture out of storage while Chris was home for Christmas, but the furnace went out at the house. Sis. Mayo's daughters, Carolyn and her sister, came for a visit around Christmas. The furnace went out the night they came. Aprille and Emell went to Raleigh the next day and stayed with someone. Chris and I stayed at the house. As soon as Robin Allen found out that we didn't have any heat, she and Mother Lee, both members of Wells Memorial, showed up at the house with a space heater. Robin had bought a brand-new, large space heater for us. I closed off the kitchen and three of the bedrooms so that the place would be warm. Of course, my mind went back to the time at Lake Wheeler Road.

Robin had been attentive to my children and me since we moved to Greensboro. She had bought everything that Aprille needed to go off to college. When she found out Chris didn't have what he needed, she got him ready also. I bought two trunks, and she bought two of everything to go in them—irons, sheet sets, towels, etc. Chris had worked that summer and bought some clothes. Wells Memorial had made him and Aprille feel special also. Their names were included in the printed program with the graduates of Wells. They were presented with Bibles with their names engraved on them during the special program held in honor of the graduates.

The next day after the furnace went out, I got a call from Sis. Mayo. She asked me if I liked where I was living. I told her that I didn't, but it was the best I could do at the time. She told me to go find an apartment and call her and she would send the deposit. After Chris and Aprille went back to school, I set out to find an apartment. I had a small window between jobs to look for a place.

Before I could find a place, we had a big snowstorm. I went to work on a Saturday and did not get home until Tuesday. Dillard's put us up at the hotel on the adjourning parking lot. School was closed most of that week because of the snow and ice. Emell was snowed in on her job also. When I got home, the pipes had burst and water was everywhere. After I had someone come out and mend the pipes, I got in a hurry to find a place to move.

I went back to the Stonesthrow Apartment Complex. Seven months after I had first tried there, I was able to find an apartment. I was told how much I needed for the deposit. I would also need to pay two months' rent in advance. I was struggling to recuperate from Christmas and had little money. I called Sis. Mayo and told her how much I needed for the deposit. I borrowed the two months' rent from Elder Leak, with the promise to pay him back when I got my income tax return. I didn't want to lose the apartment this time. So I gave them a check by faith on Friday, and they gave me the key. I went to my new apartment and sterilized it. I had my living room suit and the mattress set brought over, and Emell and I stayed at the Stonesthrow Apartment Complex on South Holden Road that night.

As soon as I got to my classroom on Monday, someone from the office came and told me that I had a telephone call. It was Sis. Mayo. She wanted to know if I had gotten the money she had left for me. I had told her where I was moving, but she didn't know the apartment number. My telephone was not yet connected, so the only way she could reach me was through the school's number. She had come to Greensboro that Friday night but couldn't find the right apartment. She recognized my car in the parking lot and had wrapped up the deposit money in a piece of paper and had put it under the windshield wiper. I told her to hold on while I ran out to the car to see if it was there. It was, so I ran back to the phone to let her know that I had it and how thankful I was for her gift. I was breathing hard from running, but I was praising God all the way. I got permission to leave campus during lunchtime, and I went straight to deposit the cash.

I knew it was the Lord's doing because during February I usually had to use the windshield wipers to clear the frost. I drove to work Saturday morning, to church Sunday morning and to work on Monday without having to use the wipers. Sis. Mayo sent me one hundred dollars towards my rent every month for one year. She was a friend spiritually and financially when I needed her most.

I moved into the apartment on Holden Road in February of 1996. But my furniture was still in storage in Raleigh. I was trying to figure out how to get my things to Greensboro when Robin came through for me again. Her father, Bro. Brown, had a trucking business. He let his men use his truck to bring my furniture to Greensboro. He wouldn't let me pay him anything. I thanked God for His favor and Bro. Brown for his compassion and prayed a special blessing for him and for his business. It was a two-bedroom apartment and all the furniture would not fit, so I had to rent a storage space. Our place wasn't far from UNCG or from my second job, so that was good for Emell and me.

As I was preparing to go to my evening job on a Tuesday afternoon in March, I received a call from Wanda. She asked me if I knew that Chris was preaching his initial sermon that weekend. I didn't know anything about it and was puzzled as to why Chris had not told me. When I hung up the phone, I called Chris. He had just heard about it. Someone had seen the announcement in the church bulletin on Sunday and had called him. I told him that I would try to arrange a bus ticket for Saturday for him. But he said that it took about two days by bus to get to Raleigh. I told him I would try to work out something. I didn't know what I was going to do.

I left for work a little earlier because I had to go by the post office. I entered the mall through an entrance that I rarely used because it was on the opposite end of where I had to park. But the entrance was near the post office. As I was walking down the corridor, I noticed an airline agency that was advertising discounted plane tickets. I went in and enquired about a round-trip fare from Jackson, Mississippi to Raleigh or Greensboro. They had two fares left flying into Raleigh/Durham. I asked them to hold the two fares for me until Wednesday at the same time, and they said they would. The next day on my way to work, I went by the agency and paid for tickets for Chris and Aprille. Then I went to the post office and sent the tickets overnight express so that they would get them in time.

Chris preached his initial message, and the service went well. It was like a family reunion because my brother Willie and some of my other family members came from D.C., my brother TJ and other family members from South Carolina and my Plaza Drive next-door neighbor, Mrs. Stewart, came for the service. It was good to be with the Upper Room saints again.

When the children got ready to go back that Monday morning, Aprille told me that she had lost her meal ticket. She needed ten dollars to replace it so that she could eat in the school cafeteria. She said that her friends had been bringing food out for her. I had put gas in the car with my last twenty dollars so Emell could take them to the airport. I would not have any more money until payday. I asked Chris to give her ten dollars for me. Chris had tried to give me some of the money that he had been blessed with from the service, but I would not take it. I told him to buy a good study Bible and a nice, black suit.

They flew into the airport in Jackson, which was the closest they could get to Itta Bena. A friend of Chris was to pick them up and take them back to school, but he didn't show. When Chris couldn't reach him on the phone, they called me for help. I didn't know how to help them. Aprille said that she couldn't miss another day of school. So I told them to call Elder and Sis. Johnson, a couple living and working at Saints Academy.

I found out later that Elder Johnson told them that he was already in bed and could not take them. So Aprille caught a ride with someone back to school. Chris stayed in Jackson that night and took the bus back to school the next day. I was furious that Aprille had caught a ride with someone she didn't know, but I was grateful that she was safe.

Later that month, I found out that Therese was ill and could not work. I was working two jobs at the time and still couldn't make ends meet. While I was praying about what to do, Emell came to me and said she was going to withdraw from UNCG and go to Maryland to help. I began to deposit money in Emell's account to help them out. Emell found a full-time job almost immediately and took care of her sister until Therese was back on her feet.

In May when it was time for the students to get out of school for the summer, Aprille told me that she wanted to go to summer school. I had paid for their bus tickets to come home for Christmas and had borrowed the money from Robin Allen to send them back after Christmas. I wasn't able to send them back after Christmas break, because I was living in a place with a stove that was not working and a refrigerator with a door that wouldn't close. I used what money I had to pay for eating out while they were home. I had paid Robin back and had purchased two airline tickets in March and was trying to save money to pay another obligation. I told Aprille that I could pay for her bus ticket to come home but couldn't afford to send her back for summer school two or three weeks later.

While I was talking to her, I found out that Chris didn't give her the ten dollars for her meal book until over a month after they got back. The cafeteria workers wouldn't let her friends bring food out to her any more. She was hurt about that, and I could tell that she didn't want to come home.

She called a day or two later, asking to go home with a friend whose father was coming to pick them up and would bring them back for summer school. The Spirit told me to bring her home. I asked her questions about the girl, the father who was picking them up and where he lived. Against my better judgment, I said ok. I regret that decision to this day.

I tried to reach Aprille from May till the end of August but couldn't. She wrote me a letter just before Chris went back to school in August. When he got back to Mississippi, he called and told me that he saw Aprille and that she looked good. Then he said something that disturbed me. He said that she was not skin and bones anymore. That's when I found out that during the time when her friends were no longer permitted to bring food to her, she had lost weight down to skin and bones. My eyes were like a fountain of tears for a while.

Emell returned from Maryland in August and re-entered school at UNCG. Therese and her son Daniel moved to Greensboro in September. Ithiel returned home after serving three and a half years in the army and later entered DeVry University in Atlanta, Georgia. JT was at A&T and was looking forward to graduation.

When the ones who were attending school out of state came home, we were all together in the same city where I met their dad, got saved, fell in love and married. Therese, Daniel, Ithiel (when he was home from school) and I were worshipping at Wells Memorial. James and Emell were worshipping at Evangel Fellowship.

I was looking forward to having everybody together for Thanksgiving. It had been years since we had been together as a family. I cooked a turkey and dressing with all the trimmings, everybody's favorite food and some of everything. Emell came in early that morning, and I could tell that she had been crying. I asked her why. She said that all of her friends had gone home for Thanksgiving. She had been driving around the streets of Greensboro all night because she didn't have a home to go to anymore.

I hugged her and told her that my little apartment was our home now and that she knew she could always come over here. She had moved out of my apartment around mid-October because, with so many of us there, she couldn't study. She settled down, and we had an enjoyable time and a great dinner. Except for Aprille, all of us were there. We had our family prayer, each of us giving God thanks for the blessings He had given us. Within a month, except for Aprille, we were all back together again for Christmas. We had a merry Christmas.

James graduated from N. C. A&T State University in May of 1996. That was another big day for us. During his first two years, I was able to help him and he didn't have to work. With the time to study, he was always getting academic awards. I would go to the award ceremonies, smiling from ear to ear. He had always studied and worked hard to succeed. He had to come out of school for a while. But he went back, sticking it out through hard times to continue his education. There were times when he couldn't buy his books. His teacher would copy pages for him to study. Bishop Clemmons bought a book for him one semester. And one year Deacon Miller and Deacon Morgan sent him seventy-five dollars apiece. His godparents, Deacon and Sis. Lawson, took him in for a while when he didn't have a steady place to stay. Elder Locket was a great help to him. He allowed JT to play the organ for the Sunday, Thursday night and noon day services, which helped sustain JT until he graduated. We were proud when he received his Bachelor of Science Degree in Electrical Engineering. I was sitting in the audience as he marched, tears of joy running down my smiling face. I couldn't help but give praises to God for what He had done. To God be the glory!

I was still working two jobs without making ends meet. I was looking forward to filing my income tax so that I could pay Elder Leak back and catch up on some bills. I would always play catch up with my bills when I got my income tax returns. Much to my surprise, this time instead of receiving a return, I owed taxes. I was crushed. I had forgotten to take three of my children off my tax form as dependents, and I was in deep trouble. I arranged a payment plan with Uncle Sam, another monthly bill that I could not afford.

I wrote checks by faith before payday and mailed them off so that they could be on time. I was trying to rebuild my credit. During that long period the Lord did not let any of my checks return. I had to keep striving and keep believing that God was going to bring me out in due season. During that time, one day Sis. Nancy had me meet her. She was a great blessing to me. I believe the Lord would do things like that for me in order to let me know that He heard my cry and would deliver me at His set time.

Chris and Karen were married in March of 1997. It was like a big family reunion. Willie and his family came from Washington, D.C., my family came from South Carolina, Sis. Wooden and some of the saints came from Raleigh. Friends and family from Greensboro and other parts of North Carolina were in attendance.

Chris and Karen Turner
March 15, 1997

JT's fiancee, Nichole, finished her studies in December of 1997. She had to wait till May for the graduation exercise. In May of 1998, she marched with her class and received her Bachelor of Science Degree in Marketing from N.C. A& T State University. When she received her degree, she gave a big shout-out to her mom, who was sitting in the stands. It was another special occasion for us, for we were able to meet Nichole's mother, Mrs. Dianne, a beautiful person on the outside as well as on the inside. We also had the opportunity to meet her other family members from Milwaukee and Memphis. Nicole continued her education and became a realtor as well as an artist, painting pictures worth thousands.

James and Nichole Turner
July 07, 1998

James and Nichole were married in July of 1998, which was another great day. We were all together again. My family including, my brother TJ and my nephews, came up from Salters, South Carolina. Nichole's father, McKinley (Mack) Gathings, came from her hometown of Milwaukee and Elder and Sis. Lockett and friends from Evangel Fellowship. Bishop Clemmons and friends from Wells Memorial, including James' godparents, Deacon Percy and Syretha Lawson, and other friends from Greensboro were there as well.

The highlight was when Bishop Clemmons attended, even though he was sick. We were moved by that act of love and kindness. Elder Lockett performed the beautiful ceremony, with Nichole's father giving away the bride. Her father was as nice as her mother, and they both seemed to love James as much as they did their daughter. James and Nichole had bought a new home in June. Nichole moved into the home, and James moved out of his apartment and in with me until the wedding. After the honeymoon, they started their new life together in their brand new home.

CHAPTER 20

Making It Through Prayer

I sought the Lord constantly for financial deliverance. I would pay my tithes and offerings, praying and fasting time and time again. But it seemed as though my situation wasn't getting any better. It had been years of struggles and challenges. As I was praying one night, I told the Lord that I didn't know what else to say. I told Him that I was His child and that I wasn't going anywhere and that I was going to take my chances with Him. After that night I prayed the serenity prayer for weeks: "God, grant me the serenity to accept the things I cannot change, the courage to change the things I can, and the wisdom to know the difference."

    I ate lunch at school most of the time because I had an account there. Once a month when I got paid from the school system, I would pay the account in full and cook a balanced meal. After that, once a week, I would buy a gallon of milk and a box of cereal for my dinner between jobs. I was off from my evening job one Tuesday night, and I was tired of eating cereal. So I decided to go to bed early and eat at school the next day. Shortly after I got into bed, the Spirit led me to go to church. I got up, got dressed and went to church. At the end of service, Dr. Wells asked everyone to come to the back for a repast in celebration of Deacon Goolsby's ninetieth birthday. There was no smell of food during the service. But when I went in the back, everything I had craved earlier was there: fried chicken drumettes, potato salad, different kinds of fruit and cheeses, crackers, etc. I ate there and had some to take home. The Lord was still doing things to let me know that He was with me.

I was sitting up in the bed one night when I decided to balance my checkbook. When I balanced it, the figures showed that I was out of the reds. Even though I was praying for financial deliverance, I couldn't believe it had come. I went over and over the figures, knowing I had made a mistake in addition or subtraction. I was about to beat that calculator to death, but it was right. I was out of the reds. I jumped out of bed and praised the Lord. "Thank you, Jesus! Lord, I thank you!" I couldn't stop praising Him for a while. During my tough times, I didn't say anything to my friends or family; I kept paying my tithes, praying, fasting, going to church and worshipping the Lord. And the Lord had not only heard my cry, but He had delivered me. Around this time I was offered the position of District Missionary, working with a newly appointed District Superintendent who was a praying man. I was still tied to two jobs, and I did not feel that I could do the position justice at the time. After much prayer and consideration, I turned down the position.

In January of 1999, Bishop Clemmons went home to be with the Lord. The home going of Bishop Clemmons left a weight in my heart. I knew him to be a great man of God. When I moved back to Greensboro, he received me with open arms and would use me to help out at times. Bishop Leroy Jackson Woolard became the interim pastor of Wells Memorial. He preached under the anointing of the Holy Ghost, and the Lord did bless. Bishop Woolard greatly helped the church during this transitional period. Later he left a wonderful man of God, Elder Herman G. Platt, at Wells Memorial.

Emell and Aprille graduated from college in May of 2000. Emell received a Bachelor of Science Degree in Nursing from UNCG, and Aprille received a Bachelor of Arts Degree in Art from Mississippi Valley State University. Aprille received a full vocal scholarship in music upon graduating from high school, but she changed her major to Art after the first semester. She had to use student loans like the others because she changed her major, but she made it. We gave praise, glory and honor to the Lord for the accomplishments the girls made through Him. Thank You, Jesus! The children and I rented a van and went to Mississippi Valley State for Aprille's graduation. We had a great time. Some of the saints came from Raleigh to see Emell graduate, and we had another joyful event. Oh! The Lord is good to the children of men!

After my two youngest graduated, I again had a strong urge to visit Colorado. So in June of 2000, I booked a flight to Colorado Springs for the week of July Fourth. I took a vacation from both jobs, my first vacation since my husband died.

Colorado Springs is a beautiful place. Its mountains are breathtaking. The Air Force Academy and the Red Rock formations are a must see if you ever go to Colorado Springs. After I had been there for three days, I noticed that I didn't have to use my inhaler or pop one cough drop after another. Back in Greensboro I had started having trouble with my breathing, and I began coughing a lot. My cough drop bill was sixteen dollars a week at the time; as soon as one melted, I had to pop in another to keep from coughing as much. I also used my inhaler–two puffs every four hours. In Colorado, I went for long walks, breathing easily. It seemed like the place to be, and the time went by quickly. I decided that I would move there. I filled out applications for jobs and for apartments before leaving.

While I was walking one day, I noticed a church that I thought I would visit for Sunday service. Later, I looked in the telephone book for a Church of God in Christ. There was a listing for Bountiful Blessings Church of God in Christ, and I called the number and arranged to be picked up for service. The pastor's wife, Mother Bettie Peterson, came for me. I walked in, and it was as if I were home. Elder Earl Peterson reminded me of Elder Turner in the way he prayed. He reminded me of Elder Clegg when he preached. Oh! He could sing and preach. We had good church. After service, Elder and Mother Peterson took me out to dinner and then back to the motel. The members were nice and down to earth as well. I knew that when I moved there I already had a church home. I left Tuesday after a seven-day vacation and came back to Greensboro, rested physically and mentally and rejoicing in the Lord.

One Friday night during service at Wells, I had given my offering and returned to my seat. Then Elder Torrain came and prayed for me. He whispered in my ears, saying he didn't know my husband but had heard so much about him since coming to Wells. Elder Torrain said the Lord was getting ready to bless me through the churches that my husband used to pastor. I received that word and went on home.

Shortly afterwards, one of the members of Wells called to let me know that Elder Whitley was trying to reach me. She had given him my number. Elder Whitley called and we talked. He told me that he was re-establishing the Founder's Day Service at Revival Temple and was going to be a blessing to me. It had been set up years ago and had continued until Elder Clegg's death. It was discontinued when Elder Cannon became pastor. The Founders Day service was set to reconvene on the same day that it had been observed during Elder Turner's lifetime and during Elder Clegg's lifetime—the second Sunday in December.

In the meantime, I received a call from Superintendent McClurkin. He invited me to be an honored guest at a banquet in October, which he, Sis. McClurkin and Greater Faith Church of God in Christ were sponsoring. Mother Cannon, Mother Hines and I were honored that night. It was a beautiful occasion. I yet remember the kind words and the slide show with my husband on the screen. The service brought back fond memories. Supt. McClurkin presented each of us with a beautiful glass plaque, which I still have in my den, and a check. I took the check to work on Monday and showed it to the teachers. I made a copy of it and put the copy in my files. Every now and then I take it out and look at it.

It was in October when I heard from the apartment complex in Colorado, letting me know that they would have an apartment ready for me by mid-November. I was finally able to pay Elder Leak back. Then I prepared to move. I put in my notice at both jobs. I had worked at Brooks Global Studies Extended Year Magnet School for six years. It was a year-round school, and I enjoyed it. They asked me to stay until we got out for Christmas, and I agreed. I was asked to stay on at my evening job also. They said they didn't want me to leave and told me to just name my price. I named my price, but I still decided to leave.

I sent the necessary paper work and the deposit to the apartment complex office in Colorado. I was set to move in November. I decided to move out of the apartment ahead of time and stay with James and Nichole until the middle of December, which would save a month's rent. Therese put in her two weeks' notice when I put in my notices, so we packed up the apartment and sent our things to Colorado. She and Daniel left a month ahead of me in order to have things set up when I got there.

The Founder's Day Celebration at Revival Temple in Troy was something I'll remember always. People from Troy, Southern Pines, Rockingham, Morvan and surrounding areas packed the church. Elder

Dock Kelly III was a member of Wells at that time, and he had preached at Wells that Sunday morning. But he made it to Troy for the Founder's Day Service. Elder Garcia Morman preached, and we had church that evening. It was like homecoming to see and rejoice with the saints again. And they were such a blessing to me. When I went to work Monday, I told the teachers about the service and showed them the check Pastor Whitley and Revival Temple had given me.

A week before I left, I shipped my car to Colorado so that it would be there when I arrived. The Lord had brought me out, and He was continuously blessing me. Thank You, Jesus!

CHAPTER 21

A Necessary Move

I left for Colorado Springs on December 18, 2000. My children, James, Nichole, Ithiel, and Emell, took me to breakfast and then on to the airport. Chris and his family had recently moved back to Raleigh, where they stayed in a motel for about six months before finding a place to call home. I missed saying goodbye in person. I knew it would be a while before I saw them again.

The plane had to be de-iced in Atlanta before it could fly into the airport in Greensboro. I told the children to go on to church, and when service was over, they could call. If I was still there, they could come back to see me off. When service was over, I was still at the airport so they came back. Some were crying and others looked sad. They touched my heart, and I was sad to leave them. But I felt like it was a necessary move. I have never gone wrong when I followed the leading of the Lord. It was when I followed my own understanding that I made mistakes.

The plane finally came. We made it as far as Chicago but had to spend the night at O'Hara International Airport because of snow. We were able to take off the next day, and I arrived at Denver International Airport on December 19, tired and hungry. Therese and Daniel picked me up, and we went to Colorado Springs. It was my plan to move out West by myself, but my children got together and decided that I shouldn't be out there by myself without knowing anyone. I found out about the conversation later. It was good to have Therese and Daniel with me. Besides Daniel had to finish teaching me Spanish. He came home from day care one day when he was about three and a half years old and said, "Grandma, I've got to teach you Spanish." He began saying, "uno, dos, tress, etc." and counted up to ten. I didn't know what he was saying except for uno.

I had given many things to the Lord while I was living in Greensboro. I had expected help from Wells Tabernacle and from Temple Church. I could not understand why the people who seemed to have loved us for so many years would not help us in our time of need. It was like I'd all of a sudden contracted a contagious disease. I would not have expected the help if the bishop had not said it would be done. A pastor came to see me at my house in Raleigh just before I moved. He told me that the Lord told him to help me. I told him that I was preparing to move, and we talked for a long time that day. But he didn't help me. Instead, he left me a little burdened because he told me things that another pastor had said about me. I had to give that to the Lord also.

There were times when things would hurt me. But I would not let these experiences turn to bitterness, a work of the flesh. Mother Hattie Williams had always told us that if we held something in our hearts against another person, that thing would not be against the person. It would be against us in the Day of Judgment. Instead, I released everything through my tears, closing the gate with a mighty prayer. I gave all those things to the Lord in Greensboro. He delivered me and blessed me naturally and spiritually. I knew that God wanted me in Colorado for a reason, but I didn't know why then.

When I moved to Colorado, I came trusting, leaning and depending on Jesus. Some of my family and friends thought I was crazy. But I'm only crazy for the Lord. I did not come as Mother Turner or Sis. Turner. My family and close friends call me Dean, and that's good enough for me. I came as Dean, a saint of the Most High God.

I planned to continue working two jobs. I had transferred on one job and had sent in a resume to the school system of Colorado Springs. I wrote to District Eleven, but I did not hear from anyone. I was then fifty-seven years old, but I was healthy. After a few days resting, I reported to work at Dillard's Department Store as a sales associate on December 24th of 2000.

When I got my first check at the end of the next week, my mouth flew open. I knew that they had made a mistake. I went to the office to see, but there was no mistake. They told me that my paperwork came in from

Greensboro with that hourly wage. The Lord was still blessing. Thank You, Jesus!

Before I left my job in Greensboro, my manager said, "We don't want you to leave. Just name your price. We just want you to stay." I named my price, even though I had already made up my mind to move. I worked a few weeks longer at Dillard's before leaving because Brooks Global Studies wanted me to stay at least until the Christmas break. So I worked both jobs until almost Christmas. When the time drew closer for me to leave, Dillard's in Greensboro called the manager of the store in Colorado several times. He never returned their calls. When they knew that they couldn't persuade me to stay, they decided to put me in the system at the store in Colorado. They told me to show up at work on the 24th. I was not due for another raise until July 2001. Yet my first paycheck showed a substantial increase. So much so that for the first time in six years, I did not have to work two jobs unless I wanted. God is a wonder!

The cost of living was much higher in Colorado Springs than in Greensboro, but God had provided. When I started working for Dillard's in 1994, I was making minimum wage. But I did my job well, by the help of the Lord, and I got a raise whenever it was time for an increase. By the time I left, I had almost tripled my starting wage. I finally went to the school system in Colorado Springs to check if their pay was any better than it was in Greensboro. I found out that the Colorado School System's pay was about the same as the pay at the school system in Greensboro. I decided to work the one job full time since it was paying a little more than the two jobs did before. I began to thank God for His blessings.

Even though I was miles away from home, I started hearing from Elder Dock Kelly III every month. Elder Kelly and I were at Wells Memorial when I was there, and he would always have encouraging words to say to me. Each month he wrote me a letter, enclosing a monetary blessing. In one of his letters, he told me my husband's labor nor mine was in vain. He was a product of Wells Tabernacle in Southern Pines, and he said my husband's and my coming blessed his soul each Sunday we were there. He was known as "Little Dock" back then. He was thirteen when my husband died, but he has grown up to be a fine young man, whom the Lord has called into the gospel ministry and is using for His glory. God has made a great preacher out of Elder Kelly. Elder Kelly graduated from UNC at Greensboro and has a coaching job at a college in South Carolina. He is also the pastor of a church in Georgia and has been accepted into the Wrestling Hall of Fame. There is an impressive write-up about his accomplishments on the Internet.

The Lord was still blessing. The devil couldn't stand it, so he went to messing. I couldn't understand why I was being treated badly on the job. My co-workers didn't want me there. They told me that they didn't need anyone else. The top man and some of the managers were treating me the same way as my co-workers did. Months later when I asked why, one of the managers told me that it was because I was making almost as much as the managers. I thought to myself, that was not my doing. That was the favor of God!

One of my adversaries got sick on the job and had to go to the hospital. She never came back to work. Two others resigned. The remaining one was still there as a thorn in my flesh. She would smile in my face and then talk about me behind my back. I was nearby when she was talking about me one day, but she didn't see me. I got angry, but I waited until I cooled down before saying anything to her. I was the new kid on the block, so I was trying to be nice. But that didn't seem to help. After months of working under so much pressure, it got to the place that I didn't want to go to work anymore. I started to walk out. As I got ready to leave, my own words came back to me.

One day back in Greensboro, my son Ithiel became dissatisfied with his job. He had a good job and was doing well. The company had sent him to Chicago–all expenses paid–for some training. Upon his return he found out that his boss had been fired. He felt like it was a racial thing and decided to quit his job. I advised him not to walk out before investigating why the man was fired. Then if he still wanted to leave, he should find another job first. Instead of taking my advice, he walked off the job without a notice. He told me that he wouldn't have any problem finding another job. Well, he looked and looked, but it took him over three months to find employment. He depleted his savings; his bills were suffering and he couldn't buy himself anything to eat. But he wouldn't say anything. There were times when I would cook his favorite foods and call him to eat. He would act like he didn't want anything. When I would leave the area, he would tear into that food. He never said, but I knew he learned a lesson from that experience. Now I was getting ready to do the same thing in the heat of the moment.

I stopped and thought for a moment. Instead of walking out that day, I went to see the top manager and his assistant. That was the best move I'd made since I had been there. I found out how many lies had been told on me, and I was able to give the facts about what happened. I encouraged them to check the computer to find out the truth about one particular incident. After checking the stats, they asked me not to leave, assuring me that they would take care of the matter. After that things got better for me on the job from the top on down.

I was still the only person of color in my department, but the girls that left were replaced with people who became good co-workers. My adversary tried to turn every new person against me before they got to know me for themselves. But she couldn't. They would tell me what she would say, and I would pray for her. I told them to judge me for themselves, which they did, and we had peace at work.

One girl named Toni, who came to work in my department, became a good friend. She wanted to know God in a more perfect way. We would talk and talk about the goodness of the Lord whenever we could. She had many questions, and I tried to answer all of them biblically. Those questions that I couldn't answer, I would find the answers and bring them back to her. She began to read and study the Bible and was excited about the Word of God. I taught the adult women's Sunday school class at Bountiful Blessings, so she would ask about the lesson. I would take that opportunity to teach the lesson again. Not only would Toni listen, but some of the other co-workers would listen. Sometimes I would have the lessons copied for her.

The Lord continued to bless me. God made me the best employee that I could be. They presented me with an Employee of the Month plaque on one occasion, and I was always winning some kind of gift. Some people would ask me how I got to be so good at my job. I hadn't considered myself as being good. I told them that I prayed every day before coming to work and used the skills that I had learned in college in salesmanship and accounting. I told them that God was the one who had blessed me to be able to perform.

One day I overheard one of my co-workers talking to the regional head of our department, who came once a month. She told the regional manager that she would just stand back and watch and listen to how I approached people. The regional manager told her that she knew I was good after checking out my stats on the computer. The manager said that I was top in the department, and I had really brought it out. When she said that, I said "thank you Jesus" within myself, knowing that it was no goodness of my own. It was the Lord. The incident also reminded me that the Lord sees all that we do and that others are watching also.

Seven-year-old Daniel and I were eating at his favorite restaurant, Family Buffet, one evening. My hands automatically went up, and I began to praise the Lord. Then I caught myself. Daniel asked me why was I praising the Lord. I shared with him the many times in Greensboro when all I had was cereal and milk for dinner; now I could go to the restaurant or cook any time I wanted. I was thanking God for His blessing.

I had settled down in Colorado Springs, and I was enjoying my new life there. Therese and I had been to Denver, and we had gone shopping in Castle Rock. I had been to Denver several times for church services and to shop. I loved Bountiful Blessings Church of God in Christ, Elder Earl Peterson Jr., Mother Bettie Peterson, their children, Takietha, Andrea and Krystina, and all the saints. I looked forward to Elder Peterson's prayers, preaching and singing, the choir's singing. I loved worshipping with the saints and teaching my Sunday school class. Deacon and Sis. Ganaway of Bountiful Blessings reminded me of Deacon and Sis. Miller, and Deacon and Sis. Williams reminded me of Deacon and Sis. Morgan. It was like I was home. Even though I came there as Dean, they began calling me Mother Turner almost immediately. So I accepted it. I also enjoyed the breath-taking mountains. I would ride down the streets, in awe of all of the beauty. God is a wonder! I got lost many times, but that was fun too–there was so much around every turn. The snow season was stunning also. The snow was so light and fluffy that it would blow at the smallest gust. I was afraid to drive in it when I first arrived. But after paying cab fare to and from work for two days, fifteen dollars each way, I began to drive. I discovered that driving was not bad, because it was snow, not ice, I had to deal with. They kept the streets cleared mostly and the altitude was high enough—six thousand feet above sea level—that when the sun came out, it melted the snow.

Back on the home front, the Lord led Elder Wooden to build a Christian school. In October of 2001, the Upper Room Christian Academy was completed. Elder Wooden invited me to the dedication ceremony and made the way for me to come. All I had to do was go to the airport and get on the plane. When I told Therese about the dedication, she bought tickets for Daniel and herself. Oh, we were excited!

As I was marching with the dignitaries on the day of the dedication of the Upper Room Christian Academy, housed in the J. H. Turner Educational Building, it was like I was a celebrity. I was marching behind our Greater North Carolina Jurisdiction Prelate, Bishop Leroy Jackson Woolard, State Supervisor, Mother Mary Love Green, Pastor and First Lady, Superintendent and Mrs. Patrick L. Wooden Sr., Prophet Shine and others. I was full of gratitude to the Lord for what He had done through Supt. Wooden.

As I sat on the platform, across from the audience of saints from Upper Room and the many people who had come to share in this momentous occasion, my heart was made glad. I had invited Elder Turner's cousin (Sis.), Pearl, and her daughter Carolyn, and Daniel's grandmother, Beverly, from Maryland. All three came. My brother Willie and some of his family from Washington, D.C., my children, Therese, James and Nichole, Chris and Karen, Ithiel, Emell, my stepdaughter, Gail, all of my grandchildren, Lee, Adrena, Micah, Daniel, Chris Jr., James, my niece Ieisha and her son Omar, were all in attendance. It was a great dedicatory service, a day which the Lord had brought to pass.

Shiloh was in progress at the Upper Room. I got to be there when Bishop Gilbert Patterson visited on Friday night. Elder and Sis. Wooden had provided a seat for me on the platform. It was the first time I had been that close to Bishop Patterson. He preached a mighty Word that night, and our souls were blessed.

On that Sunday morning, Superintendent Wooden preached under the anointing of the Holy Ghost. Talking about church, we had church. The Lord not only blessed me spiritually, He also blessed me financially through Supt. Wooden. I was blown away by the magnitude of his generosity. I thanked him, but it seemed as though the words "thank you" were not adequate. So I prayed for him, his wife, his family, the school and the Upper Room family. I stayed in Raleigh a week, and it was good to be able to dine and fellowship with the saints there again. I will never forget the many experiences I had.

When I got back to Colorado, I had a story to tell. I went to work Monday, and every chance I got, I was still talking about the blessings of the Lord. I talked about Supt. and Sis. Wooden, the school, the church, my family, my blessing and how I was treated like a celebrity, until I'm sure they could visualize it all. After a few days, I was able to settle down and concentrate on my work, a wide smile on my face as I relived all the things that the Lord had done.

Things were going good for me. The Lord was continuously blessing me at work, church and wherever I went. And I witnessed to the Lord's goodness whenever He gave me opportunity. One day while I waited to pay for my groceries, the clerk and the person who was bagging started backbiting one of their co-workers who had just left. I let them talk until I got to the register. I asked them had they ever confronted her with their concerns. They said no. Then I told them that if they had something they didn't like about her, the Bible said to go to her and tell her. I pointed out that they could be jumping to conclusions; the girl could be having problems in her body or at home. They needed to find out and then pray for her. They seemed startled, but they accepted what I said and thanked me. Not everyone received me that way, but I was always witnessing at work, grocery stores, gas stations and at church.

On February 4, 2002, Therese came to my job. I could tell by her face that something was wrong. She had come to tell me that my dad had died. I didn't believe her. I told her that I had just talked to my dad the night before. He couldn't be dead that quick. My co-worker took over for me, and Therese and I went into the dressing room. I tried to compose myself. Daddy had told me the night before that he had a terrible headache. I told him that he needed to go to the doctor. He told me that he didn't want to go because the doctor had put his friend "Prof" in a nursing home instead of letting him go home from the hospital. Daddy felt like the doctor and the nursing home were working together, so he didn't want to go to the doctor. I assured him that we would never let him go to the nursing home, even if it meant me moving back home to take care of him. He promised me that he would go to the doctor the next day. I called my brother TJ. He said that when he went to check on Daddy earlier that day, he found our father sitting at the dinning-room table, dead.

I had driven to Kingstree to tell my dad that I was moving to Colorado. I spent my summer vacation time with him before moving. We talked more then than we had talked since I was a little girl. I cooked and fed him breakfast, lunch and dinner, and he enjoyed it. I found out later that he had bragged about how I came and took care of him. I saw him again that October of 2001. Now he was gone.

We flew home to bury my dad. Our mother had died at the age of sixty-five in June of 1985, and now our dad was gone at the age of eighty-six. I was sad in my heart that my daddy was gone, but it was uplifting to think about how my brother Willie and I continued to witness to Daddy until he accepted Christ. Daddy became a different man than the one we had known as children.

A friend of my brother Willie, Deacon Hall, drove down from Washington, D.C. to see and support him. This act of kindness touched Willie. Willie and Deacon Hall served as deacons at Rehoboth Church of God in Christ, under the leadership of Elder Dupree. Evangelist Cynthia Little came from Rockingham, and her support meant a lot to me. Our family and friends from in and out of state banded together in love and support of each other during our time of bereavement. We had a good home-going service for Daddy. Even though it was a sad occasion, it was good to see my children and other relatives. After the funeral my brothers, sister and I took care of the business before I flew back to Colorado.

The Lord is a mighty good God, and He does all things well. He promised to never leave or forsake us. His presence was all around me. There were some things that I needed to do while I was home, and God had taken care of everything before I knew that He had. We serve an awesome God!

I flew back to Kingstree for the family reunion in September. It was good to see my family members again. Our family reunion on my father's side was always held over Labor Day weekend. This time there was a note of sadness because Daddy wasn't there. We focused our attention on his sister, Auntie Becka, and things went well.

Usually when I went to the family reunion, I would spend a few days at Myrtle Beach. This time Emell brought little James Michael, Chris and Karen's son, with her. We, along with my brother Willie and James and his wife Nichole, went to the beach. Little James had fun in the water and the sand. We were staying for a few days, but James, Nichole, Emell and Little James had to go back. When Emell finally got Little James in the car and strapped him in his seat, he looked at me with tears running down his face. I told him that I was going to leave too in a few days because I had to go back to Colorado. He looked at me out of those big, watery eyes and said, "Where is Colorado?" I told him where it was and told him that's where I was living now. Then he said, "I thought you had died." I told him that I didn't die and that I would be back. That seemed to satisfy him a little.

The rent on my apartment kept going up, so when I returned to Colorado, I decided to look for a house to purchase. I found one I liked, but the deal fell through on it. I stopped looking for a while. When I began again, I tried in a new area. The Lord blessed me with a two-bedroom, two-baths home in July of 2003. I got to pick out the colors for my bathrooms. When I looked out my window, there stood the beautiful mountains. I lived six minutes from my job and five minutes from my church. The Lord was continuously blessing me. To God be the glory! I was approaching my sixtieth birthday. I planned to work six more years and then move back to the East Coast in 2009 when I retired.

I flew to Jackson, Mississippi, and rented a car. Then I drove to Hattiesburg, Mississippi for Aprille's graduation from grad school on July 30. Aprille received her Master of Art Education Degree from The University of Southern Mississippi on August 1, 2003 during the 2:30 p.m. commencement exercise. It was held at Bernard Reed Green Coliseum. As I sat there watching my "baby girl," as I call her sometimes, walk up to receive her master's degree, I could hardly see to take pictures. Tears of joy flowed down my face. I wish I could say that I had a part in helping her to reach that point, but I can't. "Baby girl" had done it herself, with the help of the Lord. I gave God glory and honor for what He had done.

Emell was supposed to meet me there but could not make it. She had reserved a room, and I enjoyed that room when I was in it. Aprille and I were gone most of the time. She showed me around her school and introduced me to friends. We had a ball.

Shortly after I returned from Mississippi, I was standing outside the church, talking with Evangelist Martin. I told her that I really didn't want to leave the service to go to work. She told me that the Lord was going to fix it so that I could retire within a year. I wouldn't have to be concerned about leaving church and going to work. I told her that I received that word in the name of Jesus and went on rejoicing in the Lord. Within a few weeks it was time for our family reunion, so I flew home for Labor Day Weekend. It was wonderful being with my children, brothers, sister and other family members and friends. I stayed a week then returned to Colorado.

Shortly after I returned, I remembered that while I was living in Greensboro, my friend Ruth had told me that I could retire at sixty. I began looking into retiring. I made some calls and inquiries, filled out the necessary paperwork and sat everything in motion. I went on with my work on the job and at church while I kept worshipping, praising and rejoicing in the Lord.

Emell had been out to visit us twice. Oh, what a joy it was to have her. Once I clipped an article out of the newspaper, which stated that they were looking for nurses in my area. I sent it to her, trying to entice her to move out there. She laughed about it. Evangelist Cynthia Little came for a visit once, and that was a treat. She preached at Bountiful Blessings like two worlds were coming together. She is highly anointed and my heart rejoiced to see how the Lord used her. James and Nichole flew out and surprised me for my sixtieth birthday. It was a wonderful surprise.

The Lord truly blessed me in Colorado. I looked forward to retiring and working part time. Elder Platt and Elder Torrain had called to check on me. I received correspondence with a financial blessing from Elder Dock Kelly III and his wife every month. I heard from Elder Whitley in December of each year verbally and financially, and I heard from my children and friends often. Robert, Lue Belle and Evangelist Mose had been there for their family reunion, and I got the chance to worship and visit with them. I had never been homesick since moving. Then all of a sudden one day, the Spirit told me to go home. Well, I wasn't ready to return yet. I felt like I had six more good years out there.

I kind of put what I felt God had said out of my mind. Then my right leg and foot started turning black. I kept going to the doctor, and they couldn't find anything wrong. I told Emell about it, and she called my doctor. I don't know what she said to him. But he sent me to another doctor, who couldn't find anything wrong either. I thought about it, and suddenly I got the urge to come on home.

I called my children and told them that I was moving back. They seemed excited. Emell called me one day and asked what kind of house I wanted. I told her a house with no steps inside it. She called me about two or three months later and said, "Mama, I'm a homeowner now. Come on home." She was a homeowner at the age of twenty-eight. To me, that was a great accomplishment. I still get teary eyed when I think about what she did. She has such a big heart. I had planned to do as I did before I moved out West, put in for an apartment and wait until it came through.

My retirement papers were finalized, and I was already retired before I remembered what Missionary Martin had said to me months before. The Lord had brought it to past. God is a wonder!

When I told Elder Peterson that I was moving back home, he stared at me with an expression of disbelief. I put in my resignation as full-time employee at my job and began to work part time. I sold my home to Mr. Joe White for what I owed on it and sent my things home. I stayed a few more weeks with Therese and Daniel before leaving.

My department manager gave me a surprise retirement party my last day on the job. My co-workers were there and the top manager. My adversary was no longer my adversary but was now my friend. They gave me such a warm farewell party and wonderful gifts; I shall always remember their kindness.

Bountiful Blessings Church gave a going-away picnic for me and most of the membership was there. Elder and Mother Peterson along with many of the members gave farewell speeches, gifts and monetary blessings. It was a happy and a sad occasion. It was hard to say goodbye to all of them. They are such nice people. Therese seemed to be okay about my leaving until that day. She cried all night. I think she realized that I was really going home. My little grandson, Daniel, didn't want me to leave either. I was torn inside, but the thought of seeing my family on the East Coast and my son Ithiel's approaching wedding refreshed me.

I can tell you of a truth, the Lord has been good to me. When I moved out to Colorado, I moved on a credit card. But when I moved back, I moved with cash. I didn't have to struggle to pay my bills. I finished paying my taxes back with ease. Whenever I decided, I ate what I wanted to eat where I wanted. The Lord blessed me with a home, which helped make up for the one I had lost back in Raleigh. And He gave me many other blessings. God can do anything. While I was living in Greensboro, He had delivered me from things that had been bothering me. In Colorado, He ministered to me, gave me favor and showed me His power. Our God is great!

CHAPTER 22

Return to Raleigh

I left Colorado Springs on June 9 and arrived in Raleigh on June 12, 2004. I had a terrible flight in a little plane on my last plane trip. After that experience, I decided that I would never fly again. I traveled back to North Carolina by bus. Well, that bus ride was some trip, and I knew I had to go back to flying.

Chris, Karen, Micah, CJ, James, Ithiel and Emell were waiting for me at the bus station. My grandsons had made signs for me, which read "Welcome Home Grammie." We had a great reunion. It was good to see them and to be home. Emell had a nice three-bedrooms, two full-baths home in Knightdale. She gave me the master bedroom, which was all set up and ready for me.

I went to church that Sunday. Pastor Wooden welcomed me back with an open heart and open arms. Sis. Wooden and the saints also let me know that I belonged. It was good to be in service at Upper Room again.

Before I arrived, Ithiel had told me all about his fiancée, April, what a beautiful-saved person she was. I got the chance to meet her that Sunday. She was everything and more than what he had said. I was sure that he had found a "good thing," and I was looking forward to the wedding. He was marrying into a family where his mother and father-in-law to be were saved and in the Church of God in Christ. That was a blessing. I had a daughter named Aprille. Now I was getting a daughter-in-law named April, and they were both born in the month of April.

We got busy preparing for Ithiel's wedding. Therese and Daniel were coming from Colorado, Aprille was coming from Mississippi and James and Nichole were coming from New York.

Power to Overcome

    Ithiel and April got married on July 24, 2004, and the wedding was simply beautiful. It was like a big family reunion. April's family members and friends, along with Ithiel's friend and family members on his dad's side and on my side from South Carolina, Washington, D.C., Maryland, North Carolina and surrounding area, were in attendance. His dad wasn't there in person, but he was there in thought. It was a happy day for all of us.

Ithiel and April Turner
July 24, 2004

April remained in school and graduated from Meredith College in 2006 with a Bachelor of Science Degree in a double major—Spanish and Religion. She is a gifted gospel singer who sings under the anointing of the Holy Ghost.

I was riding down the streets of Raleigh shortly after I returned. My mind went to a time when my husband and I had ridden down the same streets together. So many memories came rushing back, and tears began to flow down my face, till the road blurred. I thought that I was through with all of that. I said, "Lord, you've got to help me." After a while and through prayer, the Lord gave me my smile back. I began to praise God for all my children and thank Him for bringing us all through those tough years. There is some of their father in each of them. I pray daily for their continued growth in the Lord and for success in their lives as well as in the lives of their children.

The life of retirement was great. I had more time to pray for the saved and the lost and for family members in the mornings and evenings. There was more time to witness and to lend a helping hand. To be able to go to every service without having to be concerned about being able to do a good job at work the next day was a delight. And what a joy it was being available to do whatever I could for the furtherance of the ministry at my local church. From time to time, I had the opportunity to drive to South Carolina to visit with family members and friends and to check on my parents' home.

Elder Dock Kelly III was still writing encouraging letters each month, with a financial blessing included. He continued to do so until 2005. Elder Whitley was still having the Founder's Day Service every second Sunday in December. It was joyous to be able to be with the saints in Troy. The Lord always poured out of His Spirit during the service. And the saints yet praised the Lord as they did when Revival Temple began.

The Lord was pouring out of His Spirit in every service at Upper Room. Pastor Wooden was preaching and teaching under the anointing of the Holy Ghost. People were being saved, sanctified and filled with the Holy Ghost, and the Lord was adding to the church continuously. Pastor Wooden, Sis. Wooden and the Upper Room saints have made me feel at home and a part of things. Elder and Sis. Wooden have been a blessing to me every year since I've been back. I am humbled by and thankful for the love, care, respect and concern they show me.

Not only is Elder Wooden a powerful preacher/teacher. He also prays for the sick, and the sick are healed, delivered and set free. I had heard about how he had prayed for Deacon Morgan and how the Lord healed the deacon of cancer. That stayed with me. Then one day Sis. Williams gave her testimony of how the Lord healed her of cancer. Her testimony stayed with me as well. I didn't know then that I would be faced with cancer a few months later. I kept praising and magnifying God and giving Him glory, honor and praise.

CHAPTER 23

My Miracle!

I had a cough that wouldn't go away, so I went to the doctor. She told me that it was a side effect from a blood pressure medication. She took me off that medication, but I kept coughing. After a few months, I went back again for the same reason. The doctor then sent me to the hospital for X-Rays. About two weeks later, I received a note in the mail, advising me to make an appointment to discuss the X-Rays' finding. I made an appointment for March 6.

On March 3, 2007, I got up early to attend a friend's funeral in Rockingham. I noticed that I was coughing more than usual. But I went on anyway. Aprille came also. She prayed for me before I went in the church. I didn't cough much until about halfway through the funeral. Sis. Wooden and Sis. Leak gave me cough drops and mints so that I could make it through the service. Evangelist Little prayed for me before we left Rockingham. I was all right until we got to Southern Pines. We stopped several times because I was coughing so much that I was choking. By the time we got to Sanford, Aprille decided to call Emell. Emell told her to take me to the nearest hospital. I told Aprille to take me home, which she did. When we got home, I undressed and went to bed. I thought I needed some rest. Later that evening, when I still couldn't stop coughing, Emell insisted that I go to the Emergency Room. After spending hours in the waiting room, the attending physician decided to send me home with antibiotics. Emell mentioned the X-Rays I had taken a few weeks prior. He decided to go check them. When he returned, he decided to admit me.

The X-Rays showed a mass on my left lung. A CAT scan was ordered. Before daybreak Sunday morning, I was diagnosed with lung cancer. The doctor said that the mass had metastasized because a cancer of that sort usually starts in other places in the body.

I stayed in the hospital eleven days and underwent several procedures and tests, all of which indicated that I had cancer. The PET scan was the last test and would determine if the cancer was in the limp nodes. At about 5:30 on the morning of March 14, I was preparing to be transported by ambulance to another hospital for a PET scan. A verse of Scripture dropped into my mind. "I am the Lord thy God that healeth thee." In my mind I was sure that the PET scan would show that my limp nodes were not cancerous. Two hours after I got back to my room at Wake Med, the doctor came. He said that my chest lit up like a Christmas tree on the PET scan. The cancer was in my limp nodes. I couldn't believe what he had said. When Emell came about thirty minutes later, I said to her, "Shall I cry now or cry later?" Her reply was, "Go ahead and cry, Mom. We have all had our cry, and we are going to believe God." I thought I was going to tell her the bad news. But she, along with her siblings, my brother Willie and Evangelist Little had already talked and prayed on a conference call over the phone. We hugged and I cried a little. Then I remembered what the Lord had said early that morning. "I am the Lord thy God that healeth thee." I grabbed a hold of that Word and held on for dear life. I was released from the hospital later that day, with surgery scheduled for March 21.

In the meantime my pastor, Supt. Wooden, and the Upper Room Church of God in Christ were in prayer for me. All who visited me on Sunday afternoon, March 4, told me that Pastor Wooden prayed a powerful prayer for me during the morning service. They believed that I was healed. Pastor Wooden and Elder Cooper came to see me after church. Pastor prayed another powerful prayer for me.

Each time I got some bad news from test results, I also received some good news. I was told that my brothers, sister and children were on a fast for me. I heard that Pastor Peterson and the Bountiful Blessings Church of God in Christ, Colorado Springs, Colorado were on an around–the–clock prayer vigil for me. Mother Crawford and her prayer team from First Church of God in Christ, Brooklyn, N. Y., Bishop Searight and the church in New Brunswick, New Jersey along with many others were in prayer for me. Thank You, Jesus!

I went to church on March 18. Pastor Wooden preached a powerful message. I began to praise God in the service with the little strength I had. When I sat down, a voice down on the inside of me kept ringing out "I am healed!" The voice kept on ringing the same three words throughout the furtherance of the service. I began to verbalize them on the way home and all that afternoon. Krystina, Pastor Peterson's daughter from Colorado Springs and her husband came to the house to see me that afternoon. I told them I was healed.

Emell took me to my appointments on Monday morning. I had to take more X-Rays at the hospital and see the anesthetist and the surgeon. The surgeon told me all of the things that could happen during the operation. He said that it was a possibility that I would not make it off the table. When he went in and took a biopsy of the limp nodes, the findings would let him know whether to go on with the operation or not. He talked to me about whether my lung function could stand such an operation; the test that I had received in the hospital showed that my lung function was borderline. He also talked about the possibility of paralysis. When he got through, I was shaking. But I got myself together. I looked over at Emell and said, "We will have the victory!"

All of my children came home to be with me. Therese, James and Nichole, Chris and Karen, Ithiel and April, Emell and Aprille were right by my side. On the night before the surgery, they along with my grandchildren, Micah, Daniel, Chris Jr. and James, joined hands and prayed an anointed prayer for me. Elder Chris Turner prayed, "This is just one more fight… What's another fight…Mom, we are going to fight it with you…Despite all, victory!" The glory of the Lord was in that living room.

When they left to go to their separate homes, the telephone rang. It was Pastor Wooden. He talked with me, prayed with me and told me that everything was going to be all right. Before going to bed, I prayed. I told the Lord that I didn't want to have to go through surgery. But nevertheless, His will be done because I wanted Him to get the glory. I went to the hospital Wednesday morning with words of encouragement on my mind.

"I am the Lord thy God that healeth thee."

"It's one more fight."

"Despite all, victory!"

"Everything is going to be all right."

I knew when I came through, I would give God all the praise and glory. But if not, I knew that I was saved.

The last thing I remember before going into surgery were my children, my grandson Daniel and Evangelist Mose standing over me. Sometime after the surgery and while I was still dazed, Sis. Valeria said, "You came through the surgery, and you did well." Before I went back to sleep, she also said that T. Lett's husband was there. When I came too hours later, my children, Pastor and First Lady Wooden, Evangelist Mose and Evangelist Little were standing around me. Oh! I was glad to see them.

The doctor came in on that Friday and said, "I don't know what happened, but we couldn't find cancer nowhere." My heart leaped, and I began to say, "Thank you, Jesus! Thank you Jesus!" I praised the Lord with all the strength that I had. The surgeon said he didn't know what the mass was, but it looked like matted gray charcoal. He said it looked very angry and had to come out. When he said that it looked angry, I thought of it as the devil, who was mad with me because I was a child of God and would not do his will but the will of the Lord.

Emell had left the room when the doctor came to remove the chest tubes. Shortly afterwards the nurse left, closing the door behind her. They had said that I should be able to breathe on my own. But I was having trouble breathing. When I thought I would lose consciousness, I pushed the button for the nurse. She offered me oxygen, but I told her that I wanted to keep trying. She left and closed the door again. I was in that room, struggling, and when I thought I was losing consciousness again, I pushed the button. The nurse came back in and talked with me. She offered me oxygen again, but I said that I wanted to continue on my own. I asked her to leave the door open. I didn't want to come home with an oxygen tank, so I prayed to the Lord and asked Him to fill up whatever lungs I had left. And He did. I came home on March 28. I give God all the praise, glory and honor for healing me. Thank You, Jesus!

After a few weeks, I was still very sore. I mentioned it to Emell. She told me that the mass on my left lung was as big as a grapefruit. They had tried to get it out by cutting it up in chunks. They couldn't get it that way, so they had to remove a rib to get to it. I didn't know until then that I was missing a rib. I told Emell that I hoped it wasn't the rib that Adam gave me. Even though I am missing a rib and half of my upper left lobe, I am breathing and doing well. And I can yet praise the Lord. Thank You, Jesus! One doctor said, "It was a miracle." The surgeon said, "It's the Lord we have to thank."

During this trying time, my family did not let me spend one night in the hospital by myself. My sons, daughters, including my chosen-daughter Cynthia, and daughters-in-law took turns spending days and nights with me. They were remarkable. I thank God for having saved, praying, believing children.

When I got home, the children had already arranged for my sister-in-law, Matilda McCrea from Washington, D.C., to come and take care of me. Before she retired, she worked in the school system and at group homes in D. C., preparing different dietary meals. She knew just how to prepare my meals according to my diet. Nichole, Bro. Vernon and Sis. Valeria cooked and helped to take care of me until Matilda got here. When she came, she prepared my meals and helped Emell and Aprille take care of me for weeks before leaving. That was a blessing.

Jesus is the same yesterday, today and forevermore. Thank You, Lord, for my miracle!

CHAPTER 24

Broken Contract

The devil has a contract out on you and your children, but God will break the contract.

Below you will find out what happened to the family of James H. Turner. We went through some trying times, collectively as well as individually, since God made me that promise. But God will do just what He said. He brought us through. When it seemed my children's grief and hardship would take them out, I kept praying. I told the devil that he could not have my children. I was reading the Bible one day when the Lord led me to the fifty-fourth chapter of Isaiah. When I read the fifth verse, tears began flowing down my face. I began to talk to the Lord. "Lord, if my Maker is my husband, then my Maker is my children's father, and they need you." By the time I finished praying and reading the entire chapter, my burden had rolled off my shoulders.

Everywhere I go, I tell mothers to never give up on their children. Moms have to continue to pray for their children because the moms might be the only ones praying for them. The Lord entrusted my children to my husband and to me. With my husband gone to be with the Lord, I had to rely on my Maker to help me. He had already said that He would; I just needed to be reminded. He did and we are all Overcomers. Praise the Lord for what He has done!

Evangelist Willa D. Turner
Retiree–Serving with the Women's Executive Team, Missionary Circle,
Mother's Board, Intercessory Prayer Team & Prison Ministry
Upper Room Church of God in Christ

Power to Overcome

Therese Turner
Political Science Major: Winston-Salem State University
Great Apologist for Jesus Christ, Mother of one - Daniel

Daniel Turner
Graduate: Knightdale High School
Junior: N. C. State University

James & Nichole Turner
Graduate: N. C. A. & T.
Bachelor of Science Degree
Electrical Engineering, Bilingual,
A Musician, Great Apologist for Christ
Husband and Father of two

Power to Overcome

James III (J3

Boaz

Elder Christopher Turner
Graduate: Saints Academy
Music Major: Mississippi Valley State
Graduate: COGIC Academy
Anointed Gospel Preacher & Singer
Father of four

Willa D. Turner

Micah Turner
Gratuate: Upper Room Christian Academy
Enloe High Shool
Junior: Methodist University, Fayetteville, N.C.

Power to Overcome

C. J. Turner
Upper Room Christian Academy
Graduate: Smithfield-Selma High School
Freshman: Cape Fear Community College, Wilmington, N.C.

Willa D. Turner

James Michael Turner
Upper Christian Academy
Junior: Athens Drive High School

Tia Turner
Middle School Student

Power to Overcome

Ithiel Turner
Served: U.S. Army
Electronics Major: DeVry University
Husband & Father of three
A Soldier for Christ

April & Ithiel
Jameson Isaiah, Noah David & Ithiel Josiah

Emell Turner
Graduate–Athens Drive High School
Graduate: University of North Carolina at Greensboro, North Carolina
Bachelor of Science Degree in Nursing
Graduate–COGIC Academy, Magna Cum Laude
Critical Care RN
Anointed Gospel Preacher

Power to Overcome

Aprille Turner
Graduate–Saints Academy, Lexington, MS
Bachelor of Arts Degree–Mississippi Valley State University
Master of Art Education–University of Southern Mississippi
Co-founder, Director and Advocate
Women Fighting Crimes Against Children (WFCAC)
"A Voice for Christ–A Voice for Children"

Evangelist Cynthia B. Little
Mother of four: Mitchell Jr., Brian,
Dorthell and Kelvin Little
Grandmother of four: "Little" Brian, Fallon and twin boys,
Carson & Aiden
District Missionary
Anointed Preacher and Soul Winner
Great Revivalist

Willa D. Turner

Gail Summerville
Studied at Richmond Technical College–Executive Secretary
Career: Member Manager
Mother of two: Adrena and Albert Nicholson Jr.
Grandmother of two: Jayln & Nasir Nicholson

Front Row, standing (left to right): Micah (holding Noah),
CJ (holding J3), Daniel (holding Josiah's hands)
Second row (left to right): Karen, Emell, Mom, James, April
Third Row (back row): Chris, Aprille, Therese, James Jr., Nichole, Ithiel

Front, seated: James Jr.,
Standing, left to right: Daniel, Emell, Dean, Chris Jr., James, Michael, Noah, Adrena, Gail, Lee, Chris Sr., Karen, April, Ithiel, Josiah & Therese

CHAPTER 25

Letters, Tributes & Poems

March 27, 1966

Dear Darling,

God bless you in Jesus' name. I love the Lord because he is so real to me. Willa, I know you have been praying because God has done great things in our revival. The greatest thing I believe I have ever seen happened in this revival. I saw a woman have a heart attack and then look as if she was dying, and then I saw how God touched her body and revised her and brought her back as if from the dead, gave her speech back, all in the same night. We are serving a miracle working God.

Willa, I thought about you all the week. I remembered the wonderful few hours I spent with you Sat. night. I enjoyed every minute of it. It was as if we had just met for the first time. I mean we had just really got acquainted with each other. Love is such a beautifully strange thing. Perfect love casteth away all fear, says the scriptures. So what we really need is perfect love. The reason I smiled so much the other night is because I have overcome something in my life, Baby. I believe I have overcome <u>insane jealousy</u>. You know what I was telling you about on the letter I wrote that time. I believe I have overcome. It's a good thing to overcome something in life. It really makes you feel free, and now that I have overcome, I feel like I could make you a better husband.

You have to excuse me for not writing more tonight, but I am very tired. I have just come out of two revivals and a District Meeting and attended a second District Meeting, so you know how I feel, also I work six days a week also. Please understand. I love you.

Yours Forever,

James

June 8, 1966

Dear Willa,

Greetings in the sweet name of Jesus, Lord and King of my soul. I thank him for what he is doing right now. God has been very good to me.

Willa, I want you to know that I certainly enjoyed being with you Sunday. I love surprises like that. You can do that anytime you'd like to. I was telling my mother today, I have never met anyone like you. I have traveled halfway around the world, met people in all walks of life, but there is not another Willa "D" in all the world. You have a unique personality; you know what you want and you certainly know how to go about getting it. You are especially endowed with beauty; yes God really blessed you, (smile) and I'm glad he did. However, I am not taken by your beauty alone. I love you because you are just who you are.

It's five minutes to midnight right now, and I just arrived from service a few minutes ago. We had a wonderful time in the service. God met us there in a great way. I love the Lord because he has heard my prayer and my supplications, because he has inclined his ear toward me. Therefore will I call upon him as long as I live (Psalm 116). This Psalm of David has been with me ever since I have been saved. Remember it and repeat it in your heart when you are burdened. God is a burden bearer and a problem solver, a way maker, a friend in trouble, bread when you're hungry, water when you're thirsty, bridge over water, you name it, God's got it.

I love you; may God keep you is my prayer.

Yours Forever,

James

June, 1966

James H. Turner, my dream come true. Is it really real? Is it happening to me? How can I ever thank God for the wonderful privilege of meeting such a fine man. Saved, sanctified, baptized with the Holy Ghost, wonderful preacher, consecrated and handsome. All these things wrapped up into one. Who could ask for anything more? Surely not I.

Willa D.

June 24, 1966

Dear Willa,

Greetings from God the Father and from the Lord Jesus Christ. Truly my soul is rejoicing in the God of my salvation. The Lord is blessing me right now.

Dear, I enjoyed the wonderful singing tonight. The Lord really has blessed the choir. I love the Lord for his goodness. Singing stirs something way down within me. I noticed during the devotional service an old lady got up and sung an old hymn, "Amazing Grace." That started me off in the spirit. I love those old songs that I can understand the words. Don't get me wrong, I love these modern, up-to-date songs also, but most of them are derived from the hymns.

Doll baby, I enjoyed seeing you, and above all, I enjoyed seeing you on fire for the Lord. I love to see you go forth in the praises of his Holy name. You seem to put your whole heart into it. That is the only way to get anything from God, with our whole heart. I enjoyed seeing that beautiful smile of yours, it is always encouraging to see you. I remember telling some time ago that you have such a strong face. It gives me more courage to see you.

I believe that when we are married that God will really bless us because I think we are both serious about our souls. I could go on, but I must close. May God bless you.

Yours,

James

P.S. Tell Francis to thank God right now for a job.

June 23, 1966

Dear Willa Ann,

Greetings from God the Father, and the Lord Jesus Christ.

Dear, it would hardly be adequate for me to say "I miss you." Those mere words can hardly describe the empty feeling within the portals of my heart when I'm not with you. You are a wonderful, young, intelligent lady, and I love you for it. I can imagine seeing the beautiful smile upon your lovely face. Those accented oriental eyes. Baby, you got it made.

I am preparing to go to church, and I am lying down, wondering about many things. I hope to see you soon, possibly Sunday, I don't know exactly. God has been especially good to me this week. I guess you noticed my pen quit on me. I have written more letters this week, I guess, than any other time I can remember. I even wrote my sister for the first time in about six years. Ok, I am sorry and ashamed of myself. I know that's what you are saying.

Darling, I truly hope that you are as much mine as I think you are. I think a lot more of you than you possible realize. You mean a great deal to me. Since I met you, you have been a great incentive to me. The spark that has caused me to go on and try to be something in life. Stick with me, Baby, we are both going places.

Yours forever,

James

Willa D. Turner

February 12, 1967

Hi Honey:

I just want to talk a little while. Do you mind? Oh, I am so glad that you do not mind. You know, Honey, my God is so wonderful. What about yours?

I feel so good right now. I feel like going on. I just came from a wonderful service, and my soul is still rejoicing. The Lord really met us in the service tonight. I feel that if I die right now, I will see my Savior's face. You know I do not even mind dying right now, for my soul is right with God. I am trying to live so I can feel this way every day of my life. Oh, I thank God for salvation.

The Lord is so good to me. He has made ways for me when there was no way, He has made my sad heart glad so many times, He has lifted up my hung-down head many times and most of all He has saved, sanctified and baptized me with the most precious gift among gifts, the Holy Ghost. He has put joy in my soul and running in my feet. He is a prayer-answering God. How can anyone help but serve a God like my Jesus!

Oh, if I had wings of a dove, I would fly above the clouds to meet my Jesus in the air. To be like Jesus is my heart's desire.

The Lord is even blessing me in Sunday school, for there was a time when I would not contribute by way of conversation; but the Lord is giving me what to say, and I thank God for it. I could go on and on, but I really should go to bed now.

Deloris Garrett Hamilton has a seven months (premature) baby girl. They are both fine. It weighted five pounds and some ounces.

May God bless you always and never forget that I love you more than I could ever say.

With all my love,

Willa "Dee"

August 18, 1967

Hi Love:

Greetings in the name of Jesus.

I am happy and bubbling with joy because I am free. God has made me free, and I am so thankful. The Lord has really been good to me, and He is pouring out showers of blessings on me whereof I am truly glad. We had a high time in the Lord on Tuesday night. The Lord came in the prayer and blessed, and throughout the service He continually blessed. I am sure that you are having a good time in the Lord this week. I hope that the entire membership is being blessed of the Lord.

You are a mighty fine man who loves the Lord and the church. I am sure that you are a wonderful pastor because you have the love of God in your soul. You are a laborer for the Lord, and I am sure that He leads, guides and directs you in the ministry. I believe God has great things in store for you. May God bless you always is my daily prayer.

I have been trying to write you all week. For the past six weeks, I have really been working from eight to five, with one hour for lunch. Things will be better now, though, with the students gone home until regular school session begins. Nevertheless, I am taking time out to write to the man who means more to me than anyone else I have ever known. The man whom I love so dearly and with whom I want to spend the rest of my life with. I love you, Darling, with all my heart. My desires are only for you. You make my days brighter and more pleasant. No one will ever be able to take your place in my heart. I love you so much.

I am looking forward to a grand Convocation. A Holy Convocation in the true meaning of the word. Not a signifying session or a fashion parade but a Holy Ghost time in glorifying God. I pray that this Convocation be the best yet, and I hope more souls are saved than ever before. God is able to do it. We need salvation in a time like this. It is time for everyone to be concerned about his soul. I believe God is going to bless just like He is blessing right now. We will be from different churches but of the same family, striving for a home in the Heavenly Kingdom.

I feel good right now. I feel that if I lie down tonight and do not wake up in the morning, no one will have to worry about me, for I will be sleeping in Jesus. I like to feel this way every day. Seems as though the higher I reach the more blessings I receive from God, yet I keep on reaching and seeking more of Him.

Pray for me for I need your prayers. I shall be looking forward to seeing you whenever you can come. May God bless and keep you now and always.

Love Always,

Willa

LOVE
April 9, 1968

My Love for my husband
Elder James H. Turner
6'3" – 194 lbs. – Very Handsome

LOVE: A very deep, strong, emotional feeling that I have for my husband. It makes
    me laugh. It makes me trust Him. It makes me want to be with him all the
    time. It makes me very comfortable with him. It makes me feel free around
    him. It makes me love talking with him. It makes me want to please him. It
    makes me sad when he is sad and glad when he is glad. It makes my heart
    ache when his heart aches. It makes me sad when he is physically ill. It
    makes me love, cherish and obey him in sickness and in health, for richer
    and for poorer. And I do mean it, for I am speaking from experience.

    My love for him is a complete love. I love him deeper than I love any other
    earthly creature. I love him because God made him. I love him because he

is truly saved. I love him because he is sanctified. I love him because he is
sure enough baptized with the Holy Ghost. I love him because he is preaching God's word, the true gospel. I love him because he is very concerned about lost souls. I love him because he loves everybody. I love
him because he is my husband. I love him because he is the best husband in
the whole, wide world.

Hurry Home Honey

I love you.
Your wife,
Willa

July 6, 1979

Hi Honey,

 Greetings in the name of Jesus.

 This leaves me tired and sleepy but enjoying the goodness of the Lord. It is about ten of three a.m., and we have just returned from service. We had a good time tonight. We went to Hollywood and to the Farmer's Market today.

 Even though I am really enjoying myself, I feel that this trip would be much more enjoyable if you were here to share it with me.

 I miss you very much. I wish I could see you right now. I love you very much, and with a room full of girls, I am lonely for you. You are a very handsome man, and you have so many good qualities. Most of all you are saved. I thank God for allowing me to spend these last twelve years with you. I am looking forward to many more good years with you. I pray that God will make me more of an asset to your ministry.

 How are the boys doing? Hope that you all are spending a lot of time together as Father and sons.

I see Braithwaite about every day. He told me to tell you that he asked about you. He said that he will be in L.A. for a month then in Detroit for a month.

Honey, I am so sleepy now until I must go to sleep. I love you and the children and the Saints.

Kiss the children for me and tell them I said hello and that I love them. Give my love to the Saints and take care of yourself.

Love always

Your Wife,

Willa

January, 1987

Praise the Lord!

God bless you, Pastor. I hope this letter finds you in the best of health. The Lord put you on my heart early Tuesday morning while I was at work. The thought came to me just to write a letter. Most of all I want you to know that I love you. You are indeed a very special man, and I really appreciate you and the ministry God has given you. I thank God that there is someone who'll cry aloud and spare not. It is joy to my soul to know someone who's living godly.

I appreciate the word and how you allow God to manifest himself through you. Pastor, I just want to let you know that there is somebody who is gladly receiving the word; yes, the word is taking root within me. Thank God for the things he's doing and how the word keeps coming.

I was reading the thirty-third chapter of Ezekiel, and all I could say afterwards was, "My God." I now more than ever realize the tremendous responsibility you have as the watchman. Pastor, I'm praying for you effectually and fervently, and I have confidence that God shall continue to strengthen, elevate, inspire and lead you. I understand Satan will always be on the attack, but thank God for the weapons of our warfare.

My desire is to go higher and to do all I can to help the church and the ministry to increase. I am with you, Pastor. I have not lost the vision. I'm following you as you follow Christ. God bless you and yours.

Sincerely yours,

Bro. Springs

August 9, 1987

Mother Turner,

Greeting to you in name of Jesus. I was thinking of you and your family and your late husband, my Pastor, a true man of God. I am so glad God saved me through his teaching the Word of God. Mother Turner, you are a very special Lady, a true Woman of God, a true friend. I love you for what you did for Cynthia, taking her as your own. I know you love her as your own, and I thank you for that. No one can ever take your place as first lady in my heart; they will have to make their own place. I know God didn't bring you this far to leave you. In my prayers I ask God to help you and your family.

I love you and will always (a Special Love)

Your Sister in Christ,

Julia

(I will come to see you sometime)

Willa D. Turner

Thursday Night
1316 E. Washington Street
Rockingham, NC 28379

Dear Sis. Turner,

Holy greetings in the name of our Lord and Savior Jesus Christ.

Please forgive me for not writing. I received your card some time ago but was sick with the flu or something. I really didn't feel up to writing, but it was nice to hear from you and to know that you and your children are doing fine. I think about you all often and pray that things go well with you all. The Lord is good to me. Let me live to see my seventy-ninth birthday August 27. Nobody can do you like the Lord.

I pray that the church family are doing good. Our church is in the worst I have ever seen it out of the forty-nine years I have been a member. Where there is confusion, there's no God. I can't take it. You pray for us. Give the children my love and please pray for me.

Thanks again for writing.

May God bless you,

Lou Mattie Kendall

Dear Mother Turner,

What we had we cherish, but what we have left we must consider.

It is true that there are times when we must pause, shed tears, bear the hurt because our hearts bleed and our body aches, so we grieve.

Yet somewhere, somehow thro that mysterious gift from God, we realize that thro our faith and thro the use of time, God heals our minds and hearts as He heals our bodies when they are wounded.

You must press now, for you have work to do. Learn to take one day at a time.

Remember that God loves you and we love you too. Cling to that which is good. God's grace is sufficient for the day. A time of rain or sorrow comes into every life, but remember sunshine always follows the rain. It may be the next day before the rain stops, but sunshine will follow.

Many are the afflictions of the righteous, but God delivers him out of them all (Psalms 34:19).

Watch and pray, for while you sorrow, the enemy could slip in if you don't.

You may feel all alone. But just remember Jesus promised to never leave or forsake us. You've got the Father, Son and the Holy Ghost. David said goodness and mercy would follow him all the days of his life. We can claim them too. Then you've got Deacon Morgan and me and the rest of the Upper Room family, not to mention Therese, JT, Chris, Emell, Aprille and Ithiel. We all need Mother Turner. We need that smile, that godly wisdom, that example of a godly woman that you project. For you are a light at Upper Room. You are a credit to our work. Mother Hallman is depending on you.

You just Hang in there. In this life we are gonna be bumped and bruised, but don't give up. Pause if you must, but don't you quit. Remember Phil. 4:4-8. I thank God for you.

Yours in Christ.

Love & prayers,

Sis. Pattie Morgan

Willa D. Turner

Tribute

By

James H. Turner Jr.

Elder James H. Turner was a man who was loved by a great many people. He was the founder of the Upper Room Church of God in Christ. He was also my father.

My father was a man who believed in God. As a father, he often used his knowledge of the Word of God as a tool in raising us as children. He believed that the answers to life's problems lie in the Word of God. I feel that God has blessed me to have had a father like Elder James H. Turner.

I feel honored and proud to bear his name.

I admire this man because of his sincerity about his Salvation and his strong will to make it into the Kingdom. He inspired me to be Saved. He also showed me by the way he conducted his life that you can stay Saved.

To me, Elder James H. Turner will never die. He shall Live in my memories and my dreams for however long that I shall live, but his presence will surely be missed.

Founder's Day Celebration–August 21, 1988

"Daddy, I wish you could have waited long enough to see me graduate. I love and miss you so much."–Therese–1988

"I'm saved now, but I'm still having problems trying to make it without my daddy. I love him. He understood me. He listened to me."–James (JT)–1988

"I love my daddy, and I sure hate that he left me."–Chris–1988

   "I need my daddy."–Ithiel–1988
   "I miss my daddy."–Emell–1988
   "I love my daddy." –Aprille–1988
   "I miss my daddy."–Gail–1988

"The best father a girl could have ever hoped for. Thank God, my hope was a reality."–Cynthia–1988

"'Honey,' as I have called him for more than twenty years, is missed so greatly. He treated me like a queen. He made me feel so very special. He was the greatest husband a woman could ever have, and as I told him time and time again during his lifetime–'I love you.' He preached a God spell on me about every time he preached. He was the most anointed gospel preacher I knew.

There is a great void in my life now, but I am going on in the name of Jesus. That's what he taught us. I am trying to take care of our children. Farewell but never goodbye. See you in Glory. Your wife, Willa"–1988

"Salute" to a Great Man of God
"Now unto him that is able to keep you from falling, and to present you faultless before the presence of His glory with exceeding joy, to the only wise God our Savior, be glory, and majesty, dominion and power, both now and ever. Amen." Jude 24th verse.

"Until we meet on Resurrection Day,

Your Family"–1988

Willa D. Turner

GRADUATE'S PRAYER

LORD KEEP HER CLOSE BY YOU
Thank you, Lord, for this day
The day of Emell's graduation
As her father and I stood before your alter and dedicated her
Life to you, so many years ago, I stand before you now
Asking you to continue to keep her in your care
Lord, keep her close by you
Even though her Father and Godfather passed away before she
Graduated from high school, you were with her all the way
Lord, keep her close by you
As she pursues a career in nursing
Lord, keep her close by you
As she cares for her patients, let her touch be a holy, healing
Touch to everyone entrusted to her care
Lord, keep her close by you
As she comes in contact with danger and with contagious
Diseases, protect her and keep her safe
Lord, keep her close by you
Use her for your glory so that her career will be
More than just a career

Lord, keep her close by you
Be with her always, even to the ends of the world
Lord, keep her close by You–Amen

Your Mom–Willa D. Turner–May 2000

REMEMBERING DAD

You stood tall among God's champions, as you
Preached to lost souls,

Many days have passed since you left, but my
Love for you has never grown cold,

As I sit and reflect about the time we shared,
Though too brief, the memories I have of you
nothing could ever compare.

It's hard to believe it's been twenty years, since I last
saw you face-to-face; my mind sometimes
wonders why you left us, on that fateful
spring day,

Your glimpse of heaven, as I understand now
helped you make your choice,

Knowing that you went to be with the LORD,
my soul can do nothing but rejoice.

Dad, I love and miss you always ...
Until we meet again,

Aprille

Commemorating the twentieth anniversary of the
passing of my Father, this 21st day of May, 2007

ERECTION OF HEADSTONE

I wanted to have a headstone erected at the gravesite of my husband. I told the children what I had in mind, and they wanted to help me with the project. We decided on the inscription, and I called to see how much it would cost. Then we pooled our monies together and ordered the headstone.

James and Nichole came home for Thanksgiving and for the laying of the headstone. We had a great Thanksgiving service at church, an anointed family prayer and a delicious Thanksgiving feast at home. The day after Thanksgiving in November of 2007, the children, grandchildren, daughters-in-law and I, went down to Southern Pines to meet Mr. Dwight and one of his workers from Eastwood Monument in order to lay the stone.

We had our different sayings and spent some time there by the grave before returning to Raleigh. Even though we don't have Dad in the flesh anymore, he yet lives because we carry his teachings in our hearts day by day.

Sometimes on special days I like to drive down to see him. Whenever I go that way for something that is happening in Southern Pines, Rockingham or Hamlet, I usually plan my time so that I can stop by the cemetery. Sometimes I stand quietly, remembering our lives together. Sometimes I talk and talk to him and then go. In the beginning, I used to drive down to be with him on special days. But now each year on September 16, our wedding day, May 21, the day he died, and his birthday, I think of him, no matter where I am or what I am doing.

Legacies of Faith and Faithfulness
By
Therese Turner

People are always admonished to "break the cycle" of behaviors in their families and to start anew. This usually means something bad. But I'd like to talk about a cycle, a legacy, that my mom has carried forward and has passed down to her children and grandchildren. This is a cycle about faith and faithfulness to our Lord and Savior, Jesus Christ.

I have a great-grandmother, Maggie Dunlap Barnes, who was a servant of Jesus Christ. She had nine children, including my grandma, Lula Belle. Great-grandmother brought them up in the fear of the Lord, teaching them about Holiness. When she'd finished rearing her own children, she taught the children's Sunday school class at Wells Tabernacle Church of God in Christ. As an adult, I have met people who've said to me, "I knew your great-grandmother. When I was a child, my parents took me to Sunday school at your church, and Mother Barnes taught me about Jesus." I have another great-grandmother, Annie Glenn Douglas Turner, who was a servant of Jesus Christ. She had ten children, including my granddad, James Turner. She brought them up in the fear of the Lord, teaching them about Holiness.

Each one stressed the importance of having a personal relationship with Jesus Christ, and each provided a living, breathing example of how to live holy.

Grandma Glenn's son James ran the streets at one point. But Grandma Glenn maintained her faith and her faithfulness, praying that God would show grace and mercy to her children. And Granddaddy didn't pass up his opportunity at Grace. He repented and gave his life to Jesus Christ. The Lord blessed him, and he eventually became Pastor James Turner, a servant of Jesus Christ, a good son, a good husband, a good father and a good friend. As an adult, I met people who said, "I knew your grandfather, and he was praying man. I never met anybody who could pray and shout like Pastor Turner."

Grandma Lula Belle was also a servant of Jesus Christ. She and my granddaddy James had a son—my dad, James H. Turner. They brought him up in the fear of the Lord, teaching him about Holiness. At one point, my dad was running the streets… falling into alcoholism, violence and mischievousness. But Grandma Lula Belle stayed on her knees—maintaining her faith and faithfulness, standing in the gap for her son and praying that God would shower grace and mercy on him before it was too late. And as far away as Daddy had strayed, when he finally came to himself, he took that opportunity for Grace and Mercy when he repented and gave his own life to Jesus Christ.

I have a grandmother, Lula Mae Darby McCrea, who was also a servant of Jesus Christ. She had five children—with Mama being the oldest. Grandma brought up her children in the fear of the Lord, teaching them about Jesus. Grandma Lula Mae was a godly woman. The Lord was with her and gave her incredible strength. She also provided a living, breathing example of how to live holy and love the Lord, even through the worst of circumstances. In some of the darkest times, she truly believed the scripture, "The Lord is My Shepherd, I shall not want." Grandma passed those lessons to her children. When my mama was a little girl, Grandma Lula Mae would have her read the Bible to her younger brothers and sister. Grandma maintained her faith and her faithfulness to God, praying for all of her children that God would grant them His grace and mercy. When I meet people who know Grandma Lula Mae, they always say, "That woman was a saint. She was the nicest lady I ever met."

When my dad had repented of his sins and gave himself to the Lord, the Lord blessed him and he became James H. Turner, servant of Jesus Christ, a good pastor, a good son, a good husband, a good father and a good friend. I meet people all the time who say, "Are you a Turner? I knew your father, and he sure was a preacher and a man of God. He was a good man." Everybody remembers him as a true servant of our Lord.

My mama didn't pass up her opportunity at Grace. She repented of her sins and gave her life to Jesus Christ. The Lord blessed her, and she became a servant of Jesus Christ, an Evangelist, a good daughter, a good wife, a good mother, a good sister and a good friend.

And now here I am…

Ever since our father passed away, Mama has been concerned about what she was going to leave for her children. But there is no need for Mama to worry her pretty, little head about that because she is giving us a legacy that spans generations. The lessons that she is teaching us will be passed down to generations to come.

Mama brought us up in the fear of the Lord, teaching us about Jesus Christ and giving us a live example of how a real Christian should carry him or herself when representing the Lord. Our parents taught us that God is real, that He loves us and how Jesus says that, "If you love Me, you will keep My Commandments," even when you think no one is looking. Mama always told us what the Bible says, especially Proverbs and Ecclesiastes. In fact, we heard some of her favorite scriptures AFTER she had brought back a switch or a belt to whip us. We may have been hollering and screaming while she was giving us a "Bible lesson." But we learned ALL of the scriptures about disobedience. And we also learned scriptures excusing all of those whippings when she would always say,

(Proverbs 22:15) "Foolishness is bound in the heart of a child; but the rod of correction shall drive it far from him."

(Proverbs 29:15) "The rod and reproof give wisdom: but a child left to himself bringeth his mother to shame."

(Proverbs 23:13) "Withhold not correction from the child: for if thou beatest him with the rod, he shall not die."

(Proverbs 23:14) "Thou shalt beat him with the rod, and shalt deliver his soul from hell."

Mama believed in 1 Thessalonians 5:21: "Prove all things; hold fast that which is good." She put a lot of effort into proving those scriptures! But, praise God, we all made it in Jesus' name!

Another favorite of hers was Ecclesiastes 3:1, "To everything there is a season, and a time to every purpose under the heaven."

Mama always added, "If you're young and healthy, it's not your season to be laying up here with your big, crusty feet all up on my couch. It's your season to get a job and go to work every day because the Bible says, 'There is nothing better for a man, than that he should eat and drink, and that he should make his soul enjoy good in his labour (Ecclesiastes 2:24).'"

But in all seriousness, Mama was our first evangelist. She represented Jesus Christ to us in the way that she lived her life in our home–away from church and away from public view. She represented Jesus Christ to us in how she treated other people–even the people who did not treat her kindly. She did it was simply because Jesus had said in Matthew 5:44, "But I say unto you, love your enemies, bless them that curse you, do good to them that hate you, and pray for them which despitefully use you and persecute you…" This was one of the most powerful lessons I have ever seen. When I had some issues with some of the girls at school, Mama said, "Kill 'em with kindness. And if you hold your peace and let the Lord fight your battles, victory belongs to you."

I remember thinking, "Mama is crazy. She's weak. Hold my peace?" I couldn't imagine holding my peace when all I wanted to do was grab somebody by the hair and punch them in the face. I followed Mama's advice, seething the whole time. But I was so focused on feeling powerless that I couldn't focus on what God was doing to work things out for me. It wasn't until years later that I saw my mother employ those lessons. It was after Daddy had died, and Mama was working at Dillard's. She was having a lot of issues with the women in her department. It almost took an act of God to keep Emell from jacking the women up by the hair. I'm sure that Mama was praying, "God, please keep my children out of this store before they hurt somebody." She was always nice, smiling and praying for people. And one by one, things began to happen to these people. And one by one, they all connected their calamity to the hurtful things they were doing to Mama. And after a while, they all started looking out for Mama, seeking out her counsel. They somehow knew that there was something special about her and that if they messed with her, they would have to pay for it—one way or another.

All Mama said to me was, this is why I pray for them—she did it because the Bible says in Isaiah 54:17, "No weapon that is formed against thee shall prosper; and every tongue that shall rise against thee in judgment thou shalt condemn." And the Bible also says in Psalm 105:15, "Touch not Mine anointed, and do My prophets no harm." She said, I pray for these women because when they mess with me, they have to answer to God for what they do to me. It was that day that I stopped praying for people to get hit by a bus and started praying that God will have mercy and extend His grace towards them and towards me.

But that's how Mama is… she actually lives what she teaches about. She has been a disciple of Jesus Christ in her own house by the way she lives, by her conversation, by the way she deals with the good and the way she deals with the bad. She has influenced future generations of her own family with her brand of evangelism.

It is because of her that I know who Jesus is and formed my own relationship with Him. My daddy was my evangelist too, and he certainly lived what he preached. The two of them together were partners in their decision to raise us in the fear of the Lord. It is partly because of Mama's faith and faithfulness that I recognized and accepted my gift of Grace from Jesus Christ, confessed my sins, repented and gave my heart to Him. I was ripping and running the streets too, at one point. And I strayed so far that I wouldn't pray—not because I didn't believe in Jesus or in His Power, but because I didn't think that I deserved any more Grace. I grew up in the presence of miracles, but turned my face so far that I allowed the devil to convince me that I wasn't good enough to ask for or expect any forgiveness or mercy. At one point, I wanted it all to end. I was on my way down Hwy 421 to Southern Pines, and I had no intention of ever coming back. But I know now that Mama was already praying for me, and the Lord gave me another chance. When I came to myself that day, I looked up with tears rolling down my face. Finally, I said, "Lord, I am so messed up that I don't want to live any more. Please save me." And immediately, the Lord moved in my heart. That day, I knew what it meant to sing the words, "I looked at my hands, and my hands looked new, I looked at my feet, and they did too." But the reason I had the presence of mind to believe that God forgives and God loves was because my Mama was my first evangelist. She taught me Romans 10:9: "That if thou shalt confess with thy mouth the Lord Jesus, and shalt believe in thine heart that God hath raised him from the dead, thou shalt be saved."

…. And now… here is her twelve-year-old grandson…

Just a few months ago, not long after we had moved from Colorado, I came home from work late one night. Daniel was crying. I went in to find out what was wrong. Daniel told me that he had been very sick. I asked what I could bring him, and without thinking about it, Daniel said, "Mama, all I want is the blessed oil that Grandma brought over here the other night." I went to get the oil. Before I could open it, he took it from me and anointed his own head. Then he gave the blessed oil back to me, laid down and said, "I'm gonna be all right now, Mama." Then he closed his eyes, turned over and went to sleep.

Willa D. Turner

To Mama:

That's the legacy you're giving to your grandchildren, Daniel, Micah, CJ, James and all of the little baby Turners that are yet to come.

You are still the first evangelist to a whole new generation. And one day their children will stand here and say, "My family is blessed because we had a great-grandma named Willa Dean Turner, servant of Jesus Christ, who brought up her children and grandchildren in the fear of the Lord."

Mom, thank you for allowing Jesus Christ to live in our home. And thank you for raising us to be receptive to His Will.

With love,

Therese L Turner
November 1, 2008

Letter to Dad
(on Father's Day)

Sunday, June 21, 2009

Hi Daddy,

How have you been? I miss hearing your voice, your singing, your laughter and your smile. I miss your footsteps through the house when you came home from a long preaching trip. I remember the nights I would fight to stay awake, just to say hello. Not a day goes by when I don't think of you in some special way. Whether it is thought, a person or place that resembles something about you, you flash before my face.

Sometimes, I wonder what my life would have been growing up with you in it. The times when I wanted to call and speak with you, just to hear your voice or when I needed your counsel in my toughest days or just when I had great news to share!

Dad, I won't keep you long, because you have much to do. But I thank GOD because he gave me ten years to share with you. The wonderful experiences we had gave me a lifetime of memories that I will always cherish.

I just wanted to let you know that I'm thankful for having had a dad like you. Thank you for your love and for your discipline and for raising me in the ways of the Lord. Thank you for giving me a solid foundation to build on.
Love you always, and I know we will meet again. Keep enjoying heaven, for I know one day I will be there too!

Happy Father's Day, Dad

Love & Miss you always,

Aprille

CHAPTER 26

Devotional Readings

A Message from the Sea

Read
Philippians 4:6-7

Thou Wilt Keep Him In Perfect Peace, Whose Mind Is Stayed On Thee: Because He Trusteth In Thee (Isaiah 26:3)

I Was Walking Down By The Seashore late one afternoon, listening to the waves as they rolled in across the deep, blue sea. There was water everywhere, and I could not tell where the water ended and the bright, blue sky began. I was captivated by beauty, in awe of the handiwork of the Lord and immersed in His presence. As I walked, there was great peace in my mind, spirit, soul and body. I was overtaken with joy, and I began to give thanks, praise, glory and honor to God. I realized that this was the kind of life He wanted His people to live every day—in a state of physical, mental and spiritual tranquility.

By accepting Jesus Christ as your Lord and Savior and by obeying His commandments, you will have a right relationship with God. You can live a life of true contentment—not just one day by the seashore but every day, wherever you are.

If we will consult the Lord through prayer when making all of our decisions, we will eliminate many mistakes, thereby causing us to live calm, serene lives for the Lord. We will be able to lie down in peace. We can experience sweet rest every night and awaken refreshed every morning, with new mercies, because our minds rest in the Lord.

Peace will bring smiles and laughter. Peace will cause you to sing hymns and spiritual songs. It will cause you to love everybody because of the joy that's on the inside.

Study Colossians 3:12-17

"Peace is a sure sign of trust"

By: Willa D. Turner

Willa D. Turner

The Fork and the Knife:

A Lesson of Faith

Read
I John 5:14

Now faith is the substance of things hoped for, the evidence of things not seen
(Hebrews 11:1)

When we are fully confident in God, the things we hope for are a reality before they become an actuality. This confidence causes us to believe in what we cannot see and to prepare for what will happen before it tangibly comes to pass.

One day a little boy, who was very hungry, asked his father for something to eat. The father was so busy doing other things that he paid little to no attention to the child. He nodded to the boy but kept doing what he was doing.

The little boy saw his father nod. So the boy went to the kitchen, opened the silverware drawer and took out a fork and a knife. He then climbed up into a chair at the table and quietly waited, the fork in one hand and the knife in the other.

After a while, the father noticed his son sitting at the table, prepared to eat. He was so moved by his son's faith that he hurried to prepare something to eat. When he placed the plate of food in front of his son, the child smiled and began to eat. The child asked, believed, positioned himself, patiently waited and he received his petition. That is what God requires of us.

The father was so inspired by the act of faith his little son exhibited that for many years afterwards he used the story in his travels as a teaching tool on faith.

Study: Matthews 7:7-11

"Faith prompts you to action"

By: Willa D. Turner

Willa D. Turner

Hope Gives Faith Something to Work With

Read
Hebrews 11:16

At a low place in my life, I knelt
down beside my bedside. My
eyes closed and tears
running down my cheeks, I
poured out my soul to the Lord.

In that darkness, there appeared a little light, about the size of a pin's head. I was amazed at how something so small could give such a bright glow. God gave me that little light, which stirred up the faith in me. Faith had me on my knees, and that little hope was magnified by faith. I knew at that moment that everything would be all right. I dried my weeping eyes and began to rejoice in the hope that the Lord had rekindled in me. That was over thirty years ago, and I have not been that low in spirit again.

Because we have hope, we keep striving.
Because we have hope, we believe in the promises of God.
Because we have hope, we continue to trust in the Lord.
Because we have hope, we keep His commandments.
Because we have hope, we know that if we live a life that is pleasing to Him in this world, we will live eternally with Him in the world to come.

We are passing through on our way to a better place, which was prepared by the Lord Himself. Our greatest desire and expectation is to gain eternal life.

Study: Jeremiah 17:7

"Hope is the glue that holds things together
while faith gets the work done."

By Willa D. Turner

Willa D. Turner

The Manifestation of Trust

Read
Isaiah 12:2

Trust in God wholeheartedly,
with unwavering confidence
in Him. Wait patiently in
faith, believing and knowing that what you have hoped for is already done and the manifestation will surely come. Waiting in faith and believing may seem like hard work, but they have great benefits.

Trust brings contentment, and contentment brings great peace. Pour out your heart to the Lord, even though He knows what you need before you ask. He will hear your cry and answer every prayer according to His will. He is our protector, our refuge, our strength, our shield and our salvation.

We are to trust God in every aspect of our lives and in every situation. No matter how it looks, we are not to waver, so that the answer to our prayer and the date of our deliverance will not be prolonged.

Take all your cares to the Lord in prayer, for He can and will do something about them. There is nothing too hard for God. Don't fret. Rest, for you can depend on Him. Believe God's Word, for His Word is true and will stand forever. Catch hold to the scriptures and hold on, while rehearsing in your mind, "I believe God! I trust God!"

Study: Colossians 3:12-17

"Trust is the work – Peace is the dividend."

By: Willa D. Turner

James H. and Willa D. Turner Through the Years

Elder James Turner (Father of James H. Turner)

Missionary Lula Belle Turner (Mother of James H. Turner)

Power to Overcome

Radio Operations Department
Intercept Graduation Class, 1958

Air Force Buddies

Gone Fishing, 1967

Power to Overcome

Willa D. Turner–Rockingham, North Carolina, 1979

Superintendent Turner preaching at last Asheboro
District Conference–March, 1987
Message entitled "Rotting Provisions"

Willa D. Turner – Colorado Red Rocks

Bountiful Blessings Church of God in Christ–
Colorado Springs, Colorado–2001
Left to right: Loretta Williams, First Lady Bettie
Peterson, Willa Turner and Liz Gannaway

Revival Temple Church of God in Christ, Troy, North Carolina (Founder's Day Celebration, 2004)

Sixty-Fifth Birthday Celebration–2008

Seventieth Birthday Celebration–2013

CHAPTER 27

Memorial Ceremony

Graveside Memorial Service

IN HONOR OF
JAMES HENRY TURNER SR.
June 15, 1940 – May 21, 1987

Devoted Husband, Father &
Servant of Our Lord
Commemorating the Twenty-Fifth Anniversary of His Passing

Sunday, May 20, 2012

Willa D. Turner

Southern Pines, North Carolina

The Children

Therese, James Jr., Chris, Ithiel, Emell & Aprille

Cynthia & Gail

The Daughters-in-law

Karen, Nichole & April

The Grandchildren

Micah, Daniel, CJ, James

Josiah, Noah, James H. Turner III (J3)

Tia, Lee, Adrina, Mitchell Jr., Brian, Dorthell

& Kelvin

Dad & Honey

(as Mom called you)

Even though you have been gone in

body for all these years, you never

left us in spirit. We rejoice and take

comfort in knowing that one day we

will all see your smiling face again,

never to be separated, but

united in love and joy forever.

Until we meet again,
Mom & Children

Opening Prayer–Micah Turner

Scripture–Daniel Turner

Songs and Remarks – "Higher Ground" &
"Fill My Cup"–Christopher Turner

Remarks–Aprille Turner

Poem and Remarks–Emell Turner

Remarks–Ithiel Turner, James H. Turner Jr., Therese Turner

Reflections, Closing Remarks & Directions for
The Family–Mom, Willa D. Turner

Willa D. Turner

I Had a Great Dad!
By
Emell Turner

It's been twenty-five years since you left for glory.
And in front of our family, I can tell my story.
Twenty-five years, the good and the bad;
I know for a fact that I had a great dad.

One who made me feel special, made me feel unique.
One who taught me that I should seek
The God of the Bible, the only true one.
You left us behind because our work was not done.

Since you've been gone, sometimes the pain still linger,
But, I've moved on with my life, and I've become a singer,
A preacher,
A teacher,
A student of the Word;
All because I believe in the God you served.

I'm all grown up now and your memory, I've rehearsed.
It was because of you that I became a nurse.
For I remember you in that hospital bed;
And I also remember some of the things that you said.

You looked at each of us, all around the room;
And I had no idea, that you would be gone so soon.
When you called me by name, you didn't scold me because I'd misbehaved.
But what you said to me was, "Emell…I want you to be saved."
Twenty-five years later, your wish has come true
I'm saved, sanctified and filled with the Holy Ghost too!

Even still, sometimes my heart still aches,
Because I have questions, like sometimes I wonder…
Would Daddy be proud of me? Or am I a blunder?
Or even sometimes I want to know what you would think of this or that.

Like would you like these shoes? Or even that hat?
Or theological questions about God's Holy Writ,
Because you had a great reputation
for your knowledge of whit

But, these questions will go unanswered 'til Jesus comes back.
I'm going to go back with him, so I keep my bags packed.
I want to see you again, but more importantly, Jesus, face to face.
To experience what you have been experiencing up close,
His love and amazing grace!
So even though there's a little emptiness since you've left me, still,
I know that your leaving was in God's perfect will.
I didn't really trust Him then, but I trust Him now.
So I just thank God for the eleven years we had,
Because I know for a fact that I had a great dad!

Emell wrote the above poem in memory of her dad. She shared it with the family at the memorial ceremony on May 20, 2012.

Willa D. Turner

Left: James, Ithiel, Karen, Chris Jr., April, Micah, Noah & Aprille
Center: Dean, Emell, & Josiah
Right: Therese, Chris, Daniel, James Jr., J3 & Nichole

Power to Overcome

Creative Works

Turner Sr., James H. Abstract painting. 1970. Acrylic on canvas

Turner, Emell. *Mannequin*. 1989. Colored Pencil on paper

Turner, Aprille. *Self Portrait*. 1999. Acrylic on canvas

Turner, Aprille. *Autumn on Mars*. 2000. Acrylic on canvas

Power to Overcome

Turner, Aprille. *Untitled*. 2004. Colored Pencil on paper

Turner, Nichole. *Creative Rebirth*. 2007. Acrylic on canvas
www.NicholeTurner.com

Willa D. Turner

Turner, April. Gospel Recording Artist soon to release CD – TrueVine Production
Natural Hair Products – YouTube

CONCLUSION

I know from the Word of God and from experience that God will give you power to overcome. I've been through many things. But I called on the Lord, and He delivered me out of them all.

The Lord promised us in I Corinthians 10:13, "There hath no temptation taken you but such as common to man: but God is faithful, who will not suffer you to be tempted above that ye are able, but will with the temptation also make a way to escape, that ye may be able to bear it." God is a promise keeper. All we have to do is trust Him. Trust is the work of faith. The peace that comes out of that trust is the dividend.

Nothing can happen to us as saints of God unless God allows it. And if He allows it, it is for a reason. Often in his lifetime, my husband said that no one was going to heaven but tried souls. We must all go through our trials. I Peter 4:12 says, "Beloved think it not strange concerning the fiery trial, which is to try you, as though some strange thing happened unto you." We have been forewarned to make sure we will not be caught off guard. Jesus suffered, so we must arm ourselves likewise. Suffering is a test of our faith. Furthermore, Christ died for us and rose again and is at the right hand of God, and He "maketh intercessions for us" (Rom 8:34). The Word assures us that He continues to go to God on our behalf. We never face trials by ourselves (Matt 28:20, Heb 13:5). Jesus is always with us.

Philippians 4:13 says, "I can do all things through Christ which strengtheneth me." It said "strengtheneth" me. It is a continuous thing, not just for one day or for one night. Christ strengthens us, day by day, for the duration of whatever we are facing.

There are two types of trials that come in our lives. The first set of trials come to show us ourselves, purify us and make out of us what God would have us to be. They didn't come to kill us. They came to press us into what we should be, to make us strong so that we can overcome the enemy. The second set of trials come from the devil to steal, kill and destroy. They come to keep us from gaining eternal life. The enemy will throw the book at you. He will use every tactic known and unknown to men. Know that if needed, God will give you power to endure and overcome by making an escape route where there is none.

When you are pressed, always stand the test through faith. Believe that God will deliver, for, "All things work together for good to them that love God, to them who are the called according to His purpose" (Rom 8:28).

There are times when you must resist the devil by applying pressure. Apply pressure by prayer and fasting, for Matthew 17:21 says, "Howbeit this kind goeth not out but by prayer and fasting." Apply pressure by making up in your mind that you are going to endure and wait until your change comes, not matter what. Apply pressure by never quitting. Apply pressure by standing on the Word. Apply pressure by giving your testimony about God's goodness, for Revelation 12:11 says, "And they overcame him by the blood of the Lamb and by the word of their testimony."

I am a sanctified witness that God will do just what He said. He will save your soul and make you whole. He will be your comfort in the midnight hour, for I called on Him and He heard my cry. He is a friend to the friendless. He will be your friend when there is none. He will bind up the broken hearted. He will minister to you when you are broken and in despair. He will encourage and comfort you when you are crushed in your spirit. He will provide food when you don't know where you're going to get your next meal. He will keep your mind in perfect peace if you will keep your mind on Him. He will heal your body, for He is the Lord that healeth thee. He will bring you out more than a conqueror. That's the kind of God I serve. The only true and living God–the God of the Holy Bible!

-I Am an Overcomer -

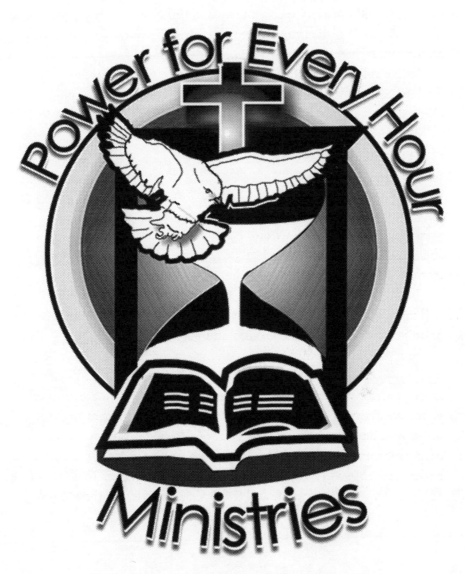

Power for Every Hour Ministry, Inc., James H. Turner Founder, Willa D. Turner, President

−powerforeveryhourministries.com

Printed in the United States
By Bookmasters